Come Spring

Come Spring

an autobiographical novel

by

Maria Lewitt

St. Martin's Press
New York

Library of Congress Cataloging in Publication Data

Lewitt, Maria, 1924-
   Come spring.

   1. World War, 1939-1945—Fiction.   I. Title.
PR9619.3.L45C6   823   82-5575
ISBN 0-312-15099-7   AACR2

First published in Australia by Scribe Publications Pty. Ltd.
First Edition
10   9   8   7   6   5   4   3   2   1

To my husband
and children

I wish to express my gratitude to Frank Kellaway, a great friend who urged me to go ahead with the book, and whose advice and corrections were invaluable.

So I returned, and considered all the oppressions that are done under the sun: and behold the tears of such as were oppressed, and they had no comforter; and on the side of their oppressors there was power; but they had no comforter.

Ecclesiastes 4:1

Come Spring

—— 1 ——

The leaves tremble above me as if a shiver has gone through the whole tree. Blotches of the sky play hide and seek, exposing bluest of blue among the clusters of green. And the sun sends its rays through, a spotlight in the theatre bringing the whole scene to life.

I screw up my eyes and rock in my hammock, encircled by colours and the appeasing quiet of nature around me. If I shut my eyes tight I can feel the dancing shadows. If I open them ever so slightly I am surrounded by a rainbow. And if I shut them again a multitude of coloured circles swims in front of me.

The late summer is still, pregnant with all the right sounds and scents, rich in shades, kind in warmth.

And there I was, half hypnotised by continuous rocking, voices and colours. A bird flew into the tree and chirped, twisting and lifting its tail up, wiping its beak in a jerky way, ignoring my presence. The wind, or rather a suggestion of it, swayed the cornfield in a multitude of waves. The shadows of the clouds moved slowly, followed by the beam of the sun's rays: the light chasing the gloom away.

Snatches of words came from a distance, fading and gaining in strength: 'Irena . . . lazy . . . selfish . . . disasters . . . worries . . . don't know . . .' I knew that my mother was discussing me; some of her words had hit

1

me dead centre. It was true that I spent most of my days in the hammock, or walking around in the fields and the forest. She was concerned about my lack of communication and my selfishness. I was moody because I wanted to be with Irma and my other friends, while my parents had decided to send my sister and me for a summer holiday away from Lodz, our home town. They were waiting for 'the political situation to clarify', as they explained to us.

But I was not concerned with the political situation, and was sick and tired of hearing it discussed at our home. I was fifteen and wanted to live, to experience, to know. And there I was, planted in that hole, my only company being Tania, my elder sister, who was beautiful and freckled. She looked down on me, which irritated me. She spent her days sun-bathing, probably hoping to tan evenly all the spaces between her freckles. The result was devastating and made her unapproachable.

There was a boy of seventeen who was my only hope for romance, and not bad to look at. My mother said he was a 'very intelligent, brilliant student'. She was right, too. He was brilliant and intelligent, always starting a sentence with, 'As you probably know', which most of the time I didn't. I felt awful, getting myself entangled with my nonchalant replies, 'Of course I know!'

He always quoted Latin, which I detested and didn't know very well; and he had a beautiful chocolate tan, while I looked like a boiled beetroot. There was one thing, however, which I knew better: poetry. So I recited to him whenever he allowed me. It wasn't easy; it wasn't easy at all. He knew exactly what he wanted to say, precise in every word, preaching all the time about obligations and self-discipline. He was an expert in every field. He called poetry escapism and memorising, a waste of time.

So we drifted apart, he on his Latin quotations, I on my ignorance — romance and companionship unfulfilled.

I wanted something to happen during that summer, something to carry me from everyday boredom. But nothing happened. What my mother called 'laziness' wasn't really laziness. It was a peculiar search for values and answers. What she called 'a lack of concern and selfishness' was really me looking at myself and trying to sort out what was going on around me.

I wasn't happy, I wasn't unhappy. I was there at that time and that was all. I didn't involve myself in philosophical reflections, but my mind was like a camera, imprinting forever the idyllic beauty of the European summer of 1939.

My father cut our holidays short. He was apologetic, but preferred to have us all together in the city. Germany and Russia had just signed a non-aggression pact. Father was very worried that the Pact would assure Russia's neutrality, making Hitler even more militant and dangerous than he had been. His next objective would surely be Poland.

My father looked tired, and his words made mother very quiet. Tania went to pack her things. As for me, I ran outside, overwhelmed with joy and, while breathing in the warmth of the late summer evening, performed an atavistic dance. I was going home to my friends, to my normal life.

When we returned the whole city was in a frenzy. Patriotism was riding high, with flag-waving and flowers for the soldiers. Troops were marching and singing:

> We're going to fight in Berlin
> where we'll kill Hitler,
> the son-of-a-bitch.

The streets carried the people along as though on a conveyor belt. It was a happy and noisy crowd, exchanging victorious glances, boasting of our strength, suspicious of spies, laughing at Hitler's army with its cardboard tanks and margarine instead of butter.

I threw myself gladly into that whirlpool. Every morning I met my friends and we would spend the day digging trenches and shelters. We joked and we sang army songs:

> Oh, how beautiful the War is,
> and when you fall off your horse,
> we won't stop.
> Because when you die,
> you'll see our beloved Poland
> in your last sleep.

It was great. Radio programmes overflowed with patriotic speeches and gay military music. Each day was eventful. In the evenings the whole family assembled at home. In contrast with myself and the life outside, my parents were strangely unenthusiastic and quiet.

One evening my mother arrived home with a big tin box, put it on the table, and said quietly: 'I want to make a wish. Let this box be always full of bread in the years to come'. She left the room in her calm way, followed by my father. Tania and I looked at each other without understanding, some uneasiness creeping in around us.

And then it started, with a noise of aeroplanes and the radio announcement. We were at war. The sirens measured the fragments of our days and nights, between one alarm and another.

We spent most of the time in the cellar; however, my father stubbornly refused to join us and the other residents of our flats in the safety of a damp and stuffy refuge. For the first time I met all our neighbours. It was exciting, because before the War I had hardly known the people around me. Our janitor was jubilant — at long last the mighty ones from 'above the ground' had come to join him and his family. He kept the door of his wretched flat wide open, not even trying to conceal his satisfaction; he would sit in his chair, his children in bed, his wife endlessly patching one garment or another, while we felt lost and uneasy in the strange surroundings.

4

Lodz was hardly bombed; but news, official and whispered from ear-to-ear, was depressing. Apparently the German army was moving swiftly; our own soldiers looked dirty and tired. The various women's committees set up hot kitchens for the boys. The soldiers were frightened to touch the food, claiming that some of their friends had been poisoned by German spies. So we sampled the food in front of them.

There were no more flags, no more flowers.

Curfew was introduced, and prices soared, but our bread bin was still full. At night we heard a constant thumping of soldiers' feet and horses' hooves. We waited for the promised victory, cursing our beautiful cloudless sky, hoping for a drenching rain which would, surely, bog and ruin the German offensive.

And then the night came when we stood in the entrance to our flats. An 'expert' in building construction came to the conclusion that the arch of the entry was the soundest structure in the entire building. Our janitor wasn't too happy. We heard approaching planes; we could hardly hear each other. Some people disagreed with the general opinion and decided to go to the cellar, which made our janitor happy and the building expert angry.

My mother put her arms around Tania and me. 'I wish your father was with us.'

'Would you like me to fetch him?'

'No.'

The noise was growing but it wasn't planes any more: it was a mixture of voices and an uneven stamping of feet. I looked through the opening. The entire width of the street was covered with people carrying children, suitcases, bird cages, pictures, bundles.

'Where are you going?' Someone fired the question.

'Running from the Germans.'

'Going towards Warsaw.'

'All men should join the Army, haven't you heard?'

5

The voices were grave, mixed-up. I didn't want to hear any more. I ran upstairs, ignoring my mother's protest.

My father was sitting in his chair reading a book. He looked up at me, his eyes questioning.

'Have you been listening to the radio?'

'No, I haven't.'

He turned the radio on, twisting the knobs with his long, nervous fingers. How I had missed him, how good it was to be with him again.

> Attention, attention. Radio Warsaw speaking. The enemy is gaining on our territories. The Army has decided to redeploy our forces in Warsaw. We need new recruits . . . This is an urgent announcement. All men are instructed to leave their homes and join our forces in Warsaw . . . Our Victory depends on you. Men of the Polish Republic, join us. Before long, you'll be back in your homes, bringing victory to your families . . . Attention, attention.

My father switched the radio off. He got up, took his raincoat, and kissed me. I followed him down. My mother and Tania ran towards him.

'I knew it.' Mother's voice was dry. 'Shall I prepare something for you? A suitcase, food?'

'No, nothing.' Father kissed Tania, then mother, then me, threw the coat over his shoulders, and left us. He disappeared almost immediately, was lost among the moving, terrified crowd, the flowing lava of an erupted volcano.

We watched the people and then went to our flat, each of us to her own room. I snuggled into my bed and, for the first time, fully realised what war really meant. My father didn't say good-bye, he didn't say that I was a big girl, he didn't tell me to look after my mother and Tania. He didn't tell me anything.

I cried.

I saw the bent figures of people marching towards Warsaw, with their indistinguishable faces; and I heard the tumult of voices, the shuffling, shuffling of feet. And my father was among them, one of them.

My father was dead. We were going to his funeral. All of us were dressed in black. My mother's face was hidden behind a veil. Her hands in black gloves lay lifeless on her lap. The only sound was the rhythmic clip-clop of horses' hooves and Tania's restrained sobs.

The carriage was going slowly. The driver hit the horses, urging them to trot. Why was he hitting them? My father was dead. They hit him, too. They hit him until he lost consciousness and died. My father was dead and the sky was blue, the sun was shining, and I wished I had a black veil; it would have deadened the day too bright and beautiful for a burial.

People were walking, trams passed by. The sound of the city grew in volume, reaching a piercing, intolerable crescendo. My city was alive, my conquered home town was coming back to reality, learning how to live under German rule. People mingled, brushing their bodies against the uniformed conquerors. My father's killer must have been somewhere among them.

Two weeks before father had returned home. He had come at night; dirty, thin and strangely quiet. He was sick with exhaustion, full of unexplained worries, his blue eyes now dull and sad. He bathed and he ate, he asked questions and listened to us. He was home, and we almost forgot that, outside, German flags hung from every door, German soldiers marched through our streets, and every day brought new decrees.

I showed him my school books, and he looked through them as always, and I promised to work really hard that coming year — though nobody asked me to make any promises. Tania kept on asking whether she would be allowed to continue her studies in France, and mother sat with us just looking at father, until he grew very tired and went to bed. The three of us stayed up very late,

7

keeping our voices as low as our excitement allowed. My father was back home, home with us, home to stay. Could there be happiness in war, joy in war?

The next day I went to school, ignoring the flags, the army and the queues. As long as we were together it didn't matter so much any more. I entered my school. Uniformed Germans were walking up and down. I went past, not looking at them. Before long I was told that the fourth floor of our school had been requisitioned by the army and must be vacant by lunch-time. All the teachers and the girls started work immediately. We carried desks, tables, school equipment, books. We felt very important.

On the following day the fourth floor was returned to us. Our joy helped us to speed up the task of returning the school's items to their rightful places.

The next day the first floor of our school fell victim to the requisition. The foreign language and uniforms, the military transports and flags frightened me once more.

New decrees had reached an epidemic stage, with printed bills posted all over the city. 'Attention, attention. Jews are not allowed to live on or to use Adolf Hitler Strasse' (the main street).

When I arrived home my father was in bed, my mother frantic, trying to get a doctor. Father asked me about school and whether we enjoyed our return to the fourth floor.

'Oh yes, very much,' I said, and it was the first time I consciously lied to him.

'We are heading for hard times.' He managed to sit up. 'No matter what happens', he said, looking at his hands, 'we have to be prepared, realistic. They might take everything away from us, except for our experiences and knowledge'. He picked up my hand. 'Your schooling is very important.' He held my hand for a while. I didn't know what to say. He let my hand go and I left his room.

In the evening he was better. Irma's father dropped in.

They had been friends for many years, since their student days. They loved to discuss and argue about politics and music. We had spent many holidays together, the Kohns and us. It was during those long summers when my friendship with Irma was cemented, long before we started school. I was very fond of her parents, especially of her father. Mr. Kohn's face was always alive; he treated me as his equal and his voice was full of music.

On this occasion both men were hungry for news, as all radios had been confiscated at the beginning of the Occupation. As usual, they got themselves entangled in political speculations; and, as a result, Mr. Kohn missed the curfew and stayed overnight. I went to sleep peacefully, listening to the familiar voices I loved so much.

Next day, during the maths lesson, I was called to see our headmistress. It surprised me. I was trying to find an explanation and, as I walked, the school corridor seemed to stretch out in front of me.

My mother was waiting for me, and she looked stiff. I sat next to her. The squareness and coldness of our school benches made me feel even more uneasy.

'Your father is gravely ill.' Mother's face was throbbing.

It couldn't be, I thought. He was better last night; he told me about values, and I hadn't said a word and left him. What was she saying, my mother? My father beaten up? No, no. An SS man came to take my father away, accused him of being a lazy, dirty Jew? No, no, I must have been dreaming. What was my mother doing at school? She should have been at home and I should have been in my class, because schooling was important. Why was she turning her face towards the window? Yes, she was crying.

'I told him your father was sick. "I know Jewish sickness; all Jews are sick when they're asked to work", he said. And he kept on kicking your father, methodically, coldly.' She waved her hand as if she wanted to

9

chase something away. 'We had better hurry home.'

'My books?'

'Leave them till tomorrow.'

It was strange to return home at such an early hour and in the company of my mother. She kept on talking in a detached, disjointed way, allowing herself short spells of silence.

'He asked me if I was Jewish. "I am his wife", I said. "You shouldn't be living with a Jew", he said. He was young. I tried. I really tried to stop him. He laughed, he pushed me away, and left only when your father collapsed.'

We went home, trespassing on Aryan grounds.

My father died the following morning.

All mirrors were covered up; there were hushed voices around us, sounds of weeping, and black stockings and dresses for the three of us.

I sat in my room alone, stunned, wondering where our mourning garments had come from. People kept on coming. 'Will you please accept my most sincere expressions . . .' I couldn't distinguish faces any more; my eyes were dry. My great-aunt shook me, tears streaming down her wrinkles. 'Why don't you cry, child? Your father is dead, don't you understand?'

My father was dead and I didn't cry. My father was dead and the world was alive. Our carriage turned towards the Jewish cemetery. Once upon a time, or was it just a few weeks ago, the entrance had led through an avenue lined on both sides with old trees, their branches meeting, forming a green roof. Once upon a time. Now all the branches were chopped down, the trunks stripped and naked. And young people were standing between them, shouting, bending down, straightening up, waving their hands. 'Down with Jews! One less, good riddance, hurray!' The stones hit our carriage. My mother lifted her black-gloved hand to her face.

My father was dead, the sky was blue. Merciless bright sun.

The sky should have been black, with the threat of a downpour to make the stone-throwers stand still, to wash their sardonic grins away and leave their faces wet, as a sign of sorrow for a man who had died.

—— 2 ——

On the way home from the funeral I experienced a feeling of relief. My father's body was buried. The finality of that act made the whole situation clear and irreversible.

As a sign of mourning we stayed home for a week, receiving endless calls; our faces were wet from other people's kisses and tears. I thought of my father, regretting the talks we had never had, pitying myself more than anybody else.

And then the morning came when all at once I noticed the crooked seam on my black stocking, when Tania whistled while feeding our canary Macius and when I realised that mother was using her lipstick again.

It was the morning when Kazia came back home.

Kazia was our servant. She had been with us as long as I could remember — making our beds, cooking meals, cleaning, answering the door. She was slightly cockeyed, her straight hair was mousey and pushed severely behind her ears. Of medium build, she was always on the move, first to get up, last to retire. She came to us directly from her village, hoping to find an easier and more secure existence. She addressed my parents as Madam and Sir, and my sister and me as Miss, while all of us called her by her first name, never suspecting that it was wrong to do so.

From time to time she would pronounce: 'When young Miss marries I'll go with her, I will.' She made me feel very important.

Kazia was illiterate but she always wanted to know what was going on in the world. Every evening my governess used to enlighten her by reading aloud choice pieces from the daily press, while I would nestle quietly in a dark kitchen corner. I was most impressed by a report of a murder where the entire family had been killed except for a servant. I listened to Kazia's comments with horrified fascination.

'She was pretty; that's why they left her alive. Prettiness, as if it was the most important thing. With my face, I wouldn't stand a chance. What a rotten world!'

Kazia's reflections influenced me greatly; throughout my childhood I had heard constantly about Tania's beauty, while nobody had ever mentioned mine — although my hair would receive complimentary remarks. So I reached my own conclusion, and decided to sleep with my face hidden, leaving only my hair uncovered. Everyone at home was puzzled by my newly acquired sleeping habit.

I loved Kazia; she was a born story-teller. The kitchen was a fascinating place, full of tempting odours and curious activities, and whenever I was in trouble I would look for a refuge in Kazia's domain.

Kazia had been away when my father died. My parents used to 'spoil' her by allowing her to visit her village once a year. The whole family suffered then from the inefficiency of Kazia's substitute.

She endured great hardship by rejoining us in those first months of the War. By the time she returned to us, Lodz had been renamed Litzmannstadt after the German general who had conquered the city in the First World War, and had become a part of the great German Reich. Kazia had to cross the frontier and was subjected to search and insults by military customs officers.

'I dreamed about you all in black', she announced on arrival. 'I knew something terrible had happened. I had to come back.'

She set to work at once, talking to herself, grumbling. She did it all the time, perhaps because nobody had ever listened to her, except when I was very young. She took charge of our life once again, attending to our needs. She ran from one queue to another, bringing provisions, feeding us. 'Eat, eat now', she said. 'Take what's yours. Tomorrow, who knows? Eat now.' She spread her mother hen's wings all over us.

My school life had been constantly interrupted and had stopped being the centre of my activities. Latin declensions, maths problems and the construction of cells explained beautifully by our biology teacher seemed irrelevant. But for some illogical reason my true passion to learn started then.

I sat late at night reading, copying my favourite poems and quotations into a thick exercise book, my very own anthology. The rumours reached us that books would be confiscated. I wanted to preserve forever the eternal beauty and wisdom of my cultural heritage. Nobody could take it away from me, my father had said.

Winter came suddenly, with snow flakes dancing in the air. It was white all around, the streets became quiet, German soldiers walked briskly with collars pulled up and hands in pockets.

It was snowing when the Jewish tenants were evicted from our flats. People were thrown out on the spot without any belongings. Kazia opened our doors to them, helping them to settle down, refusing to accept any tips.

'What are you, crazy, or what? You think the War is over? Sit down. I'll bring you something to drink.' And she would disappear, only to come back with a cup of tea, or a chair, grumbling under her breath.

Most other servants stayed behind in their former employers' flats. Kazia kept on trying to retrieve a few necessities from the usurpers — but in most cases she returned empty handed.

Seven families moved into our flat and, shortly after, the janitor delivered a note advising my mother to get rid of them immediately. Our block of flats belonged to a German family. After my father's death our landlord had come to pay his respects: 'Your husband knew when to die. It will be so much easier for you without a Jewish husband'. My mother must have remembered his words when she said to the janitor: 'My guests will stay with me as long as necessary, unless our landlord can think of alternative accommodation'.

Kazia smiled and slammed the door in the janitor's face.

Our guests were everywhere; sitting, talking, crying. Kazia organised some beds and mattresses, served sandwiches and mumbled under her breath.

Outside it snowed: snow flakes in the air, falling down, drifting up again, hesitant as if not wishing to touch our troubled earth.

Eventually, the lights were turned off and human misery found outlet in the spoken word, from a whisper to an open cry.

'Go to sleep Frida. Go to sleep.'

'How can I? I haven't even got my night cream', cried the woman. Someone laughed — a short, dry laugh. And later came the mixed breathing and the stale air.

We decided to leave for Warsaw. A general exodus had started; already, our friends the Kohns had left. Once Lodz was annexed to Germany, hardly anyone we knew wanted to live in the German Reich. Somehow, people felt that life in Occupied Poland — now called the Generalgouvernement — might be easier. At least in Warsaw we would be able to communicate and to live in the hope that the German authorities wouldn't interfere much with the civilian population.

15

We spent our last day in the German Reich packing and walking in circles. Kazia's eyes were red, her nose dripping. 'It's that damned cold, I'm sorry to say', she explained, turning her head away.

My father's German friend had arranged a permit for us. It said: 'Permit granted to leave Litzmannstadt for business purposes'. We were grateful to Albert; he had been urging us to leave the Reich for some weeks, pointing out the danger of our situation. Loneliness and uncertainty, almost palpable, were growing within us, making us silent and jumpy.

Everything was prepared, suitcases packed, my father's books stored in cases in the loft. The washer-woman had accepted money and promised to look after them — a dubious agreement.

'Go to sleep', nagged Kazia, but we were not sleepy.

'I don't mind so much that strangers will move in', declared mother, 'but the idea of them handling our personal papers is repugnant to me'. Her arms were full of letters, photographs. We followed her to the dark kitchen. The dying flames in the wood stove came to life when she threw in, one by one, recorded on paper, the fragments of her life. Something gripped me, and I left the kitchen where the flames played crazy games with forms and shadows.

First the corridor, then the dining room. The lights were off but it didn't matter, because I knew exactly how to manoeuvre around our furniture. I knew the contours of the high-backed chairs, the buffet and the grandfather clock, which had been silent since my father's death.

Once a week, every Sunday, there used to be a clock-winding ceremony. My father always took the key from the top of the clock (hidden from Tania's and my hands), and opened the slim, narrow door, exposing the chains and the heavy weights. He pulled the chains down and the weights moved up, accompanied by a winding noise.

The clock was always fast by three minutes, and that was where the whole fun would start.

'You can't move the arms back', my father would say.

'Why?'

'Because you can't bring back the time which has passed.' He would smile at me while his fingers moved the large hand of the clock around, stopping at half an hour — 'bing', moving towards an hour. One o'clock, two o'clock, not very interesting. The true excitement started with six evenly measured chimes.

'Faster father, faster!'

The clock would ring and move forward.

Kazia would be setting the table, clattering the cutlery.

'Bing bong, bing bong.'

'A real nut-house', she would say, tapping her forehead with her finger. 'A real nut-house.'

Remember, never backwards.

But now the pendulum hung still. I reached for the key and clenched it in my fist. My father had held that key only a few weeks ago. Rattling the lock, I opened the door. 'Remember, never backwards', my father said many lives ago. So I turned the large hand in the opposite direction, feeling the resistance of the movement. Faster, faster. I cried for my father. Silent anger couldn't bring back to me the times which had passed, so I pushed the hands backwards until they clicked and hung loosely, swaying lifelessly.

It was my father's clock and, before him, his father's. I wanted to stop it forever. I locked the door and put the key in my pocket. Yes, my mother was right; we shouldn't leave our personal things to others.

I went to my room stifled, broken. I sat in front of my desk and pulled the drawers open, one by one. There were old exercise books, letters tied together, an old purse, cuttings from magazines, ribbons and pins, rubber bands and clips, some scattered pieces of an old watch and loose chain links, crayons and broken pencils,

17

and stones collected during some holiday, mixed with crushed shells and pencil shavings. My desk was waiting for the clean-up I had kept on postponing. My childhood treasures, pieces of coloured glass, full of magic: you put them to your eye and the whole world changed . . . red, amber. Stamps waiting to be put in the album. Favourite nibs and useless, dissected fountain pens. They were all my things, never to be touched by strangers. I emptied the drawers and, loaded with masses of papers, went back to the kitchen.

Kazia sat on a stool, stiff and immobile; my mother's face was glowing and serious; Tania's head was bowed.

It was my turn. I watched the fire curling the pages up — the letters were still visible and distinguishable — until the yellow flames shot up, changing to red and white and black. I looked until my eyes hurt, and when I turned my face away I saw bright spots all around me, even with my eyes shut. And when the flames died I threw in another photograph; the familiar faces became distorted, bubbled, scorched, then burst into flames and disappeared.

Big shadows surrounded us. Our faces were red and hot in the glow of crazy flames. Black and grey ashes rustled in the grate.

'That damned cold's getting worse and worse', said Kazia and left the kitchen. The three of us stayed until the fire died. It became cold all of a sudden. Mother shivered. We sat silent and empty.

It was early morning: grey, misty and cold. The taxi ran through the empty streets. Good-bye Lodz; good-bye the landmarks of my childhood. Would I ever walk her streets again?

Mother, Tania and I sat in the back of the car, each lost in our own reflections. The taxi was loaded to the brim with our worldly possessions; cooking utensils were clattering at our legs — Kazia had put them in at the very last minute.

'You must take cooking pots. All you are good at is burning papers all night long. How will you cook? Take this and this and this.' She had kept on running up and down, bringing us little pieces which she considered would be useful.

We had parted with a hug and hand-waving, with a promise to keep in touch, with Kazia's blessing and few words.

Tania held our canary on her lap, the cage covered up. She made a little hole in the brown paper and informed us that Macius was all right. My neck felt cold and naked. I had cut my plaits only the day before, after hearing of incidents of women's hair being searched by customs officers. No-one was going to rummage through my hair.

'See the huts on the horizon?', asked the driver. 'That's the frontier.' We were driving through flat country. The fields covered by snow were bleak and empty. The sun was hidden by haze, the road in front of us straight and forbidding. The cottages were scattered unevenly with not a sign of life, all white, quiet and chilling.

'All that district was evacuated some weeks ago; too close to the frontier', our taxi driver informed us.

Winter: there was some unique beauty in its dismal melancholy. The trees kept hitting me at even intervals. They sat by the road naked and lonely, some branches covered by patches of snow, making the rest of the trees even more black and lifeless. The crows jumped in the fields, covering the snow with a birdish pattern. They flew away and their cawing seemed to magnify the gloomy emptiness.

How I loved to walk through the freshly fallen snow, leaving my caved-in footprints, experiencing the special joy of being the first one.

The taxi came to a stop.

'Here we are', said our driver.

The guards stood in front of the cottage, their faces hardly visible under scarves, their bodies distorted by their stuffed uniforms.

'Outside', came the command. We walked briskly, my neck felt freezing. I pulled my shoulders up. My mother tried to find the permit and there was panic in her eyes. Tania carried the cage. We were ushered into the hut, before men in greenish-blue uniforms.

'Your papers?'

It was warm inside and our Macius chirped.

'Business trip with a canary?', asked the customs officer, and winked. I wondered if he would have smiled if he had known that we were not Aryan, that the Nuremberg Laws had put us beyond acceptability.

We were on the road again. It had all gone so quickly and uneventfully. Why had I cut off my hair?

'Another hour and we will reach Warsaw.' Mother was all smiles. I put my hand in my muff and felt a cold object. I pulled it out — a silver salt dish. 'Look.' I showed it to mother and Tania.

'Kazia', we all said simultaneously, and laughed. The taxi driver stepped on the pedal, the car went quicker, there was no time to be sad. The trees, the cottages flicked past the car window. 'We are going to Warsaw, to my aunt and uncle. I'll see Irma again, I'll see some of my other friends; we have left Litzmannstadt and the German Reich behind', I kept repeating to myself.

Tania made a bigger hole in the brown paper. Macius was sitting on the floor of his cage, his wings outspread. 'Poor Macius, don't worry, we'll be home soon.' He turned his head to the side and jumped onto the perch. 'Good Macius!'

The scenery was changing: more farms and more activity. There were people drawing water from wells, their bodies and faces covered up, only their eyes visible.

Slivers of smoke were rising from the chimneys. The sun was trying hard to come through but somehow couldn't manage. I could hear dogs barking. My mother spoke to the driver, who was rather pleasant. Tania put her scarf around the cage.

There were people around; they stopped and waved to us. Little children's faces were plastered to the windows of the houses, their noses flattened. The windows were covered by frost, except for the children's framed faces.

'Go faster, driver, please go faster', I repeated to myself. I put my hand in my pocket and there it was — my father's clock key. I pulled the window down; the freezing air took my breath away.

'What are you doing?', Tania complained. 'Macius will catch a cold.'

'Shut the window, this very minute', commanded my mother. I let the key go and then pulled the window up. My hands felt numb and frozen; I put them around my neck. Why had I cut my hair? All that was left now was this bristled nakedness. I closed my eyes and rested my head on my mother's shoulder.

When the snow melted, someone may have found the key and wondered.

—— 3 ——

My uncle belonged to the Polish aristocracy. The estate of his forefathers was situated on the Polish-Russian border and, after the Russian Revolution of 1917, all the land which belonged to the Boyarski family was confiscated and several members of the family were killed.

My uncle found refuge in Warsaw and, because of his family name, received a high-ranking government position, where he worked until the beginning of the Second World War. He married my aunt a few years before the War. It was the second marriage for both of them; uncle was a widower, and aunt had left her first husband and a young daughter in order to marry Boyarski. They settled down in a small house at Zielonka, some sixteen kilometres east of Warsaw.

The contact between our families had been very limited. My aunt would visit us twice a year, and sometimes my mother went for a short visit to her, taking either Tania or me. With my father the relationship was rather cold. Uncle was a declared anti-semite, blaming the Russian Revolution on the Jews. He respected my father, however, pointing out his exceptional, un-Jewish characteristics. That special treatment wasn't fully accepted, so the families stayed apart.

The Boyarskis had no friends. They lived an isolated life, with my uncle despising the commoners around him, making people feel uneasy in his presence.

His house was set in a beautiful garden, made up of

English lawns, with trees and shrubs which, except during winter, were constantly in flower. All the plants were ornamental, some very exotic. The garden was landscaped with winding paths and stategically situated benches. The house itself was small but built like a citadel. It consisted of four rooms. One was a bedroom with walls covered by some old etchings and a family portrait of a very stern, haughty looking woman. A huge brass bed dominated the whole room. The second room was occupied by three parrots.

The green parrot from the Amazon had a squashed, square head and red circles around his yellow eyes. His wings were lined with scarlet. He called himself 'Coco' and cawed constantly. 'Terrible influence', my uncle would remark. Lolo, a pink and grey Australian Galah, would dance on her perch, swaying her body in every direction, stomping from one leg to another. All this was done to an old Polish patriotic song with a rhythmical tune and words full of pride.

> Never despair, God is watching over us,
> Never despair, our Motherland will be saved.

My uncle would sing and Lolo, 'the enchanted Princess', as he called her, stretched and shrank her body up and down.

Laura was a commoner. Boyarski had bought her from an organ-grinder one day because he couldn't stand the idea of a parrot spending its whole life picking up winning tickets for the stupid crowd. Alas, sometimes he regretted his hasty decision. Laura couldn't dance, she was just plain green, and the language she used wasn't suited for Coco's and Lolo's sensitive ears. Laura's cage stood apart from the others. Uncle treated her the same as her companions, or so he said. I don't think that Laura believed him.

The fourth small cage belonged to a canary whose name was Hippolit. He sang all day long, interrupted

23

from time to time by Laura's rude, 'Shut up, you bastard'. He would stop and sit still, a subdued fluffy ball.

The largest room was a combined lounge and dining room. It was a severe room, with a bare table in the centre and eight chairs standing against the walls (never touching them) at carefully spaced intervals. Once more there were small etchings on the wall. There was also a standing lamp without a switch, the kind you had to screw the globe into or out of, to turn it on or off. To complete the decor and to add even more to its stoic bareness, a dull-coloured Gobelin hung over the settee, with two crossed swords secured to it.

I often wondered, but never dared to ask, how my uncle had managed to bring the swords with him; although the etchings, the Gobelin, and the family portrait never worried me. I believed that he would have been quite capable of carrying them in his hands all the way to Warsaw when he ran from his estate. He was a tall quixotic figure, proud and forlorn.

A corner of the living room belonged to Shelminka [little rascal], a wire-haired terrier with a family tree probably as long as her owner's. Her name suited her; she was full of life and mischief. Three times a day she was fed a mixture of porridge, vegetables and meat. Her meals were served on a special mat, changed daily, and she wouldn't eat unless my aunt went on all fours, pushing the plate to and fro, pretending to threaten her: 'Give it back to me, I will eat it. Give it back'. Only then would Shelminka kindly oblige everybody and eat. She was never allowed to leave Boyarski's garden, and led a very virtuous life. No dog ever managed to jump over the high fences and hedges, though Shelminka tried to provoke them many a time.

'Slut', my uncle would thunder, ordering her inside where she would sit in her corner whimpering, turning her head to one side until my uncle's heart overflowed with compassion and she was forgiven.

The kitchen was sterile and clean; it was run by Stasia, who was an important part of it. She was the last and the least regarded member of the household.

On our arrival Stasia kissed our hands, carried the luggage inside single handed, and then disappeared. Seeing our embarrassment, my uncle reacted with an explanation that a servant must be treated as such; otherwise she would lose all respect for her masters. 'Don't put any stupid ideas into her head. You will make her even more lazy than she already is', he said.

Stasia was ordered around all day long. All I ever heard from her was: 'Yes madam, thank you madam, yes sir'. She slept in a recess in the kitchen, with all her personal belongings stuck under her bed in a wooden chest. She was not allowed to use the interior toilet and had to use the one at the remote corner of the garden, even during the bitter Polish winter. Her strong peasant bottom wasn't good enough to occupy her master's toilet seat, but her strong peasant hands were good enough to clean it.

The whole house had a monastic quality. It was isolated and belonged to the past. The only touch of real life was the freshly cut flowers arranged in a unique way by my aunt Olga.

At the beginning of the War my uncle had made a statement: 'There is no War in my home. I don't wish to hear about it'. The statement was followed by a decision: 'I will not work for the Germans'. Boyarski's resources were limited, his principles unlimited.

My uncle's day was well organised. He would always get up at 7.30 a.m., shave, and wash. Breakfast was served at 8.30. The table was set in an elaborate way; even when there was very little to eat he still insisted on preserving 'the values', as he called them. My aunt's role was that of a stage director, organising life in her invisible, quiet way, telling us how to fit into their household without offending her husband.

We knew exactly what time to get up, what time to use the bathroom and toilet and, most important of all, what time to stand behind the chairs in the dining room, waiting for Boyarski to arrive. He would walk in precisely at 8.30, dressed in his smoking jacket. The greetings were brief: a kiss on the hand for the ladies, followed by a brushed touch of his firm lips on the girls' foreheads. Neither myself nor Tania dared say a word beyond a very polite 'Good morning, uncle'. We had to wait patiently until all the adults were seated; first my aunt, then my mother, followed by my uncle, my sister and, in the end, me. Leaving the table we were equally regimented, with me waiting, resigned, for all the others to leave the table before I was allowed to get up.

My uncle spent the rest of the morning with Coco, Lolo, Laura, and Hippolit. He would take them one by one from their cages, making them walk and fly, talking to them; then he would feed them on apples and biscuits especially sent from Warsaw, disregarding my aunt's weak protests.

'These poor enchanted birds didn't start this wretched war and shouldn't be denied the things they need', he used to say, kissing and stroking Coco's shining feathers.

Our Macius was excluded from their company. Apparently he had learned certain bad singing habits from common sparrows. But Coco and Lolo were strong enough to resist Laura's bad influence because one had to remember, parrots had a superior intelligence. My uncle dreaded the possibility that Hippolit could lower his standards by associating with our Macius.

In the afternoon uncle would disappear into his bedroom. Later, at tea-time, he would emerge in all his splendour: clean-shaven, with a white shirt, tie, dark suit and shining shoes. Somehow, at tea-time he was more approachable and really charming, telling us anecdotes, recalling interesting events in his life, but never,

never referring to the present.

I thought that he felt better when dressed properly.

Aunt Olga told us the secret. Uncle had three suits: one for evening meals, one for Christmas and Easter, and one untouched to be buried in. 'That is why he wears a smoking jacket all day long. Please don't ever ask him about it.' The stage manager guided her stage hands to protect the hero from embarrassment.

In the evenings we all sat at the table with my uncle reading from medieval books, explaining to us the beauty of 'ye olde' Polish language and its historic background, with his eyes shining and his voice reserved but showing definite signs of excitement. As for the women-folk . . . Our heads bent down, our fingers busy, we were preoccupied with sorting seeds for the bird-folk. Who knew, one might find a glass splinter or some dirt. The seeds were not what they used to be, so one had to look through them carefully to prevent the ever-so-trustful birds from feeling any indisposition or unnecessary suffering. Prevention was better than cure.

All we ever found were mice droppings. Uncle kept them in a matchbox and from time to time showed us the collection to make us more eager and thorough.

Outside, life was going on with tangible fears and problems. We lived in hibernation.

'The gallant knight is fighting a duel to defend the honour of his beloved maiden', my uncle's voice informed us. Shelminka was asleep, her feet running; dreaming of what? The bird cages were covered up for the night. Stasia invisibly served cups of tea. There were more bird seeds to be sorted out.

There was no war at Boyarski's hermitage.

I wanted to join Macius, my very own lovely birdie.

My mother was in love and I didn't like it. Neither did

Irma. I could tell by the way she looked at her father. Mrs. Kohn shifted her eyes from my mother to her husband, then dropped her head and concentrated on her broken nails, touching them one by one with her chafed fingers.

My mother's hands were soft, her fingernails long, her eyes responsive, her laughter full of life.

We were sitting around the table while Mrs. Kohn's mother served tea and, unaware of the whole situation, complimented my mother on her looks.

The ersatz tea was good and Mrs. Kohn offered us a recipe for a cake without any sugar or eggs.

'I don't think it's needed', smiled my mother, swaying her hair in a semicircle. 'Soon the French will start the offensive, the War will end, and there will be plenty of eggs and sugar. I would never learn how to cook anyway; Kazia does it so much better.' Her voice was different, her manners were different. Mr. Kohn looked at her all the time. I felt ashamed.

'Shall we go?', I asked Irma.

'Sure.'

The Kohn family had also landed near Boyarski's place, at Wolomin. Wolomin was a small settlement, with just a few shops and houses. The population was poor: low-grade public servants, railway workers, labourers. I was glad to be close to Irma; she was teaching me. We knitted together, walked together. Her family lived in a house on a hill. The small white box had two torn, weather-worn pine trees at one side.

'An ideal place for a poet', Irma said one day; so we tried. We sat under the trees waiting for inspiration. It was very still; only the branches swayed. There was sky and there were clouds. We were loaded with emotions but our pages remained blank. In the end Irma got up. 'Nothing', she said, more mockingly than regretfully.

'Before long', said Irma, 'we'll move to Warsaw. It

should be easier. The large city has more to offer but I'll miss our walks and the fields. I'll miss our pines.'

We made an arrangement for the next day. My mother and Mr. Kohn went to Warsaw to find accommodation for both families.

Irma and I started on our way in the early afternoon. The road to the station led through the township itself. We passed narrow, cobbled streets where the houses were small and the shops plain. People hurried, horse-carts moved along. An old couple sat in front of their house staring at the one spot, maybe day-dreaming of the good old days.

Only a few Germans were around, marching in pairs. 'Fraulein', one called after us, somehow uncertain.

Jewish people were wearing arm-bands, white with a blue Star of David. A child was in a pusher, already branded. The arm-band covered almost his whole arm, for the entire civilised world to see. The child was not concerned. He said something and found approval in his mother's eyes. They laughed, both of them, he openly, she with a dose of restraint, even fright. 'My treasure', she called him. Or was it only my imagination?

The air was still chilly but spring was visibly approaching. The branches of trees were pregnant with bursting buds, and the birds were noisy and never still. The dogs were everywhere, sniffling, yelping, running, mating. I felt embarrassed. I looked at Irma; she smiled briefly and turned her head away. For us, the city-dwellers, it was a new experience. Perhaps our bodies, too, were susceptible to the birth of spring.

'Wonder how long before the train arrives?'

'So do I', was all we managed to say.

No-one was certain when the train from Warsaw would arrive. With priority given to the military transports, delays were common.

The Wolomin station was old and as weather-beaten as its station-master. The waiting room was crowded;

29

people squatted next to their bundles. The air was vile. Irma and I resigned ourselves to waiting. It seemed unreal that outside the spring air was so pure.

People were already getting up, securing bundles to their bodies, pushing, shouting, swearing, cursing, lining up on the platform. A few German gendarmes appeared from somewhere and the station-master hobbled around. The train rolled in, puffing and snarling. The people stood alert. Smugglers were determined to get their goods to Warsaw. The gendarmes led German Shepherds through the crowd. There was a mixture of voices and cries, and a barking of dogs.

'All aboard', shouted the station-master. The engine sent white steam hissing; the whistle shrieked. Above all, human voices were entangled and threatening.

Irma and I stood on the side, incapable of moving. People everywhere were getting on. Gendarmes dragged a young woman away.

'Jesus Christ, save me! All I have on me is bread, God be my witness', she lamented.

'You Polish dog, you'll never smuggle again', one said, and they pushed her roughly. At the same time one of them patted his dog.

I could see my mother. Mr. Kohn was trying to protect her, his arms around her.

'Where can they be?' Irma sounded puzzled.

'I don't know.'

My mother was crying and Mr. Kohn stroked her hair. They had eyes only for each other.

'We'd better be going', I proposed.

'Let's.' Irma stared at me. 'Oh, how I hate your mother', she added. 'Look at them.' She pointed.

They were in front of us, walking slowly, closely.

I shouldn't cry, I wouldn't. We walked in silence, only Irma kicked the stones, furiously, painfully. People passed us, carrying packages. Someone said, 'France'. 'Capitulation', said somebody else. A man walked jerkily from one side of the road to the other; his coat was unbuttoned, and he swung his hands, singing at the top of his voice: 'Poland won't perish as long as we're alive'.

'You stupid bastard, shut up. With that song you won't last long', a passer-by advised. 'Go home and never sing in public places.'

'What a drunken idiot.' Irma aimed at a stone and missed. She kicked the ground instead and the dust lifted up.

It was getting cold. The mist rose from the fields and drifted towards us. Irma walked quicker and I followed her. 'What a stupid idiot', she kept on saying. We took a short-cut and arrived at the Kohns' place.

'Where is your father?' asked Mrs. Kohn.

'I don't know'. Irma looked at me and I looked at her. 'There was a big crowd; we couldn't see much.'

'There was a raid on smugglers. They took one woman from the station.'

Mrs. Kohn looked at us. 'Poor soul. Without the smugglers all of us would starve, so we should be thankful to them . . . Where could they be? I only hope they are all right . . . As you know, no-one can live on German rations', Mrs. Kohn explained. At the same time she set the table, efficiently, mechanically, watching the entrance door.

'I think I had better go.'

'Wait till your mother arrives', suggested Mrs. Kohn. 'They shouldn't be much longer.'

'I'd better be going', I repeated. Irma took me to the gate.

'Thanks for backing me', she said.

'That's all right', I said.

'You're O.K, but I really hate your mother.'

'What about your father? Oh, it's pointless anyway. See you.' I ran away revenging myself on all the loose stones on the way home.

My mother was home; she sat at the table. Mr. Kohn

stood next to her, comforting her. Aunt Olga moved around silently while uncle thundered.

'I told you not to bring me any outside news. We can't help the course of events, anyway. So what difference does it make if France has capitulated or not?'

So France had capitulated. That was what people were talking about at the station. Mother cried. France had been our only hope. How could we keep on living without it?

'France has capitulated?' I had to know.

My mother looked at me, her eyes red, her hair disordered. She nodded her head, and Mr. Kohn put his arms around her again and said something I didn't want to hear.

'We went to the station to meet you.' I addressed Mr. Kohn.

'Oh, we didn't see you.'

'We saw you.'

'Oh.'

'Irma is back home. They are worried about you. I think you had better go.'

'Yes, of course. I will be going.' He kissed my mother on her head and then kissed me on my forehead. 'Look after your mother. She is very upset.'

I wanted to say: 'And so is your wife. Your wife is upset, your daughter is upset, I'm upset'. But I said nothing.

France had capitulated, people were being arrested, people were being branded. The War would go on and we would need the recipe for a cake without sugar or eggs. German troops were marching through Paris, 'the City of Enlightenment', as my father once called it. Our whole world was tumbling and my mother sat at the table and cried — either because France had capitulated or, more likely, because she was in love . . . with Mr. Kohn, my father's friend. Mother got up from the table and went to bed without eating.

While we ate, uncle remembered some holidays of long ago. He was annoyed by our passive response. The evening dragged on. I went to bed when I realised that Mr. Kohn wouldn't come back. Mother was asleep and Tania read. The carbide lamp threw a cold, bright light.

'Where have you been all day? What did you do?', asked Tania.

'Leave me alone. I am tired.' I shut my eyes and turned towards the wall.

—— 4 ——

We moved to Warsaw where my mother rented a furnished room from a Mrs. Stein.

The Boyarskis had opposed our plan, pointing out how irrational it was to go and live in the Jewish quarter. Uncle had jumped on his hobby horse, accusing my mother of being stubborn beyond reason, of ruining her life, firstly by marrying a Jew, then by not breaking away from the Jewish people.

But for us the decision hadn't seemed irrational. What the Boyarskis wouldn't understand was that the prospect of staying in Wolomin without the Kohns was less than attractive to us. We had wanted to be with our own people; we couldn't relate to the Boyarskis as we did to our friends and my father's relatives. Mother must have felt the same; the final decision was in her hands, after all.

Aunt Olga had cried when we left. 'What are you doing? People are talking about a closed Ghetto. The Jews are doomed. Don't go.'

It was true that the Jewish sector was surrounded by walls; they were tall, grey and guarded at the top by broken glass or barbed wire. There were small openings at the bottom which allowed rainwater to run through. The walls were everywhere, cutting the streets into sections, forming a city within a city. We were learning to live with them, in the same way as we had accepted the presence of the huge posters declaring the Jewish quarter a 'danger area infected with typhoid fever'.

Unfortunately, this didn't prevent the Germans from entering and looting.

There were new decrees being pasted all over the city daily. There were so many that they couldn't be taken very seriously; rather, one had to learn to live in spite of them. The death penalty was mentioned in all of them: for trading, for buying, for teaching, for learning, for having more money than allowed, for not stopping in front of the uniform, for not taking one's hat off, for running a business, for mingling with Aryans, for not wearing arm-bands — just to mention a few.

The weekly food ration consisted of 14 ounces of bread, 4½ ounces of meat, 1¾ ounces of sugar and 1 ounce of fats. It was hardly enough for one meal. So we were left with a choice: either to obey the law and starve to death, or to break the law, buy the food on the black market and risk the death penalty.

There was always an alternative.

By the end of October 1940 all Jews were forced to move into a prescribed area and all Poles had to move out. Sentries were posted at strategic places and the closed Ghetto became a reality.

From our window I could see the Aryan side. It looked normal — people and traffic, I mean. Hardly anyone ever looked in our direction. Our room was not bad: there was even a tree in front of our house with rickety, bending branches. It was naked now, ready for the winter, half dormant. We were lucky to have one; a tree was a rarity within the Ghetto walls.

Autumn brought rain; quiet, dribbling rain which made everything look grey and slowed down. I looked at the world through tear-stained window panes.

We put some crumbs on the window sill. The rain made them soggy and washed them away. Our birds wouldn't come that day.

Mrs. Stein was my mother's age. Her husband, a Polish officer, was now a prisoner -of-war. He sent home letters from the Oflag; brief, uniform letters which made her silent.

Mrs. Stein lived with her mother-in-law, who was all grey and pink. Every evening the old lady got excited. She prepared the meal in the kitchen, complaining of a lack of necessary ingredients for the preparation of a proper meal, because she was sure, 'Yes, quite sure', that her son would come home that very night. She would set the table for three and refuse to eat. Mrs. Stein fed her with a spoon and recalled happy incidents from their past. We hardly saw Mrs. Stein senior from one evening to another.

Apart from us there was another tenant. Mrs. Stein called him Kuba. He was full of fears, lonely and uncommunicative. His tie was always spotty and his collar curled up. Mrs. Stein cleaned his room and brought his provisions upstairs. He prepared his meals in the kitchen and urged Mrs. Stein to place her mother-in-law in a mental institution.

'How could I?', she said. I could see that she was rather annoyed. 'How could you suggest such a thing? You know what is done to sick people.'

Later I questioned my mother, but she refused to answer. She went to the window and folded her arms.

'I have great respect for our landlady', she said. She pressed her forehead against the window pane.

Because my mother had never learned how to cook, Tania volunteered to be in charge of our household. She was a health fanatic, a strong believer in vitamins. Our meals were half cooked, and, after ten days of experimenting, she went down with severe gastro-enteritis. The doctor prescribed a diet of grated apples, boiled chicken and broth. He must have come from another world, or else he had been hibernating since the beginning of the War.

My mother disappeared for several hours and came back empty handed, crying. Someone had snatched her precious morsels of chicken. Mrs. Stein came to the rescue and brought a plate of something. Tania moaned, then drank the grey fluid while my mother apologised.

It was time for me to go to my lesson. Our pre-war teachers had organised an illegal school. We had to be very careful, because teaching was punishable by death. So we met every day at a different place, coming in one by one, the books hidden under our coats, watching to make sure we were not followed.

Our teachers' room was crowded with furniture and had one small window. Their eighteen-month-old son played silently with his blocks as if he knew not to disturb us.

Irma, Bronka and two more of my school friends sat at the small, wobbly table, with a naked globe hanging over our heads. Every time someone got up the globe started to sway, shifting the circle of light away from us.

The voices of other tenants were always present, invading our sacred hour of learning. But we were used to it by then. We were there for one reason: to learn, to forget for a moment about the outside world. How good it was to see the orderly regimentation of grammar, even if it was Latin, and the logical conclusions of the sciences.

It was still raining when we left, and we made an arrangement to meet at Irma's in a couple of hours.

The streets were always crowded. People were pushing, hurrying, gesticulating — a nervous crowd. There was a lingering, acrid odour of wet clothes and poverty; a persistent, penetrating odour, always there, a part of our reality.

The street vendors, the epitomes of misery, carried in their hands goods for sale. And what goods! A pair of darned gloves, a dented cooking pot, a bent spoon. The 'professional' ones offered pumpkin seeds and flat onion rolls, shielding them from the rain. They whined and called out, hoping for someone to stop and buy. The streets were lined by half-dead kids who sat on the slushy pavements and stretched out their lifeless arms. My eyes scanned them, not really seeing, not wanting to see, afraid to feel.

The Ghetto covered one and a half square miles. With the exception of the houses bordering the Aryan side, it was the poorest district of Warsaw. There were no parks, no squares, hardly any trees. The majority of houses were built around well-like courts with windows facing each other, as if the builder had paid no regard to people's craving for privacy.

The orthodox Jews plodded along. They were dressed in traditional long caftans, had their heads always covered and hardly knew the Polish language. They carried in their eyes the fear of pogroms and in their minds the endless memories of organised persecution. They seemed to step directly from the Middle Ages, not belonging to the time of *Blitzkrieg* and constant changes.

The Ghetto was their original territory. They had lived there all their lives; small shopkeepers, tradesmen, devoting every spare moment to the study of the Torah. Passive and resigned, accepting every misfortune as God's will, they waited patiently for the Messiah to come.

All of a sudden their streets were invaded not only by the Germans but also by assimilated Jews, even Jewish converts. They didn't like that intrusion.

Many times they made me feel uneasy. They looked at me from the pedestal of their almost mystical, ancient wisdom, half mocking, half pitying. Our presence confirmed them in their belief. What good was it to change, to masquerade in other people's clothes, to run away from your own God? The time came, over and over again, when someone pointed a finger at you and blamed you for all the misfortunes of mankind and the world just for one single reason — your Jewishness.

38

They knew.

I thought about my lesson and let the rain fall straight on my face. A poem we had just read compared the limitations of Nature with the unlimited horizons of the human mind. Rivers and seas were confined to their banks, mountains were restricted in height; but the human mind could break all barriers and, through tears, longing and pain, look into infinity, holding some illogical belief in its capacity to conquer the world.

'Miss, I haven't eaten for three days. You have a good heart, Miss. I'll ask God for you to survive. Give something to a poor sinner. I left my mother and five sisters at home. All sick and hungry . . .' The young boy held on to my coat, pulling at my sleeve. And he talked incessantly, his eyes feverish, pleading and jumpy.

What could I do? I didn't have any money. I looked at him again and tried to free my hand from his amazingly strong hold. I felt pity and revulsion at the same time. I pulled my hand free and pushed my way through the crowd.

'God will punish you, you selfish bitch', I heard my brother screaming at me. Nobody even looked in my direction.

The rain came in handy. I could cry in the rain without apologising.

I stopped at Irma's place. Mrs. Kohn was knitting as on any other day, but her needles moved faster than usual.

'Where is Irma?', I asked. 'We made an arrangement to meet here.' Mrs. Kohn stayed very still, not even lifting her eyes from the work.

'They are all out. You had better go.' I couldn't understand. Why should I go? We were to meet there. I felt all cold and small.

'What has happened, Mrs. Kohn? You can tell me. What is it?' I pressed her.

Mrs. Kohn's needles moved faster, clicking unevenly.

'The girls were picked up by an army car. I pray they

will return home unharmed. Go, please go. You've just missed them by ten minutes.'

Back in the street, it was raining as before. I choked with unspoken words. For a moment I walked automatically, incapable or afraid of thinking, fearing to return home, dreaming of privacy.

I entered our staircase, to the persistent stench of cabbage and rotten potatoes. A young couple were kissing on the landing. They came apart upon hearing my footsteps. 'Hello.' Loud voices came from the flat next to ours. Why did they always quarrel?

I took the arm-band off when I entered our flat. Mrs. Stein senior invited me to see how nicely she had set the table, and informed me that, 'Tonight, for sure', her son was coming home.

Irma and the girls were back home!

The same army car which took them away delivered them back, after three hours' absence. I didn't know any details, but the main thing was, my friends were safe at home.

Mr. Kohn had come early in the morning to tell us the good news. He had changed tremendously. It was strange that I hadn't noticed it before. The collar of his shirt was gathered by a tie, emphasising even more the scrawniness of his neck. His eyes were bigger now, and he watched my mother as a man would when suddenly stopped by a German.

He arrived just in time for a morning performance by our neighbours. Our Prima Donna, as we called her, would invariably deliver her arias in a very strong contralto. There was almost no variation in the libretto and the musical score. The voices rose in crescendo, mixed together, and one had to listen attentively in order to distinguish who was who.

'Lazy; like father, like son.' Prima Donna took the lead.

'And what did you ever do?', cut in a timid tenor.

'Eat, eat, eat', trilled the female.

This was followed by a moving duet, entitled 'Grumble, nag', sung superbly by the daring males. Our diva's lyrical voice reached its utmost height in a beautifully delivered aria: 'Don't eat so much; earn more money instead'.

And then their voices blended, not so much in harmony as in a discord, which undoubtedly was the most significant strength of the whole performance. The curtain fell. We heard a loud banging of doors being shut and the shuffling echo of the male performers leaving the stage.

I couldn't take them seriously any more. That woman didn't know how to speak; she always screamed. The husband and the son were very much alike. Dressed in the same slovenly manner, they seemed ageless. They never looked at you; they just went past, stooped, with their heads pulled in. They dragged their feet as if every step was an effort.

Mrs. Stein told us that they were employed by the German-appointed Jewish Council in work gangs, cleaning the roads or whatever was demanded by the authorities.

She tried to justify their behaviour: hunger plus hard work, plus lack of security, plus lack of privacy brought out the worst in everyone. War seemed to be the excuse for the most inexcusable conduct.

It was hard to come to terms with it. The woman was a terror, plain and dirty, her hair hurly-burly, her nails framed in black. Her eternal grey skirt carried samples of all the meals they had ever had. The hem was always undone and in places touched her crooked, shapeless home-made clogs. The resonance of her steps drove everyone crazy.

Whenever she met Tania she smiled at her, if you could call it a smile.

41

'Why don't you come to visit us one evening?' Her hair was in her mouth as she spoke. 'You're a nice young lady.' Her teeth were matt-yellow. 'My Harry is such a good boy.' She scratched her hair. 'Come. I'll make some potato cakes, especially for you. You can bring your sister with you.' Her eyes rested on me as if I wasn't there. 'Young people should meet. Harry went to high school too . . . You should've seen me before the War!' Her hands were busy now, pulling her skirt up, touching her hair and ending on her flattened breast, nails hidden.

Tania managed to find some idiotic excuse. The whole situation was hilarious. I asked Tania how her fiance Harry was and, because she reacted in a violent way, I kept on pestering her.

'Don't you have anything else to do but pick on each other all day long?' It was mother's turn to deliver her favourite lines. 'Why don't you go for a walk? You look pale, both of you. The fresh air will do you a lot of good. It's not a bad kind of a day.'

I looked at Mr. Kohn. He should have clapped his hands and shouted with admiration, 'Bravo, bravo! What a performance!' But he sat still and watched our birds fighting over a few miserable crumbs.

I rushed forward and knocked at our window pane. A moment of confusion: the birds flapped their wings, chirped, hung in the air for a short moment, and returned to the window sill, wings spread out, agitated. I tapped at the glass again. They fought over a few remaining crumbs and flew over the wall to the Aryan side. I was sure they wanted to finish their meal in peace.

'Don't frighten them! They will never come back.' Tania was almost in hysterics. She put her coat on.

'Don't forget the arm-band, and give my best to your future mother-in-law', I said, and immediately felt uncomfortable. I never planned to be bitchy; it just happened. I felt sorry when Tania left the room crying.

42

My mother covered her ears, her eyes shut. 'I can't stand it', she said.

I really felt dreadful.

'Why don't you go out?' Mr. Kohn offered a solution. I looked at them both. This was exactly what they would have liked: to be left alone, to say things they wouldn't in my presence, to do things that my presence prevented them from doing. I saw them as strangers. I even felt sorry for them.

I, too, would have liked to have been left alone from time to time. If I had been a bird and could have flown away to some remote place, I was sure I would have been much happier. But I couldn't. There were no magic wings that I could attach; there was no place of seclusion for me.

'I don't want to go out. I'm going to stay home. I want to keep you company.'

'Do as you wish.' Mother was disappointed in me.

It served her right.

I didn't really know what to do with myself. I picked up a book of poetry.

> I beseech you
> Let the living hold to their trust
> And raise to the Nation the torch of enlightenment
>
> But if commanded
> Let them go to their death one by one
> Like stones thrown by God on the ramparts.

A poem with a message — that was all I needed. I shut the book. Those two kept on whispering. They built an impenetrable wall by turning their backs on me.

Our room had elaborate wallpaper, torn in places, showing finger-marks and greasy spots everywhere. The bulging, monstrous shape of our clothes wrapped up in a white sheet was stuck to the wall like a fungus. On the darkest of nights I could still see it and feared that someone might be hiding there. Our beds, pushed against the walls, two on one side, one on the other, left only a narrow plank of a passage between them.

Next to the window an iron stove occupied the place of honour. It was cylindrical in shape and sooty in appearance, zig-zagging its pipes through the empty space to end just above my bed. We treated it with gentleness and understanding but, because it was destined to share the room with three frustrated females, it had become temperamental too. From time to time it objected and started to fume and spit soot around. There was nothing we could do — even Mrs. Stein couldn't help. The only solution was to open the window and leave the room before we suffocated.

This was exactly what our iron genius wished.

Next to it was a small table covered by a table-cloth: our table-cloth from back home, packed with our luggage by Kazia. Somehow, she must have known that a glance at that piece of material would remind us of home and would mellow our moods.

Kazia, our Kazia. How was she? I missed her. I even missed my uncle Boyarski. I wondered if there was still no war at his place.

Aunt Olga wrote often, urging us to leave the Ghetto. Her letters brought confusion, because they offered an alternative. The news about labour camps and resettling filled us with fear.

Apart from aunt Olga, letters came from my paternal family. Uncle Vitek, aunt Inka and Marek, my nine-year-old cousin had all found themselves in Eastern Poland, then occupied by Russia. Aunt Inka's twenty-three-year-old brother Julek was staying with them. Marek was going to school and learning Russian and Ukrainian. He was making good progress.

I was glad they were not with us, although I missed them all very much. Marek's schooling would have been as crazy as mine and Vitek wouldn't have worked as a civil engineer as he did under the Russians. His professional work had been always very important to him. His work was his life, and I just wasn't able to imagine Vitek being idle.

From time to time they had sent us a food parcel. But not any more — we stopped them. The parcels had to be collected from the post office and then inspected in our presence. The clerks were always very thorough. The last time the clerk was more efficient than normal. He cut the sausage into minute pieces. Evidently he was concerned with our well-being. It was his duty as an officer to make sure there wasn't any concealed poison.

He scattered the sausage all over the counter and the floor, then swept it into the dust pan and placed it back in the box. He searched through the sugar, flour, salt and lard in a similar way. In the end he mixed it all up and handed the parcel to us. We had to pay an exorbitant amount of duty and were lucky to be allowed to leave. Once in the street we placed the box on the pavement. Before turning into the side-street I looked back. Our parcel was surrounded by five young children, with big bellies and cadaverous limbs, shaking with excitement, eating manna sent from Heaven.

Mr. Kohn and my mother were still whispering. I had almost forgotten them.

'Tell me about Irma, I have to know.' I threw the question. Mr. Kohn stuck two fingers inside his collar and turned his neck from side to side.

'Irma is home. She wanted to be left alone. I will give her a bit more time to herself and then I will go home.'

He told us the whole story. Then I knew.

Irma and four more of our friends had to carry coal from one side of the yard to the other, under the watchful eye of a young officer and his chums, to the tune of German military music, and jeering. Stripped naked.

Now the Kohns had to find other accommodation.

I went out and walked the streets for hours. But, before I left, I took with me my father's photograph. And we walked together. We absorbed all the misery and mystic vitality of our people.

45

5

I was killing my mother and there was nothing I could do about it.

'I'll go to Russia', I said.

'How? You must be out of your mind.' Tania paid me a compliment.

'Child, what are you talking about?' Mother's voice was as nervous as her fingers and as full of concern as her eyes. 'There is a frontier between us and Russia, a well guarded frontier with soldiers and guns, barbed wire, dogs and mines.' She came to a stop; she looked empty, with nothing else to say.

'We are experts in crossing borders, mother. Have you forgotten the barbed wire between the Ghetto and the rest of Warsaw, as well as the soldiers with guns and dogs? We've always managed somehow.'

We were living in Warsaw by then. We had left the Ghetto in early 1941. Aunt Olga had bombarded us with letters, prepared a flat and arranged some papers which allowed us to register with the authorities as Russian Orthodox.

The situation in the Ghetto had been deteriorating from day to day and, thanks to aunt Olga, we had somewhere else to go; however, our decision, once reached, left me with a most uncomfortable feeling. I hated the Ghetto in the same way that I would have hated staying in a sick room watching someone very close suffer, but mostly I hated myself for leaving the place. Rats always leave a sinking ship.

46

There had been a lot of talk and advice from our friends and relatives. Illogically, people believed that the War couldn't possibly last much longer. We had sunk to the lowest depths of degradation and misery; the situation had to improve. One day, 'Next spring', the War would end, and our duty was to withstand it all and stay alive, if for no other reason than that the Germans wanted us all dead.

'Hitler wants to destroy us, right?' My father's uncle Miron put pressure on us. 'We can't fight him, but we have our spirit. We shouldn't oblige him and simply vanish. We have to stay alive; the War won't go on for ever. You have a chance to make it easier for yourselves; don't hesitate; go. Go and stay alive.' Good old uncle.

My father used to tease him: 'Who is wearing your clean shirts?', he would mock. Miron never took offence. He stayed with us all night after my father was killed, and he was always worried about his son who was somewhere in Eastern Poland. We promised to meet again as soon as the War ended, on the very first day.

The time for discussions was over: the words meant nothing because we kept on hiding what was really on our minds. Shortly after, we left the Ghetto and moved to the Aryan side.

I carried on a lot about my total separation from Irma and other friends; they couldn't even write to me. Of course, a letter from the Ghetto would have unmasked our identity immediately, for we lived in times when contact with Jews was considered a capital crime.

I was disheartened, and then a Mr. Stokowski came to us with letters from the Kohns and Irma. He introduced himself in flawless Polish as a Rumanian Jew whose mother was smart enough to give birth to her only son while holidaying in Rumania. Because of that accident, he, his wife and their two little sons were allowed by the Germans to stay outside the Ghetto and were treated in the same privileged way as all other friendly aliens. They were given choice accommodation, the best food-ration coupons and complete freedom of movement. Letters from the Ghetto didn't bother Mr. Stokowski: the authorities knew he was Jewish and, besides, his wife was corresponding with her parents who lived behind the Ghetto walls.

'She writes to them daily. What can I do?', he said.

We thanked him a million times. I was so grateful, I nearly kissed him. How lucky we were that Mr. Kohn had established this contact for us. The irony of the whole situation was that our 'Rumanian' didn't know his 'native' language at all.

Mr. Stokowski was a man with the face and body of a clown; he looked like a second-rate comic who had been suddenly forced to take part in a tragedy.

He loved good food and his little sons, and constantly squabbled with his wife. She was his intellectual superior, but could never appreciate his culinary talents and his unique ability to present a nicely arranged dish of salt herring without a single bone.

He visited us often, bringing us letters, but mainly using the visits to complain about his wife.

'All my wife wants is to bring out her parents from the Ghetto. She should demand to go to the French Riviera instead. See, I am frightened. If the Germans start digging into my papers we are finished. Listen, Lydia Petrovna', he addressed my mother, 'I prepared a beautiful egg-plant dish today. You might have thought she would appreciate it? No such luck. I chopped the onion really fine, didn't help. She just ignored it. What shall I do?'

'Things will work themselves out.' My mother looked amused. Mr. Stokowski brought us letters from the Ghetto, and German chocolates.

'I want to go to Russia.' I fired another shot at my mother.

'So do I, so do others.' Mr. Stokowski's voice was full of amazement. 'How will you do it, tell me?'

I had been planning it all for some time and knew exactly how to go about it. I had thought of my plan before falling asleep and dreaming of freedom. I had planned it while walking alongside the Ghetto walls, not daring to look up at our window on the other side. I had planned it in the lift going up to our sixth-floor flat.

Many a time I would open the grille of the lift and stay suspended between the floors, looking into an old, spotty mirror and talking to myself. I would stay very still, stare at one point and evoke whomever I wished. 'Hello', I would say, 'remember me?' I spoke of our isolation, my pains and dreams. And they would listen without interrupting, without reproaching, patient and understanding. One blink of an eye and all would vanish.

My lift 'meetings' would usually end with heavy bangs, curses and shouts that someone had forgotten to close the grille properly again. I would press the button and travel to the nearest floor, never to ours, to cover the traces of my secret meetings.

I explained to my mother my plan, step by step. I pictured for her the train journey to the Russian border, followed by a search for a friendly peasant who undoubtedly would know the movements of the German guards. Crossing the border wouldn't be too difficult if one were careful enough. The main thing would be the choice of the right moment — a dark moonless night, or maybe a cold, rainy night with a strong wind which would muffle my steps. All there would be left to do would be just to walk straight to a Russian post, explain the whole situation, offer my watch — not as a bribe but rather as a sign of appreciation — then board the train to Lvov and join uncle Vitek, aunt Inka, Marek . . .

'Before you would have a chance to say one word, you

49

would be raped by the entire Russian regiment.' My mother moaned and almost cried. Mr. Stokowski declared that I was foolish beyond all reason. 'She is killing me.' My mother wiped her eyes.

I didn't want to kill her but I wanted to be free. It made me sick to see German decrees plastered all over the streets proclaiming the death penalty for hiding and assisting Jews. We constantly heard of people being denounced to the Gestapo. I hated the streets without one single friendly face. 'Russia is different; people are all equal there; I want to live among them', I said.

'If you think that equality exists in Russia you are heading for another disaster. Millions of people are imprisoned in labour camps there', mother answered.

'I don't believe it. And if they are, there must be a good reason for it. Not just because they are Jewish.'

The Boyarskis had hardly any money left. To ease the situation they dismissed their servant, Stasia, and aunt Olga found herself a job as a cashier in a coffee house in Warsaw. She commuted between Zielonka and Warsaw every day. Apparently, uncle never queried her daily departures as long as his enchanted birds had their biscuits and fruit. Sometimes aunt Olga would stay with us overnight. She did it either to give herself a bit of a break, or to point out to me my lack of consideration and my selfishness, especially as it affected my mother.

Beata, her nine-year-old daughter from her previous marriage, had been placed in a convent boarding school by her father. On Beata's name day aunt Olga took me along to deliver a present for her daughter: it was a doll dressed as a schoolgirl. Aunt Olga had made the clothes herself. I was looking forward to seeing Beata again. My little cousin: I was sorry for her; and I was sorry for aunt Olga; they should have been together. I knew little of the whole situation, only that Beata's father was impossible' to live with. He had fought for Beata to hurt aunt Olga, so I was told.

The walls of the convent were high, and inside it was quiet. Under huge trees early spring flowers bent down; I would have loved to see them a few days later standing erect. Our steps were noiseless. The trees were full of buds; I craved to see them burst open. It was a different world. Hush. Two nuns stood among the trees, their white-winged head-dresses swaying like branches of the trees, like our steps, like flowers. It was the closest to God I had ever felt. Serenity. Maybe, I thought, I should stay there, leave my Russian dream, walk in secluded gardens and be kind.

I absorbed the stillness and remembered a lesson delivered by our science teacher about the symbiotic association between plants and microbes; what about plants and humans?

The building was old; twigs of some kind of vine embraced it in a protective gesture. We entered the hall, which was tall and dark, and saw a nun, whose smiling face was mounted between a stiff collar and hoisted sails.

'May I help you?' It was a kind voice; it was a kind place. The nun listened to my aunt's subdued voice, got up and disappeared behind the doors; a black, fleshless figure.

Apart from the desk and two chairs there was a willowy statue of Holy Mary holding in her arms a minute Baby Jesus. Someone had left a bunch of flowers in front of it. Aunt Olga must have held Beata like this; my mother must have held me like this, and now I was killing her.

'What can I do for you?' Another nun stood in front of us, tall, with austere features.

'It is my daughter's name day today. I've brought her a present. May I see her, Sister, please — Beata?' Aunt Olga was nervous. There was no need to be, I was sure.

'No, you can't see your daughter, now or ever. Beata's

51

father told me all about you and your family. The Good Lord will protect that innocent child from you and your influences. It was you who broke the vows of the Holy Church. It was you who left the child, let me remind you.'

I clung to my aunt. I hoped she wouldn't cry. The statue of Holy Mary stood as before. The Mother looked on Her Child.

'Please, let me see Beata.' Aunt Olga's voice was quite steady. 'God in his mercy will forgive all my sins. Please.'

'You should have foreseen the consequences. There is nothing I can do. And who is that girl?' She pointed at me. Aunt Olga twisted the doll in her hands and I felt that she was still full of hope.

'It is my niece; her father was killed at the beginning of the War. She also would like to wish her cousin all the best.'

'Oh, *that* niece. Your rightful husband told me about your sister and her Jew. How dare you. How dare you bring the child of a Christ killer within our walls!' She turned her back on us in a judging, accusing way. 'If you won't leave now, you will force me to call the Gestapo and report your niece. You must be out of your mind, as Beata's father warned me, to bring the child of a Jew to our Holy sanctuary!'

'Let me leave the doll for Beata.' My aunt pleaded and cried, but the nun was gone. The young one led the way, not looking at us. She took us to the gate, through the garden, which was now barren and hostile.

'I'll tell Beata you called', she whispered.

'The present?'

She took the doll and hid it in her habit and then shut the heavy gate behind us.

The tram was overcrowded. No, aunt Olga would not stay in Warsaw that night; she was going back home; she had some titbits for the parrots.

I kissed her wet face and left the tram. People rushed

past; paper boys called out newspaper headlines. Street vendors sold fresh, illegal bread; its penetrating aroma made me feel hungry. I wanted to be home as quickly as possible.

'Hey you, your bloomers are showing', a paper boy called and laughed. My underpants were indeed sliding down; it must have been that damned elastic, ersatz rubber. I put my hands in my coat pocket and tried to catch my pants. It would happen just as I was crossing the junction, where there was nowhere to hide.

'You there, in the navy coat. You blonde one, want my help?'

'Grand dame with panties falling down', another one called.

I let my pants fall to the ground, picked them up and ran home. That day the tenants of our flats had to wait a long time for the lift.

After the incident with the nun I was more than ever determined to leave for Russia.

My political awareness didn't amount to much. I simply knew that fascism was all wrong. I had grown up in a home where politics was discussed. I remembered my father listening to Hitler's speeches and how much they would depress him. I used to sit in the same room feeling very small and, although I didn't understand German very well, the thundering delivery of Hitler's rhetoric used to fill my whole being with horror. The discussions which followed seeped into my mind. I was aware of the Nazis' principle of racial supremacy, of their contempt for any human being who didn't belong to the Germanic race. It was little wonder that I turned to the extreme alternative. Soviet Russia was an answer, a Union of Nations where people, as I believed, were free; where racial discrimination didn't exist.

My mother didn't see it my way. She would use the

fact of Russian labour camps as proof that freedom didn't exist in Russia. We quarrelled a lot. I felt that my mother consciously chose to sabotage my plans. She couldn't or didn't want to understand that my craving to go to Russia wasn't part of a premeditated plan to destroy her; rather, it was a determination to exchange the blind hatred of racial discrimination for freedom and equality.

I wasn't very popular.

My only ally was aunt Olga's friend Jadwiga. She came to us one day.

'Good morning', she greeted us. 'I have to leave a message for Olga.'

'Please do', my mother said, in her Mater Dolorosa voice. Jadwiga scribbled something, gave my mother the note, and smiled.

She was a tiny woman and her protruding chin reminded me of Toulouse-Lautrec's caricature of La Goulue's dancing partner. When I spoke to her, I addressed her chin; but when I discovered that she had two very warm and very blue eyes, her chin suddenly shrank and I stopped noticing it.

Jadwiga lived with her teenage son and her very old mother in a detached single-storey house. I never knew what had become of her husband, most probably because I was constantly bombarding her with my own problems.

'So you want to go to Russia?', she said. 'Now, let's look at the situation in a rational way.'

'Aunt Olga asked you to talk to me; you want to change my mind.'

'Yes, Olga did ask me to have a word with you. But, believe me, I don't want to change your mind. I know how you feel. I belong to the socialist movement myself and have always considered that young people can only be fulfilled by developing a social conscience. I, at least, try to understand.'

'So what's wrong with my plans?'

'Nothing, only the timing is wrong. It's too risky. You have only one life. Guard it.'

'Life is cheap.'

'To the Nazis, yes; not to us. You just feel sorry for yourself, that's your real problem.'

I listened to her. I didn't scream, I wasn't defiant, and gradually I learned to trust her.

She introduced me to a librarian who had somehow managed to hide books banned by the Germans. She opened a treasure chest for me. I read Remarque and Zweig, Ludwig and Roger Martin du Gard, Tolstoy and Wasserman, Kafka and Gorki. I looked for humanism and learned second-hand what it meant. My reading reassured me that sorting people according to their nationality or religion didn't make sense.

'The War will end', Jadwiga kept on saying, 'and sanity will triumph again.'

It's strange, Irma wrote to me, *but the sun and the warmer weather play a tremendous part in our disposition. Sometimes, all of a sudden, when I feel a wisp of spring around me, my thoughts turn towards nature. I think of the air full of sunshine, of summer, of heat and sluggishness, of bees and the colour of the sky. My only wish is that next year won't be any worse, and if my wish did come true things would get better because it's impossible for our situation to deteriorate even more.*

Jadwiga introduced me to two teachers who were willing to give me lessons. It was illegal, since the Germans allowed only trade schools to exist. But underground high schools, even universities, were very much alive both in the Ghetto and on the Aryan side. My mother was afraid, and it took Jadwiga's great persuasive powers to make her see how important it was for me to start learning again.

Spring came and I found, as Irma had, that the warmer weather made me feel better.

55

On the way home after my lesson, I came across a woman selling an abundance of field flowers. Lilly-of-the-Valley, picked somewhere around the forest, found its way into my hands. I breathed in again and again, then got frightened that there wouldn't be any more perfume left for my mother and Tania to inhale. On my return home we put the flowers in a glass and my mother dissolved a fraction of an aspirin into the water.

'They will keep longer', she explained. The white flowers, little and perfect, brought happiness into our home. Tania prepared some ersatz coffee, beat an egg-white, divided it carefully into three equal parts and mounted it on our coffee.

We sat, drank, inhaled and it was easy to talk; it was easy to make plans and think in terms of 'When the War ends . . .'

We have organised a puppet show for the kids from the depths of the Ghetto slums. It makes our life more worth living. One four-year old asked, 'What does it mean, a tree?'

The peaceful moments at our place were rare. I had little patience for Tania's preoccupation with herself, or for my mother's attitude, which treated the War as a temporary situation. For me, every passing day was only too real and irretrievable. Though the streets frightened me, very often I would leave home and walk for hours just to be left to myself.

I came back to life fully when Germany declared war on Russia. I wrote letters to Irma and all my friends in the Ghetto. 'It won't be long', I spread the good news. I was more than sure that the War would end within a few weeks, and in turn transmitted my enthusiasm to everyone around me. In reply Irma wrote:

Thanks for your letter which is so much in your vein. Your rosy account of current events, so full of optimism, frightened me. We have dreamed about it for so long, put our whole confidence in it and now if our hope collapses we will be left with

56

nothing. Nevertheless, I trust that in the end the righteous cause will be victorious and only wish it would eventuate before we turn into bitter, apathetic, lethargic, indifferent people.

By the way, my grandmother and Mrs. Stein senior were deported together with your Prima Donna. When her husband and son returned from work the pot of soup was still warm.

We miss their, what you used to call, 'daily performances'. It's dead quiet now. Nobody knows where they were sent to, but we fear for their safety.

I went out and once again wandered through the streets, not knowing where I was going. It was a clear summer's day. There were puffy white clouds and a deep blue sky above; the trees were rustling as if wanting to draw everybody's attention to their splendid crowns; and the crowd was colourful and very much alive. I walked; the church bells rang in the distance; it was getting warmer and my feet burned.

'Carrots, lovely crisp carrots.'

'Tomatoes, tomatoes! You can walk to the left, you can walk to the right. What will you achieve? Sore legs! Because you must return to me. You ask why? Because my tomatoes are the firmest, the sweetest and the cheapest in the whole German Province. Tomatoes, tomatoes, hurry, hurry. If you leave it too long all the best ones will be gone.'

The market. How did I get there? I wasn't sure. The market . . . and, next to it, the Ghetto wall.

I must have wanted to be closer to Irma.

I walked through valleys with mountains of fruits and vegetables on both sides. People bargained, touching and smelling whatever they wanted to buy.

We earn enough to cover three-quarters of our budget. To bridge the gap we have to use magic . . . As you know, there is no magic . . .

Next to the wall I came face to face with a tightly

packed crowd. People, with their necks outstretched, stood on tip-toe. Some faces were amused, some terrified; the majority were indifferent, unmoved. I heard the sounds of someone crying and someone hitting.

I pushed my way through.

'A Jewish smuggler got caught', someone whispered.

A Polish policeman, his back turned to me, was shaking something. A bag, I thought. It wasn't a bag. It was a boy with the wrinkled face of an old man and hardly any flesh.

He stood there, his eyes petrified, uttering spasmodic cries. And the policeman was shaking, hitting, shouting. Next to them, on the ground, were smuggled goods: a few potatoes, a few carrots and a half-loaf of bread — they must have fallen from the child's clothes.

'You dirty Jew. Developed a taste for smuggling, eh? I'll teach you!' And he gave him a lesson with his fist, and a kick and a thundering yell. Suddenly a German soldier pushed his way past me. The crowd moved a few steps back, just in case, ready to flee.

'What is this?' The German pointed to the potatoes and the policeman dropped the child and saluted. The little one seemed even smaller. His eyes were enormous and dark and looked in every direction, as if exploring whether there was any possibility of escape.

'You swine.' The German hit the policeman till he swayed and fell to the ground. He picked the boy up and helped him across the wall. Then, one by one, he threw those few potatoes and carrots and the bread over the wall too. Nobody moved; everyone was watching, and the policeman didn't dare to get up, but kept wiping the blood from the corner of his mouth. The German looked around, his eyes shining and angry; he moved swiftly towards the stalls, grabbed whatever was at hand, and sent it flying over the wall. He muttered something under his breath and left the scene before I even had time to think.

The policeman was back on his legs, brushing his navy-blue uniform. He waved us away and shook his white club in front of our faces.

'Disperse', he screamed. 'You think it's a circus, or what? I'll get the bastard, don't you worry. You can trust the police force!'

I went on my way home. A man was pasting an official announcement on a circular post. The odour of glue hit my nostrils; it reminded me of my early school days. The glue smelled sour and sweet. Kazia often used to be angry with me because I always managed to smear my uniform with it. How remote it all was, remote and irrelevant. The freshly pasted posters were covered with names. They announced that, because of an act of sabotage, the derailment of a transport train, the authorities were forced to take into custody the hundred hostages listed below. If the act was repeated, the hostages would be killed. It was so painful to see all those names. When I had left home, all I had wanted was to go for a walk, to mingle with an ordinary, normal crowd. But nothing was normal any more, the time of normality had vanished. I read the names one by one, faceless names. I felt for all those who would find the name of someone they knew.

My teacher had witnessed an execution. She told us how the Germans hadn't even bothered to keep it away from the civilian population. A huge military van had pulled up in the centre of Warsaw. The hostages had their heads covered with paper sacks. They stumbled when they were pushed against the brick wall; they must have been either drugged or gagged, not even one of them produced a sound. As soon as the prisoners were lined up, the black-uniformed Germans shot them. Then they ordered a few passers-by to load the bodies back into the van, and were gone. The whole operation took no more than a few minutes. There was nothing left of the people; only the brick wall bore the marks of bullets.

I was lucky never to have seen an execution but, like all

Warsaw people, I knew how to recognise the location of one: it was usually marked with a few flowers, left there by an unknown hand. What frightened me was the fact that we had learned to live with all these savage brutalities. We were all scarred. Like Irma, I was frightened that if we survived we wouldn't be able to relate to another human being any more.

When I was a child I had known how to react when I saw a kitten being attacked by a dog. I picked up a stick and chased the attacker away. My father had praised me. 'You are a brave girl', he had said.

—6—

My mother was sick. I couldn't accept it because I had
never seen a sickness like that before. She had no temperature, no cold, no pains. In the morning she didn't
want to get up; at breakfast time she didn't want to eat.
There must have been something radically wrong with
someone who didn't want to eat in the Warsaw of 1942.

Winter arrived early that year and somehow I took no
pleasure in it. The snow and the crisp, cold air went well
with full bellies, warm clothes and heated dwellings.

People rushed through the streets, all wrapped up,
with only their red noses sticking out. Long queues stood
in front of food stores. The sounds of church bells were
mixed constantly with the prolonged siren of Gestapo
vans. The monuments were stripped of statues. On the
base that once carried Copernicus someone had written:
'Because you took me away I declare an extension of
winter by seven weeks'. It was signed 'Copernicus'.

Fuel, electricity and gas were heavily rationed, so
people ran in the streets to keep warm. They seemed
crazy, waving their arms, clapping their hands. 'It's cold
enough for us', they winked at each other. 'Wonder how
it is on the Russian front?'

All furs had been confiscated from the Jewish population. The Third Reich army at the gate of Moscow was
waiting for the Russian winter to end; Jewish children's
rabbit bonnets were sitting on soldier's heads. The officer

giving a command was dressed up in Mrs. Kohn's persian lambskin, tight at the waist, flared at the bottom.

'How about it, mother?'

My mother was sick; she couldn't even smile. If it hadn't been for us she would have stayed in bed all day, unwashed. We combed her hair and she let us do it. She cried a lot; the tears ran down her face noiselessly. I dried her cheeks and her nose.

'We must have a doctor', we urged aunt Olga.

'It's nerves, it will go away. Be good to her. You will see, she will be better before long.'

My mother's depression had started when Mrs. Stokowski committed suicide. She arrived at our place early one morning along with her sons.

'My parents have been deported', she announced. 'Look after my boys for a couple of hours or so. I have to attend to a few things. You see my dear husband is shopping as usual. Take the boys over to our place. Forgive me . . .' And she left.

Mother didn't even have time to say how sorry she was and not to worry about the boys. We played with them, and then on the way home we came across Jewish children begging. It had become quite a common sight in Warsaw. Kids like these were always being driven out from behind the Ghetto boundaries by hunger and despair. They would sit on the pavements, wrapped in rags, supporting their limp bodies against walls. They waited passively for human compassion, risking their lives all the time — for there was no place for them in the new order of the Third Reich. They were doomed to die at any time at the hands of a Nazi stooge. Sometimes they would just die.

'Why do they sit in the snow? They will get all wet! Look! They are dirty like soot', the elder son of Mrs. Stokowski observed. My mother pushed something into the young beggar's hand. He didn't even move. 'My remorse-money', mother said, with great sorrow.

'What did you say?', pressed the elder boy.

'Never mind, we are almost at your place.'

I averted my eyes.

We had some difficulties with the lock. The boys were jumping on the landing.

'Mummy, our mummy.' They skipped in circles.

'Oh, you'd better shut up', I shouted, and was surprised that they stopped. My mother opened the door and shut it immediately. I caught a glimpse of feet dangling in the air.

'Take the boys to our place', my mother ordered me.

'I don't want to go to your place, it's awful. I want to see my mummy.'

'Mummy', the younger one joined in.

'Your mother is not home yet. I tell you what we will do. I will wait for her here and you go and show Irena the toy shop around the corner. See you all at our place.'

The boys, although reluctant, ran down the stairs.

'Be careful', I shouted, 'you'll hurt yourself, or something.' They took me to their favourite toy shop, and were mad at me because I didn't buy them anything.

'You are mean, really mean. My mummy and my daddy always buy us something, whatever we want.'

'Yes, they always buy . . .' echoed the younger one.

'Oh you, can't you ever keep quiet?' I didn't know how to handle the situation and they must have felt it.

'We will tell on you when mummy comes to pick us up. You are awful.'

'Yes, we will tell on you . . .'

What can one do with two brats whose mother has hanged herself? If she had been still alive, I would have murdered them, I was quite certain. The dangling feet were constantly on my mind and I couldn't shake off my sense of the agony that that woman must have gone through. So I played with those two brats, or rather they ran amok and turned our flat into a disaster area, while I shouted at them.

63

After hearing what had happened Tania decided to use our entire weekly ration of meat. She was right, too; the future had become an abstract concept. My head didn't feel my own. I wasn't even sure if I would be able to eat, although the aroma of cooking made my stomach feel almost hollow.

'Tonight we'll eat to bursting point.' Tania was determined.

Mr. Stokowski arrived at our place towards the evening and told the boys that their mother had gone to join her parents for a few days. The upper left corner of his lip twitched in an uncontrollable, funny way, although his face was dead serious and his voice was constantly breaking.

'Would you like to have something to eat?', my mother offered. Mr. Stokowski agreed; he sat at the table and ate.

'No harm in dieting from time to time.' He was absolutely serious. By the time he finished there was hardly anything left for us.

Diet indeed.

Mr. Stokowski hurried to reach home before curfew, his stomach packed tight with our meat and cabbage.

On the following day, after obtaining the authorities' permission, he buried his wife at the Jewish cemetery. One lonely mourner. In the evening he came to collect his sons, his arms full of shopping. He asked me to come to take care of the boys, starting on the following day, which I promised I would do. But when I arrived the door of their flat was sealed by a round stamp with a swastika in the middle.

The caretaker informed me that the rest of the Stokowski family had been arrested during the night.

'There was another Jewish foreigner living in our block. Got arrested at the same time. Pity the flats are sealed. Must be plenty of good things inside, plenty of food. It will all go to waste. Pity.' He gave me a letter which had arrived that very morning, from Irma.

'Take my advice; put an end to that letter writing. Might fall into the wrong hands, one can never tell', he said.

I have become a fatalist. Everyone must experience a certain degree of suffering. If my theory proves right the War will end very soon. There are more agonies going through every household than food. I have started work in a candle factory, unheated of course. You can ring me up if you want to risk it. My phone number is . . .

My mother cried for a long time. 'The children, what are they going to do with the children?', she kept on asking until I could have screamed.

We finished our meal from the previous day and I thought of Mr. Stokowski and how he had dieted the night before. I wondered if he had envied his wife at the moment of arrest. I was full of remorse regarding his little boys.

The brats also had the right to live.

That night I dreamed of the Gestapo knocking at our door and us jumping to the floor below. There were dangling feet wherever I looked. The Gestapo knocked again and I jumped to the lower floor once more, but this time on my own. I thought how good it was that mother and Tania stayed up there, because the knocking on the door was more urgent and noisy and I saw more and more feet dangling. There was a constant banging of fists on the door; the door was just about to give in. I tumbled to the lower flat and the forest of feet swung like a hundred pendulums. I tried not to look up, fearing I might recognise faces of people I knew.

I shut my eyes, I covered my ears, but it didn't help. The banging terrified me and with my eyes shut I saw Mr. Stokowski. He held a huge plate of steaming cabbage. 'It's good to diet from time to time', he was saying.

65

There was a long row of swaying bodies. They didn't frighten me at all; they just swayed. Then I recognised the face of uncle Vitek, then Marek's, Irma's and, in the end, the two little boys. I screamed and the boys laughed. 'Push us up a bit higher; our mummy always did.' I ran and stumbled, howled and jumped down, heavy steps right behind me.

I woke up all wet both with tears and perspiration.

It wasn't really a nightmare.

It was dark. I stood in front of the window. It was freezing cold; I shivered. I deliberately chose to prolong the physical discomfort. The streets were deserted; it snowed; and from time to time a car or a van went past, on the way to round up some enemies of the Third Reich. I heard dry, short shots, and the puffy quiet snow fell down, as it had before the War when I used to jump out of bed full of expectation, thinking 'It's going to be a super day for skating.' The snow was like it was before the War, but there was no joy in it. The people were shut in their dwellings, their bellies rumbling, their hands and legs frost-bitten, not thinking, not planning, just existing from day to day.

What a waste of dry snow.

My mother was sick and I didn't know what to do. Some distant relative of uncle Boyarski, a psychiatrist, visited us and talked with my mother.

'Her mind is very clear, very logical and very vulnerable. We can't place her in a hospital, which she obviously needs, because of the risk involved. The Germans might clear the whole place out, as they do from time to time.'

My mother's doctor had very steady, penetrating eyes.

'We could help her but we will have to do the treatment at your place. Electric shocks would be ideal. Unfortunately, we must rule out the hospital. By using an intravenous injection we can produce a tremor similar to that of an electric shock.'

He was studying our reaction. We said nothing; my mother pretended to be asleep.

'What I am proposing to do is illegal, therefore I can't use an outsider. I will need the assistance of one of you.'

He scanned our faces, our hands, all of us.

'It's just a matter of holding the patient when necessary to prevent the breaking of a limb, or an arm; to hold the head to eliminate the possibility of injury.'

My mother moaned.

'Think about it and let me know. The sooner the better.'

He was ready to leave; I went after him. 'When will you start? If you think it's going to help her.'

'There is a good chance we will help your mother. See you tomorrow at three. Get hold of some lemons — your mother will be very thirsty after every session. And I have to warn you: it's not a very pretty sight. She might suffer a temporary lack of memory. But in the end all should be well.'

I wasn't sure any more what reality meant.

My mother's twitching body.

Two Jewish children being killed by a German officer; 'What a shame', he had said, after firing two shots.

We were lucky to get twenty kilograms of frozen potatoes and, when we brought them home, they were reduced to a weeping goo. They tasted sweet. We grated them and made pancakes.

My mother's jaw jumped out of its sockets. I couldn't recognise her distorted face, and the doctor reprimanded me for being hysterical and threatened not to come again if I didn't pull myself together.

In the spot where the children were killed the snow melted and the red turned dirty brown.

67

There were names of hostages pasted on every corner. Jadwiga told us that once the list was printed the people were already dead.

We fed my mother with ersatz tea and lemon. The liquid dribbled down her chin. Several times she asked when my father would come back.

I rang Irma from the public phone, I was that brave.

A lot of our mutual friends have been deported. Yesterday it was them; tomorrow it will be us . . .

'How can you say a thing like that? It can't be true. Don't give up, you'll be all right', I interrupted her.

You don't realise. I know what our prospects are. There is no need to lie to me . . .

There was a click and a silence. And that was all. I wanted to tell her about my mother's sickness. I couldn't.

A click, a silence and nothing more.

'Anything wrong, dearie?', a woman asked me when I left the phone booth.

We received a few letters from uncle Vitek, sent from eastern Poland, which was now also occupied by the Germans. He indicated that he would like to join us. He was concerned: 'It's not a good place for Marek, I want him out of here along with his mother. Later on, if it is possible, I will join you and so will Julek' [Vitek's brother-in-law]. He asked for advice and a speedy reply.

My mother slept for hours after every treatment; we watched her all the time. Aunt Olga worried about her own husband. Uncle wasn't well; he suffered from pains and refused to see the doctor. When the pains became unbearable he sang an old folk song:

> I'll kiss youuuu
> And you'll kiss meee
> I'll never tell on youuuu
> You'll never tell on meeeeee.

Spring came, the ice on the Vistula cracked and the torrent of water broke loose.

Spring came. On the Eastern front the snow melted and the might of the German army broke through deeper into Russian land.

The Germans planted loud speakers throughout Warsaw and, several times a day, we were subjected to reports from the front line preceeded by the opening bars of Beethoven's Fifth Symphony.

TA, RA, RA, RAAA,
TA, RA, RA, RAAA . . .
THE GERMANS ARE WINNING ON ALL FRONTS. HEIL! HEIL!

Just when everything seemed lost, mother's health improved. The doctor was very happy with her progress. She came back to life, started to go out and to look after herself.

One evening she returned home with two members of a Russian folk choir plus one guitar and one balalaika. They stayed overnight and sang 'Dark Eyes', 'The Volga Boat Song' and many others. Mother joined in. She laughed and cried and was happy.

In the morning she told us: 'Poor Shura lives in a rented room, in a terrible place, where his wife is most miserable. They pay an unheard-of price for the so-called dwelling; therefore I have decided to offer these good people one of our rooms. One can't be selfish during the War; one has to think of others. They will bring a bit of sunshine into our lives, I am sure'.

'Mother, mother. We don't even know them. What happens if our own relatives arrive, as uncle Vitek is planning to do?'

'The Popovs are my friends; I can trust them. Anyway, I will think about it when the time comes. Remember, the doctor told me not to worry.'

So Mr. and Mrs. Popov moved in. He sang old Russian songs; she cooked 'bliny' and borscht. A lot of friends visited them, including a man called Chechachoff, an old

69

Tsarist colonel. They stayed up until all hours of the morning recounting the good old life and drinking vodka.

The doctor said that my mother was going through a state of slight over-excitement which would normalise before long. 'Don't worry, it is quite common', he said.

Communication between the Ghetto and Warsaw hardly existed. The Germans resettled part of the Ghetto population, and the rumours of extermination camps were stubbornly repeated.

Another message, this time a very urgent one, arrived from my uncle Vitek. It was delivered in person by his previous employee, a Ukrainian. 'Please come', it read, 'the situation is desperate. Time is running out. I beseech you to save Inka and Marek'.

Aunt Olga went to Lvov immediately to rescue Inka, my aunt, and Marek, my eleven-year-old cousin. I promised to look after uncle in her absence.

I returned to the house where the War was not allowed to be mentioned.

Aunt Olga had instructed me to tell her husband that she had been forced to go to hospital because of a very complicated pregnancy which most probably would have to be terminated. I never understood how she could have conceived that extraordinary lie.

At night I was awakened by my uncle's haunting chant, full of suffering.

> The gee-eese waddle paa-ast the brook
> The du-ucks waddle paa-ast the brook
> Ru-u-un quick my lovely mai-aiden
> So they won't ha-a-a-arm you.

I covered my head with a pillow and wept.

——— 7 ———

The days were long at Zielonka. My uncle looked saintly: tall in height, earthy in colour, the incarnation of a medieval painting. His ineffable suffering carved deep lines all over his face, hollowed his cheeks and impressed dark circles under his eyes. His skin was shrivelled.

He was as well disciplined as ever, his daily routine almost the same as I remembered it from our previous stay at his place. The parrots and Shelminka were his main preoccupation.

As for me, I spent my days cooking, cleaning and pumping water. Boyarski's house was one of a few in the district which had an interior toilet and a septic tank, but the water had to be pumped. There was a pump in the kitchen with a wooden handle, and one had to move it forwards and backwards thousands of times in order to keep the water running.

Spring had come and the garden had to be watered. Uncle stood high on his stilty legs, hose in hand, and gave his beautiful plants a good soak. He talked to himself or to the plants — I wasn't sure which. The pump was noisy in its wooden way and my heart beat hard.

Food was scarce, that is, for us humans. Shelminka, as usual, had her wholesome meal served on a mat; the enchanted birds enjoyed an apple a day and the best seeds available.

For the evening meal uncle would emerge as before in his dark suit, clean-shaven and charming. In the absence of aunt Olga he would wait for me to sit down and kiss my hand before sitting down himself. He insisted on the proper setting of the table, although most of the time our meals consisted of so-called Eintopfgericht, a single dish containing a concoction of whatever was available.

The room was lit by a constantly percolating carbide lamp. While we were eating, Shelminka sat on her cushion in almost as exemplary a way as I did. The birds would utter some parroty noises which uncle would translate, oblivious to my insensitive, indifferent self.

Uncle never forgot to compliment me on the superb meal, no matter how terrible it was. By the time I finished cleaning up, uncle was already waiting for me with an open book in front of him and a heap of bird seeds ready to be sorted.

Nothing had changed.

His choice of books was as limited and as boring as ever. His voice somehow hadn't changed much; only at times he would come to a stop, straighten himself even more, and then apologise for the 'unnecessary interruption'. I knew he was in pain, although he never spelled it out.

But when he read the words flew out from his mouth as eagerly as his parrots would from their cages, given a chance. My mind was bombarded with images of noble knights whose only preoccupation seemed to be with their never-failing ability to defend the honour of their country, church and women-folk. And the maidens, of course, were all beautiful, with fair hair, small feet, dainty hands, and waists which would turn wasps green with envy.

The climax was reached when the knight put his firm, crimson lips on the maid's transparent hand when she was just about to die from consumption. In a weakening voice she would accept the knight's love and devotion, which usually lasted for a page or two, and then her soul would go to a better place. From time to time one could see the heart-broken knight on his faithful chestnut horse, riding somewhere along the horizon, and holding to his bleeding heart the lock of his beloved's hair.

I felt like a goose being stuffed with ancient glory.

'It's raining. It's raining. IT'S RAINING.'

I stopped sorting the seeds and raised my head.

'It's all right my dear. I simply wanted to test if you were paying any attention to my reading', he said. Reassured, he would continue.

He would finish the session whenever he felt bad; so, in some crazy mixed-up way of mine, I preferred to stay and listen to his reading — the longer the better. Otherwise I feared my sleep would be saturated by his painful singing.

A week had already gone and there was no news from aunt Olga. I did all my worrying while pumping the water. It was much harder to push the handle forward, but once past the half-way mark when the point of resistance had been reached, it clanged with some hesitation and let itself be moved with more ease.

'They will . . . come?'

'For sure.'

'And if . . . not?'

'Can't be.'

'Sentries . . . there.'

'With guns.'

'Will they . . . come?'

'Let's hope.'

I would usually stick to the same phrase or the same theme and keep on repeating it like a worn out record.

When uncle suggested that I should go to Warsaw for a day or two to visit aunt at the hospital and find out when she would be strong enough to return home, I accepted his proposal with relief.

Going outside Boyarski's property was like stepping

into another world. The trains were packed with people. Military transport trains were going in the opposite direction, covered by heavy tarpaulins which outlined guns and army vehicles, just as uncle's trousers outlined his fleshless, angular limbs.

By the time I reached Warsaw there was nothing left of the flowers my uncle had picked and arranged for his ailing wife. I walked through the bustling station holding limp stalks in my hand.

'Lovely lady with lovely flowers.' A young soldier pointed at me.

My mother was all right, or more than all right. She was enjoying the Popovs' company. Our flat had become more like an inn, with people coming in and out at all times.

There was no news from Lvov, which troubled me and Tania very much.

'Mother', I pleaded, 'you have to ask the Popovs to leave. Look at all these people. They might denounce us to the Germans when Vitek and the others arrive.'

Mother promised us, although reluctantly, to ask the Popovs to look for alternative accommodation.

On the following afternoon I left for Zielonka once again, my mind burdened with worry.

Train-load after train-load of German and Italian soldiers was heading for the Russian front. They sang, clicked their cameras and some waved towards our train.

It was a warm, late spring evening, sluggish and slumbering. The train chuffed; the young men on it would soon find themselves bridging the gap between life and death. They had eager faces, healthy bodies and poisoned minds. They carried with them guns and memories, ready to sacrifice themselves and to kill for their Führer or Duce, for their Vaterland. They leaned out the windows, holding a licence to kill and a few photos of strange people. I wondered if the soldier who had helped a Jewish child over the Ghetto wall was among them, and hoped he wasn't.

Uncle was full of surprises. He gave the soup I left for him to a Jewish boy, and cried when a Polish ruffian tipped it over the child's head.

The little boy had probably crawled out of his hiding place somewhere in the forest, where he must have been squatting since the liquidation of the Ghetto in the township nearby. All ghettos in the district had ceased to exist; instead, their inhabitants were shifted to the Warsaw Ghetto, which swelled in population to about half a million.

'What will become of us? That child was hungry, all I had was that soup.' He cried openly, not even trying to wipe his eyes; and when they dried he demanded that I prepare some food for him.

'I am hungry, hurry up. I don't like Jews, but what is going on now should cause a protest to rise straight to Heaven.'

He didn't touch what I cooked and I heard him toss and cry long into the night.

The next day I returned to Warsaw. Inka and the rest of the family had arrived at last. Aunt Olga brought them safely to us and then went back to look after Boyarski. The Popovs were going to move to another place. Meanwhile we all lived together, pretending that our family was not our family but some friends. They had new names, too. Uncle Vitek had managed to buy the Aryan papers of a family which had been deported to Siberia. So he was not my uncle any more: his name was now Konstanty; Inka was Jozefa; Marek was Jurek; and Julek was Jozef. I just couldn't adjust, and mixed up the names. I called them by their real ones in front of the Popovs and then made unconvincing excuses.

In the evening we sat around the table drinking vodka. Popov, prompted by my mother, sang old Russian

romances and, although I didn't trust the man, I had to
admit that he did it well.

> Look in the mirror
> A grey hair curls
> Into a silver ring
> And you want to cry
> Because your heart is so much younger
> So much younger than your age and your face.

Popov crooned, and hit directly at my mother's ageing,
stale nostalgia. She wiped the tears away, asked for
more, more, more, and he obliged.

Chechachoff, Popov's friend, was a little sparrow of a
man — small, grey, nimble. He hovered constantly
around Inka.

Chechachoff preferred to talk, to recall yesterdays —
women, food and his army career in good old Tsarist
Russia. 'Da' [yes], was the first word of every sentence.
Marek got tired, left the room and went to bed, where he
read Verne and drowned reality, becoming an eleven-
year-old again.

Chechachoff talked a lot. A cavalry colonel, he was.
Da. After the Revolution he ended up in Poland, working with horses in a circus. Da, da . . . And now war
again.

Julek (sorry, Jozef) looked at me.

I liked it.

Popov strummed his guitar. Da, Chechachoff went on.
He once wrote a poem, we learned, about cranes, crossing the borders without passports. Da. Julek looked at
me and his eyes were puzzled.

I liked it.

'Da, women.' Chechachoff galloped around the table.
'Beautiful women, but none as beautiful as you.' He
came to a halt in front of Inka. 'Gracious one, oh thou
fairest among women. Thy neck is as a tower of ivory,
thine eyes like the fishpools in Heshbon . . . I have
always worshipped biblical beauties.' He stepped

slowly, then poured himself another glass of vodka. Da.

'What a poetic outburst', said Vitek.

Popov put his guitar down and stared at Inka as if he had never seen her before. His wife's eyes were round, pink-rimmed and as pale blue as Inka's were black.

'Colonel, you have had enough; no more vodka. Time to go to bed', Popov prompted his friend, and helped him to their room.

Some shots were fired, as on every other night. I should have been used to it by then, but that night the sound was more threatening, and I felt cold.

'It's all your fault', I attacked my mother. 'How could you let them stay? Biblical beauty; they have guessed already; they know.'

'What shall we do now?', asked Vitek. His voice should have been tired, or angry like mine, but it wasn't.

'They are good people.' Mother's chin wrinkled in a pleading way.

'Tomorrow morning I want Marek, Julek and Irena to go away to Olga's place, if she agrees. We can't take chances. Popov drinks, he works in clubs, he might tell someone. We can't take risks.'

Inka's eyes were darker than ever, the upper lids shed a shadow of sadness over them. Jewish eyes.

'Maybe aunty should blonde her hair', suggested Tania.

Inka made a little gesture, an impatient, dismissing gesture. Inka, Vitek and Julek grouped together.

'Sorry', mother kissed them one by one. She put her arms around Tania and me, and we all went to bed.

I thought of Popov, Chechachoff, of the way Julek looked at me, of my mother — and I wondered why my eyes were blue.

The Boyarskis had agreed that we should come to their place. We were to leave for Zielonka in the evening from a little-used western Warsaw station. The crowds, and the possibility of being recognised and denounced, frightened us.

In the morning the Popovs moved out, wished us luck and promised to keep in touch. Chechachoff lingered on.

'Da, da. That's life for you. Of course I knew you were Jewish. You can't continue like this, unprotected. I give you my word of honour, my word as a Tsarist colonel, no harm will come from me.' And he outlined a plan, a master plan: a hiding place.

'I was chased by Bolsheviks, I was chased by Mensheviks, I was pestered by sentries; I know how you feel. Once I was in love with a Jewess, looked like you. Maybe it was your mother?' He turned his bulging eyes on Inka. 'Are you sure your mother never lived in Moscow? Maybe she kept it a secret. Are you absolutely sure? . . . Da.'

During the upheaval of the Russian Revolution he crossed the Polish border dressed in an ermine coat, carrying a Stradivarius under his arm. The coat was too long and he had to hold it up, especially when he had to run. He tripped over a few times and noticed that the fur moulted. Never mind, he thought, once across the border, all troubles will end; he was planning to sell the coat and the violin and thus become rich.

'Da, guess what happened? The fur happened to be that of rabbits, the violin a fake. Da, da . . . Are you sure your mother never had a love affair with a Russian officer? Are you? . . .

'Well, as I said before, you must have some hiding place of one kind or another. Once when I was in trouble a beautiful peasant girl hid me in her bed. She called me 'my little one', her hair was thicker than a broom. I mean a good quality, pre-revolutionary Russian broom, not like the rubbish they produce now . . . Hiding place, Chechachoff is telling you.'

And he carried on and on, allowing us only to nod our heads. He left when Jadwiga arrived.

'Never liked Poles. One shouldn't trust them, Polaks!' He winked at Inka. 'Remember, a hiding place, take my advice. Da . . . Do you understand? . . . God have you all in His mercy.' He jumped in his birdish, springy way and left us, but not before he kissed Inka.

Da, da, da, da?

Jadwiga brought us bad news from the Ghetto. People were being deported, nobody was sure where. Some said to labour camps, some mentioned concentration camps. She had spoken to a man who worked as a train driver, who reported transports of Warsaw Jews going East and branching off the main route. On the outward journey the cattle wagons were full of people; but they returned to Warsaw empty.

Jadwiga offered to register Vitek, Inka and Marek, as her tenants.

'You must have ration cards', she said. 'Don't thank me, don't tell me of the risk I am taking. I want to do it; hungry friends are impossible to deal with. And if you send the young ones to the Boyarskis' you'd better hide Marek's Jewish features — put a scarf on him so that he looks as though he has toothache. I will take them to the station anyway. It will be safer.

She took us as planned, and, while waiting for a train, talked about Marek's tooth infection in a loud voice. Later, someone even offered him a seat on the train.

Our sixteen-kilometre journey took us more than two hours. The train stopped several times to allow army transports to go through. The three of us arrived safely and were greeted warmly by aunt Olga and Shelminka. Uncle was very formal and the parrots couldn't have cared less.

—— 8 ——

There was a new terminology among Jews living on Aryan papers: 'good look', which meant that the person looked like a Pole. A lot of women blonded their hair and wore crosses around their necks. The men grew moustaches and made a point of remembering to take their hats off in front of every church. Some, to avoid the risk, preferred to go around bare-headed.

'Butter on the head', was the code for people who were in trouble. 'Lard on the head', meant denunciation and involvement with 'navy-blue police', the Polish police force working under German command.

There was a new and a very profitable profession — collaboration with the Germans. It attracted a special breed of men. Ruthless hunters, experts in spotting Jews and communists, concentrated on the Polish Underground. They worked in gangs, or single handed, blackmailing victims, often torturing them. The worst were the so-called idealists who acted from idealistic motives, to make Poland free of Jews, communists and the Underground.

We learned all this at Boyarski's when aunt Olga brought home an Underground Socialist Party Bulletin. Treblinka was mentioned as a special camp for the extermination of Warsaw Jews.

We listened to uncle reading the Bulletin. So the War had penetrated Boyarski's walls; I couldn't believe how he had changed.

Where had all his knights gone?

Uncle stopped, and looked at Marek. 'Youngster, I order you to leave the room. This material is not suitable for a boy.'

I followed Marek, who was quite shattered by this new experience in human relations.

Uncle wasn't well; he even allowed aunt Olga to call a doctor. The diagnosis was cancer. Uncle refused to go to hospital, refused to consider an operation, and kept to his daily routine; he looked ghastly.

The doctor advised aunt Olga to get him as many morphia injections as she could. 'Your husband will need them badly in the not-too-distant future', he said. 'Call me at any time — though I won't be of much use. Sorry, but this is the situation as it stands. I can't even help you with pain killers, you will have to secure them on the black market. That's war for you.'

Aunt Olga started on her daily trips to Warsaw in order to obtain drugs for her husband.

It was a time of happiness for me. I had loved Marek since he was born. He was my favourite cousin and, though he was seven years younger, we had always understood each other. At eleven he was skinny and dark, all legs and all eyes. He never discussed Boyarski with me; never objected to his newly bestowed title of 'Youngster'; he kept quiet, and laughed only when Shelminka put her head to one side, or licked him all over.

Uncle was almost invisible. He stayed in his room, probably gathering strength for aunt Olga's return.

He allowed us to use the garden.

'Be very careful. Remember, nobody should see you. To be shot by Germans doesn't appeal to me. I would rather die in my bed. And you, Youngster, keep your voice down and put a kerchief over your head. Your hair doesn't blend too well with the Polish countryside.'

The weather was perfect by then. We always managed to find a secluded spot in the garden, where we would spread ourselves on the ground and talk. Shelminka kept us company, while the parrots enjoyed fresh air on the back terrace. Uncle stayed indoors. He entrusted me with watering the garden, so it was Julek who did most of the pumping; I often wondered if he, too, chose to kill the boredom by repeating sentences, as I always did.

Once the cooking, watering and washing-up was done, there was time to be together; there was time to talk to living people, instead of shadows invoked from my memory in that mirror. There was time to recall pre-war days, to exchange war experiences, to think in terms of, 'When the War ends . . .', and to make crazy plans.

I told Julek of Irma, and of my mother's romance with Mr. Kohn. Julek would constantly refer to his parents, who were left alone in the Lodz Ghetto, separated from their children.

They had lived with us at the beginning of the War, until we left for Zielonka, but had rejected my mother's suggestion that they leave Lodz. Julek's father had been in a partnership, first with my grandfather, then with my father, in a textile concern. He stayed behind to keep an eye on the factory after the Germans had commandeered it. 'No, Lydia, we can't go', he had said to my mother. 'As long as I am here I will guard the business. We have to think of the future and of our children.'

When I went to bed, I thought of Julek's parents. Our family had always celebrated Jewish holidays at their place. Suddenly, I remembered one of those occasions. I could see Julek's father praying in Hebrew and me giggling. Julek's mother put my head on her knees and stroked my hair till I calmed down. The table-cloth was very white and the candles flickered. Julek's mother was all radiant and silvery. I must have fallen asleep, and then I heard someone say that in any future war the civilian population would suffer because poison gases and bombs would be used over the cities. I nearly cried, but I got up and said that I would invent a huge, protective canvas, to cover the entire city, every city in the whole world, so nobody would get hurt, ever. My mother laughed, but Julek's father picked me up and declared that he believed me. He hugged me and his moustache tickled.

Julek, according to Boyarski, had a 'good look'. For me he was good looking. We spent every spare moment together. Once, on a warm night when we sat outside, he cuddled me and I was almost sure he kissed my hair; but maybe it was only wishful thinking, maybe it was the light wind, or maybe simply my imagination. We stayed in the garden just looking around, thinking, just being; words were not needed.

Aunt Olga continued her 'drug mission' with her usual stoical calm, and every night brought us news from Warsaw. Mother and Tania had turned our flat into a refuge for numerous friends with either 'butter' or 'lard' on their heads — a refuge for a night, for a day, for as long as was needed. Jadwiga was constantly in touch and, through her connections, had found a job for Julek; he was to return to Warsaw soon and start work on the railways. The Popovs were keeping away, but Chechachoff would come for a chat from time to time. My mother was well and Tania missed our company. Albert, our German friend who helped us to leave Lodz, had sent a letter announcing his intention to visit Warsaw soon.

So all was well on our domestic front.

Both Marek and I felt sad and lost when Julek left to go to work. The days dragged, and I urged aunt Olga to take us back home.

Uncle had a talk with me while I was making macaroni. I was rolling the dough and Marek was pumping water.

'What do you think you are doing?'

'Preparing the meal.'

'I know that. I am not blind yet. You and Mister Jozef, you are keen on each other. Take my advice and keep away from him. Look what a mess your mother made of her life. Don't get me wrong; I have nothing against Mister Jozef personally. I have your future at heart. Don't complicate your life, child. Find yourself a fine Polish boy. You should know by now that Jews always complicate life', he said, and walked out.

Marek never stopped pumping, I kept on rolling the dough until it broke in several places, and then I kneaded it again. I tried not to cry, but I did. I couldn't see very well. The dough got wet and I had to add more flour.

Marek kept on pumping.

That night we heard distant bombing coming from the direction of Warsaw. We sat at the window, Marek and I, and wondered what it meant.

Aunt Olga worried; uncle sang the whole repertoire of his songs.

The following morning, before she left for Warsaw, aunt Olga tried to soothe me.

'He is a good man. He loves you. You shouldn't take to heart what he says. Think of his sickness. He means well.'

'I want to go back home', I insisted.

In the evening, on her return to Zielonka, aunt Olga brought good news; Warsaw had been bombed overnight by Russian planes. It meant the Front was approaching; it meant the Russians were able to spare a few planes away from the front line; it meant we were not forgotten; and it meant the War would end one day.

I nagged aunt Olga to take Marek and me back to Warsaw; she promised she would discuss the matter with my mother and Vitek. I couldn't stand Boyarski any more. The whole atmosphere became chilly. We hardly spoke with each other. Every day which passed seemed longer than the previous one.

Marek and I waited for permission to leave Zielonka and, when the day of our departure for Warsaw arrived, I was so ecstatic that I even kissed Boyarski good-bye.

It was good to see Warsaw again, to be back with my mother and Tania, Vitek and Inka, and Julek of course. Marek was glad to be with his parents again, and enjoyed his newly rediscovered freedom. He would slump at the table whenever he wished and take a vivid part in all our conversations.

I resumed my lessons and my teacher agreed to teach Marek as well. She came to our place because we felt Marek was safer at home. Warsaw was full of denouncers whose preoccupation was Jew-tracking.

One night we were woken by a siren. We heard doors slamming, hurried footsteps running down the stairs, and panicky voices. My mother jumped out of bed. 'Another night's bombing — we'd better rush to the shelter.'

There was a knock on our door.

'May I come in?' It was Julek.

Mother looked us over, all three of us in nightgowns. She made a funny face. 'Oh well . . . before the War, definitely no; now, who cares . . . oh, come in.'

Julek walked in and his eyes rested on me. I liked it.

'You should be in the cellar already.'

'What about you?' Tania was struggling with her dress which she was pulling on over her nightie.

'We're not going down. Vitek has decided that it's safer to stay upstairs. We are too exposed in the shelter.'

The house shook.

'Where is Marek? Where is he?' Mother ran along the corridor. Inka stood in the doorway. 'He is staying with us', she said.

The night sky was alight. There was a deafening explosion and the old walls swayed. Julek pushed us towards the door. We ran down to the cellar. People sat along the dank walls, some holding hands to their ears, some praying, some already asleep; all dressed as if for some crazy fancy-dress party. They watched me, or maybe they didn't. I couldn't have cared less, I knew that I belonged upstairs. In a whisper mother called me an egoist; an obstinate, selfish, pig-headed egoist.

I ran upstairs. My father never went to a shelter. Marek was up there and I wanted to be with him. I took the steps three at a time, and it reminded me of a time when I was at school running up the steps.

Vitek was angry with me, Inka was angry with me, Julek was angry with me — only Marek ran to me and gave me a kiss. We sat in an inner room, first on chairs and then on the floor. The bombs seemed to explode near us; it was incredible to be swaying with a solidly built seven-storey building. I held Marek's hand.

'When I was a boy', Vitek spoke loudly, 'we — my parents, your father and I — used to visit our grandparents in a small Lithuanian township.' He looked at me in such a way that I knew he wasn't really angry with me, and I was happy and less frightened.

Booboom, booboom. Turra-turra-boom. The anti-aircraft battery wanted to, but couldn't silence either the planes or Vitek. The doors swayed open and the walls screeched.

'It was a sleepy Jewish township. My grandfather, who was your great-grandfather, was a learned man. The whole day through he would sit over the ancient Hebrew text and write commentaries. He was respected by all. While he sat lost in his thoughts, his wife ran a little shop — a few lollies, some sort of soda water — ran the household, and looked after the never-ending additions to the family . . .'

Booboom, turututututura, booboom, booboom.

Vitek sat between Marek and me; he put his arms around us; he smiled at Inka. 'These are family matters. Do you know that your father had two uncles younger than himself . . .?'

Boobooboobooboom, booboom.

'One day we decided to go fishing. There was a little river running through the town. Everything was little, the town itself, the houses, the people.'

Booboom, rarararaboom.

'We spotted a horse grazing near the river and we made an on-the-spot decision to pull a hair from his tail and use it as a fishing line.'

Smoke had forced its way into our flat. Inka went to investigate. Flames reached high into the sky, windows shattered, and suddenly Inka's arm was bleeding. Vitek handed her his handkerchief, then Julek made a funny face and bandaged her arm.

'My younger brother Michael volunteered. Your father spoke to the horse.'

Vitek's voice was drowned by the piercing siren of a fire-engine. Thick smoke filled the room. Marek coughed. I wondered where the smoke came from and whether our block of flats was on fire. And then the wailing siren announced the end of the raid.

'What happened then?', Marek wanted to know.

'To be continued.' Vitek went to the window and we all followed him. The fire across the street was under control.

I recognised my mother's quick steps among the others. Doors were banging and agitated voices broke off.

We started cleaning up. Tania and mother attended to Inka's cut, Vitek put Marek to bed, and Julek and I kissed till my mouth was sore and hot.

Life was coming back to normal, if one could put it in such terms. Julek went to work and came home late, while Vitek, Inka and Marek stayed home because of their 'bad look'. The three of us shopped. I attended my lessons and my teacher kept her promise and came to our place to enlighten Marek. Aunt Olga took yet another job as a cashier to cover her additional expenses. She arranged for a nursing sister to visit uncle a few times a day and to give him injections when necessary.

The Germans started issuing Kennkarten [identity cards]. Everyone had to register: name, date of birth, baptism certificate, photo, fingerprints, a sworn declaration stating racial purity, that is, that one is not a Jew in the first place, and, on the other side of the form, that one is not a half-Jew.

Jadwiga pacified our minds to some extent; she told us that the Underground had infiltrated the Kennkarten Office and that the clerks assigned to the job were very helpful. She advised us to place our applications without fear. One couldn't really exist without a Kennkarte anyway; one couldn't move around or get ration coupons.

The first step was to have our photos taken. The photographer retouched the photos and provided each of us with a 'good look'. Mother went with Tania to put the application form in, signed on one side only.

'You have forgotten to sign on the other side.' The woman gave the sheet back to my sister.

'I haven't. My father was Jewish.'

'There's no need to speak so loudly; I'm not deaf.' The woman looked at Tania and mother, consciously ignoring Tania's 'confession. 'Here you are. The pen. Please sign as indicated', she said, as if the Nuremberg laws didn't exist. Tania first gasped and then, prompted by mother, signed the declaration.

So Jadwiga was right; this rare species, people who were ready to take an enormous risk and help Jews in obtaining identity papers, really existed.

Encouraged by what had happened, my mother gathered all her courage. 'I have another daughter', she said in a very low voice. 'She hasn't even got a birth certificate.'

The woman bent down and handed a copy of the declaration to my mother.

'If your daughter is indisposed', she said in a clear voice, 'I'll accept the signed document by tomorrow . . . Next please.'

When mother and Tania returned home and told us what they had accomplished, we all felt euphoric.

What a break!

I was the only one who, through stubbornness, didn't have false papers. Tania had a baptism certificate; I had refused to get one. To accept would have been an act of rejection of my father. I knew it was stupid beyond all reason, because no piece of paper could ever change people. The best proof was my mother's case. Although she had converted to Judaism, as a gesture to please my paternal grandparents, she had always remained a true Russian — her songs, her vodka, her nostalgia were constant reminders of her readiness to display her Russian nature.

And now, through more luck than I deserved, I was going to receive a German document, containing my own name, my own date, and my own birth place. The only lie was my religion, Russian Orthodox, but that was already an old story.

Mother went three more times to the Kennkarten office with Inka, Vitek and Julek. They placed the applications in the hands of the same woman.

I received a letter from Bronka, my school friend, hand delivered by a young Polish man we had never met or heard of before.

It read:

> The situation in the Ghetto is beyond description. My parents have been deported. Irma, Lusia, Yvetta are all gone. You name them and they are no more. You can trust my friend, he wants to save me. If not for him I would've died from starvation a long time ago.

The names changed to people as I read, and I couldn't accept what Bronka said.

Mother, Tania and I sat with that young man in our dining room. Behind the closed door Vitek, Inka and

Marek froze in whatever position the unexpected visit had found them, and they kept so still and silent that I wondered if they were really there.

'I have connections with the Ghetto', the young man said. 'All of them in there are doomed. I'm in love with Bronka, I want to take her out. Such a nice girl, with a "good look" and all, it would be a pity to let her go. She told me a lot about you, about how rich you are. So what about helping? Financially, I mean.'

'Let me remind you it is 1942; there are no rich people left now', mother said hesitantly. 'But I will do everything possible to help. You must give me time.'

'Not much time left.' He looked around. 'You live here alone?'

'No, we have a tenant, a young man. He is at work at present. What about yourself, do you have a family here in Warsaw?' mother asked.

The go-between was well dressed: high boots, leather jacket, leather gloves. He looked well too; definitely not starving.

'Sure I have a family. My parents run a shop.'

'Where? Where do you live?'

'Too far for you to pay me a visit. Powisle.' He picked up his gloves. 'It's not important, is it? Better give me an answer. Haven't got much time, always on the go. Say yes, or no. Having Jewish children, you should . . .'

'Hold on a second!' Mother left the room, and I was sure that she had gone to consult with Vitek and Inka.

'Irma', I said.

'What Irma?' He stretched his body until the chair tilted.

'You knew Irma?'

'Nope.'

'How is Bronka?'

'Great, just great. Looks more Polish than you two. Have you got a boyfriend yet? Let me guess . . . that

90

tenant of yours.' He pulled the chair closer to the table.
'. . . You, or you, or both?,' he laughed.

'Nothing of the sort, not what you think!' Tania defended our honour.

Irma, I thought. Irma, Irma.

'Where does he work, anyway? I'd like to meet him.' He stopped when mother returned.

'That should buy some food.' She handed him a few banknotes. 'Now, about bringing Bronka from the Ghetto.'

'Yes?'

'Where will she live, what about her Kennkarte?'

'You're a kind of nervous lady. It's all taken care of.'

'You mentioned that your parents run a shop; they must be well-off. Every shopkeeper is nowadays.'

'Yes?'

'How much money is involved? I will have to sell something.'

'It shouldn't be a problem for a wealthy woman like you. Bronka told me. Two, three thousand; more like three than two, I would say.'

'I want to save her life. I will give you money. My conditions are these: borrow the money from your parents and bring Bronka over to the Aryan side, but not to our flat; we will be going away soon to spend some time with my sister, so I wouldn't want you to come for nothing.'

'You're considerate, aren't you. It really would be bad, to come here and find the doors shut . . .'

'Stop interrupting and listen. Where are we to meet? Name the day and the place. I will come and bring the money. What about it? If you love her, your parents must be willing to help.'

'Oh, they are. O.K. Next Tuesday. At the corner of Marszalkowska and Zbawiciela. Bronka will be there, as sure as day. No worries. Nice to do business with you.'

He counted the money and put it in his inside pocket.

'Ta ta girls', he said, and left.

Irma, Irma.

Vitek, Inka and Marek joined us. They read Bronka's letter.

'I don't trust that young man.' Vitek pronounced his judgment.

'Neither do I. He frightened me with his questions, his attitude. If he has access to the Ghetto his work must be connected with the Germans.' My mother added her bit.

'You never trust anyone, do you?' I exploded. 'It's not him I am concerned about. He has one great asset, he's not Jewish, he'll survive without your miserable three thousand zlotys. Are you all blind? Bronka wants to live, like us, under false pretences in order to survive. Look at the letter: there is nobody left, all my friends are gone. I feel responsible for their deaths. We must save her.' I shouted and cried.

'Calm yourself. Nobody said we shouldn't help', said Inka, 'but it must be done cautiously. No problem would be solved if we all perished in the process. Calm yourself; try to understand.' Inka kissed my face. I wanted to stay with all of them, but instead I slammed the door and buried my face in my pillow.

'I haven't finished telling you the story of our holidays, when we were children.' I heard Vitek's voice. 'When Michael pulled the horse's tail the jaded hack kicked, and our youngest brother landed in the little river, unconscious.'

'What happened then?' Marek prompted.

'Michael regained his senses; he was all right. But it was all very dramatic and the little township kept the incident alive for many, many years. Boris and I were not too popular, especially with our grandfather. Our grandmother was more forgiving; she gave us a lolly each as a truce.'

Irma, my Irma.

Julek was briefed on the 'Bronka affair' in detail. Plenty

of comments were thrown in, gratis. From my bed where I lay in darkness I thought of Irma, of my friends, of my people and of our times. At night I woke, terrified, having experienced once again the dream of dangling feet.

Bronka and her friend arrived on our doorstep a day before they were supposed to meet my mother.

'I instructed you not to come here.' Mother wasn't pleased.

'What's the problem? You wanted Bronka, here she is. Now, money', the young man said.

I was glad to see Bronka; she hadn't changed much. I remembered how she sat behind me at school and how when she copied my work once, the teacher blamed me.

'Tell me . . . everything.'

Bronka seemed nervous, uncertain.

'Where can I begin?', she said.

Mother reminded the young man that they were to meet on the following day; she said that since she had made arrangements to get the money then she didn't have any to give him straight away.

'It had better be as you say.'

'Are you threatening me?'

'Please don't mind him', said Bronka. 'He sometimes says things he doesn't mean. He is the only friend I have. Thanks for being willing to help me. You must know it's not easy to leave the Ghetto on a prescribed day. It happened to be possible today and here I am. Thanks once more for buying my life.' Mother hugged her. They were to meet on the following day. The exact sum of money had been agreed upon.

As soon as they left Vitek walked in. 'Girls, you'd better catch up with them. You must separate that young man from Bronka and find out whether or not she is being used. Perhaps she is in trouble.'

Tania and I ran fast and caught up with them. I took

Bronka's hand and Tania walked behind with the young man.

'Are you all right, Bronka? Is there anything you would like to tell me?'

'What d'you mean?' She smiled all the time.

'I don't know. Is he good for you? Will he marry you? He is not using you, is he?'

'I told you before he's the best friend I have. If not for him I would've joined the ranks of our friends a long time ago.' She kept on smiling. 'Aren't you afraid to walk with a full-blooded Jewess? Your mother forbade me to come and visit you. If you ask me, the street is much more dangerous, even though you're only half Jewish. Come along, Stefan, the deputation was sent to find out if you maltreat me.' Bronka and her friend walked off hand-in-hand, laughing.

Tania and I returned home. I was full of unspoken fury; I didn't bother to answer a single question.

As always, my mother was the easiest target.

'Why d'you object to Bronka coming here? Why didn't you give them money today? She was right to feel rejected. She didn't say much after the welcome you gave her.'

'What if they were followed?', mother said. 'Think of our own family; their lives are at stake, too. When will you see things as they really are? What do you know of that young man, what do you know of Bronka? She sat behind you in the classroom when times were normal. What do you know of her now?'

I shut myself away and brooded for the rest of the day.

Mother delivered the money as promised.

'More is needed', said Stefan.

'I am giving you exactly what you wanted.'

'It's not enough. It's nothing to do with me; the guy who helped wants more. He's threatening to denounce me for helping Jews. You should know how I feel, you having Jewish children.'

94

'You asked me for a certain sum, I gave it to you. I haven't got any more, that's final.' Mother walked away and returned home quite perturbed.

I was blamed for giving Bronka our address.

I had given her the address ages ago, as I gave it to all my friends; she was the only one who lived long enough to use it. It wasn't a crime.

Our teacher was arrested. I was just leaving for her place when a friend of hers arrived to warn me not to go. The place was being watched by security men.

Later, I learned that she was sent to Auschwitz.

Another person to miss; another person to grieve for.

Albert came to visit and brought things that Inka's and Julek's parents left with him before they moved to the Litzmannstadt ghetto — a fur coat, cufflinks, their mother's watch on a chain, Julek's college medal, some letters and photos.

Albert was in Warsaw on official, undisclosed business. He told us that, as far as he knew, 'the Final Solution' was definitely under way. He assured us that once the War ended our lives would be different. He promised to send a message, through his contacts, to Inka's and Julek's parents to let them know that the whole family was with us.

'My brother collects money for gas and electricity in the Litzmannstadt ghetto; he will tell them, I am sure. It will brighten their lives. You shouldn't worry about them, they are old people, nobody will harm them.'

He couldn't tell us much about the Ghetto. It must have been pretty bad because even in Litzmannstadt proper there was a shortage of food. He once went for a walk beside the barbed wire to see how the Ghetto looked. It wasn't a pleasant sight. He even saw, or thought he saw, a Jewish girl he had known. Thinking about it later, he had told himself it wasn't her, it couldn't have been, there was a one-in-100 000, 200 000 chance, he wasn't sure. On the other hand the girl did look at

95

him; it was just for a second or two. It was idiotic; it really was . . . There was a chairman in the Ghetto who used to be in charge of an orphanage in pre-war days. He was running the Ghetto very efficiently. People worked in factories, and everything they produced went to Germany. The Ghetto even had its own currency. As long as the Ghetto was useful, the Lodz Jews should be safe. Food was the problem, even in Germany. 'You are lucky', Albert said. 'One can buy everything in Warsaw, from Russian caviar to French champagne. Remind me to take some home.'

The Lodz Ghetto was quite safe, according to Albert, as long as the Jews behaved. The situation of Warsaw's was another kettle of fish; it was very overcrowded, squalid. The German authorities wanted to help. They had proposed a scheme to resettle part of the Ghetto population in the East, in the country. A special train siding had been built so the volunteers would have easy access from within the Ghetto. For those who came forward there was a whole loaf of bread waiting. Initially, there were lots of volunteers; but someone must have started to spread anti-German propaganda, and the numbers dropped drastically.

The authorities who had gone to so much trouble and expense in preparing a new location, not only living quarters, mind you, but also industry to make the new project self-sufficient, had to fulfil the quotas for resettlement anyway. An 'action' had to be undertaken. Now people were being systematically rounded-up. Once they reached their destination, they would realise how foolish they were to resist. There was work waiting for them, and accommodation, and they were allowed to take all their possessions. There were special quarters for the oldies and for kids, and for those who had lost their families.

'There is work for those who until now have been

unemployed', Albert declared. 'All the unproductive elements will find something to do.'

Albert, I just couldn't believe it. He sincerely trusted the German government and in the process had lost the ability to see and to question.

When he left for Lodz, his suitcases were loaded with all the goodies available in lucky Warsaw. My mind was loaded with uncertainty. I feared for the people of the Ghetto. I wished Albert's account was true. On the one hand he spoke of a 'Final Solution' and, on the other, of a simple resettlement programme. The 'Final Solution' filled me with an unspoken horror, but my logic couldn't accept that such a scheme was physically possible to implement. We were aware of concentration camps, of endless German atrocities. Regardless of what I knew, I just held to my belief that even Nazis wouldn't dare to exterminate the Jews; or would they?

Julek took a day off from work to help Albert carry his luggage to the station. Albert had changed. We constantly reminded ourselves that he had helped us to leave Lodz; it had been decent of him, it really had been. But we felt uneasy in his presence; his mind was already contaminated by Nazi propaganda. The end of the War meant a German victory for him. The thought was quite horrifying to us, but we were afraid to contradict him.

I wasn't sorry when he left for his Litzmannstadt, and I was quite unhappy about Julek's mission to carry Albert's suitcases, loaded to the brim with caviar and French champagne, to the station.

Julek hadn't come back. Where the hell was he? Albert's train was long gone.

'He might have gone to work.'

'Maybe something has happened? It's over three hours since he left. Dear God, make him come home unhurt; if you do, I'll believe in You again', I said to myself, and remembered that I had said the same thing when my father was dying, and when the German

97

pulled his gun and pointed it at the wretched Jewish children. Before I had had time to finish there had been a sharp, dry noise. The children were still sitting, their backs to the wall, but the snow around them was soaked with blood. I had said it so many times before, so now I stopped short and waited.

—— 9 ——

Time crawled; our ears were tuned to the highest pitch.

The door bell rang.

Julek struggled in, white and confused. 'Quick, ransom money. I got caught. A Polish policeman, he's waiting downstairs. Quick.'

We all stayed still for a second, as if turned into pillars. Then mother grabbed her bag and ran down the stairs Inka hugged Marek, Vitek picked up a cigarette and I followed my mother. Julek ran after us.

The policeman stood in front of our flats, swaying on his legs, club in hand. My mother faced him.

'What do you think you are doing, harassing a good Polish boy? You should be ashamed of yourself. He was entrusted to me by his parents, and now it's brother against brother.'

'It's nothing to do with you, lady. Mister Jozef, if he wants, can come to the station with me. All he'll have to do is show his private parts. And if he has nothing to hide, we'll let him go.' He put his arms over his chest.

'I know your game', my mother shouted.

The passers-by stopped, looked and listened.

'Hiding your number, are you?' Mother pulled his arms apart. '861, I'll remember, let us all remember. The War won't last forever, Mr. 861. I won't allow the boy to go to the station, but we could all go to the Germans to report you for blackmailing innocent people.'

'Nothing to do with you, lady, as I said before. You

keep out of it. Mister Jozef and me, we had reached an agreement. Someone said he was Jewish. It's our patriotic duty to clear Poland of Jews. We don't need them, do we?'

'Leave him alone. He hasn't got a work permit. You should know. Do you want him to be sent to Germany, what do you want?' Can't you understand the simple fact that one doesn't have to be a Jew to refuse to go to the police station? Can't you understand simple Polish, Number 861?'

'Yes lady, I want nothing, God's my witness. I'm doing my duty. Disperse everybody, disperse.' He waved his club. 'Disperse, don't try my patience.' He pushed his way through, and went away.

We went back upstairs. My mother-lioness was agitated and Julek seemed bewildered, so I held his arm.

Vitek, Inka, Marek and Tania were waiting at the door.

'What happened?'

'All is fine. The policeman went away, empty handed.'

'Mother was superb.'

'Yes, if not for Lydia . . .'

'The best policy is to attack, before the other party has a chance to attack you.'

'Yes.' Vitek looked worried. 'But what happened in the first place?' Julek dropped to the chair. 'I took Albert to the station.'

'He should have taken a riksha.'

'Does it matter now? Let him speak', I said.

'On the way back I stopped at the chemist shop. There was a queue. I had to wait. A man pushed his way to the front and looked at me. I wanted to tell him off but then I realised that we had been at school together; another one trying to survive, I thought. He had a small Italian emblem in his lapel. He must have managed to get good papers. He didn't buy anything; he just stood there and looked. I was sure he was waiting for me, maybe to tell me something important. When I left the shop, he left straight after. He walked in the same direction, but didn't approach me.' Julek cleared his throat and coughed, and kept on pushing his fingers through his hair.

'And then I went past the police station, and when I glanced back my school-mate was gone. I felt something was wrong, so I ran towards the first block of flats, and found myself upstairs in front of somebody's front door. I decided to wait till dark, till . . . I wasn't sure what. Someone opened the door.

'"Haven't seen you before. What d'you want here?" I told him I wanted nothing, that I was just visiting.

'"Whom?"

'"Mr. Krajewski."

'"Nobody of that name lives here." He looked at me.

'"Oh, Krajewski is just renting the room on the third floor, I stopped to have a bit of a rest."

'"Did you indeed? I'm telling you there's neither a tenant, nor a sub-tenant of that name. What is it? Are you trying to hide, or what. It's not a comfort station. If you want to piss, find yourself another place. You'd better go, there is a police station nearby; don't force me . . ." So I left.'

'You should have hidden in the attic.'

'I know, but I couldn't think properly, I didn't know what to do.'

'Does it matter now?', I said.

'Anyway, when I left the building the policeman was waiting for me.

'"Hey mister, someone told me you're one of them. You don't look Jewish to me but, you understand, I have a job to do. Your papers?" He was slightly confused when he saw my papers, he wasn't prepared to see a school report and the result of a urine test, as well as the birth certificate.

'"If you have nothing to hide, pull your trousers

101

down, show me your dick, it's as simple as Pater Noster." I told him that I was in a hurry, that my family was waiting for me at home, that my underwear wasn't very fresh.

'"Say no more, I know, I know, I wasn't born yesterday. I tell you what we'll do . . . I'm a reasonable man but times are hard, one has to live. You give me a bit of money and the whole incident will be forgotten."

'"How much?"

'"Not much. For a young man like you . . . say two thousand zlotys."

'Of course I didn't have that much money with me, so he followed me home. Please don't say anything, I know only too well that I shouldn't have given him our address; he dragged it out of me . . .' Julek's voice broke. 'You know the rest. Lydia scared him away, but for how long?'

'What you say now is unimportant', Vitek said. 'All we have to do is find the best solution. First, your Kennkarte. You must go and collect your Kennkarte before our policeman recovers from Lydia's treatment. Second, you mustn't stay here; you have to go away. You and Marek and Irena must leave Warsaw this very evening. Zielonka is the obvious choice.'

'I won't go without you', said Marek. 'What about you?'

'Don't worry, the rest of us will go to Jadwiga till the situation is clearer. I promise you we will join you at Boyarski's as soon as possible.'

It made sense; once the police knew of a Jew they would not give up on him readily. Our 'law-and-order' man had missed out on his ransom money, and he had been humiliated. The chances of him not coming back were minute.

Julek received his Kennkarte without a hitch. Once again we bandaged Marek's head, and arrived in Zielonka towards the evening.

The Boyarskis had a visitor; a Jewish woman whose accommodation had become too 'hot'. She had lived for over three months with a Polish woman who stayed indoors all the time. Aunt Olga's friend was obliged to give her landlady a detailed account of every sermon in the local church. When the woman remarked that her tenant behaved in strange ways and put lipstick on in a Jewish fashion, aunt Olga's friend left all her belongings behind and begged the Boyarskis to give her shelter for a day or two, until Jadwiga could arrange some alternative accommodation for her.

Uncle was in bed when we arrived. He had become frightfully thin; the nurse was now coming two or three times a day to inject him with pain killers. Aunt Olga watched terrified as the stock of morphia dwindled.

We spent the night sitting up. There was only one bed and no one wanted to use it; everyone insisted that the other needed it more. We talked; we dozed off; our companion laughed a lot.

'Jewish way indeed! Have you ever heard of a special Jewish way of applying cosmetics? And if there is, so what?', she said.

In the morning she left. Aunt Olga was relieved that she went of her own accord and spared her the unpleasant task of telling her to go.

Boyarski agreed to keep Julek and Marek. 'Though the Youngster gets on my nerves — he has no manners, sits at the table without permission, asks far too many questions, wants to know too many things.' But he firmly refused to hide Vitek and Inka. 'I worry for you, Olga, Jews always spell trouble. If they were discovered it would mean death — not only for them, but for us also, and for our neighbours. It doesn't matter to me, I am dying anyway . . . Is my suit ready? And remember, before I die I want to convert back to Catholicism . . . Yes, it is easier to hide two people than four. There is not enough room for everybody, anyway. Because the choice was given to me, the decision is mine; I would rather save the young.'

When he had finished he shut his eyes and either pretended to, or really did fall asleep.

Aunt Olga was of a different opinion. Uncle was confined to his room except when he needed to use the bathroom. He had expressed the wish that Julek and Marek should keep away from him, so aunt Olga didn't see why Inka and Vitek shouldn't join us.

'Frankly, it doesn't make much difference if the Germans kill me for keeping one, two, or four Jews. We will have to be very careful; the nurse has the key for both the gate and the front door and comes whenever she pleases. We will have to bring all of our provisions from Warsaw because the local shopkeepers know what we usually buy. You will have to keep quiet, use the toilet wisely, build a hide-out. After all, it would be nice to survive. All will be well; you will see.'

So aunt Olga went to Warsaw and in the evening smuggled Inka and Vitek into Boyarski's household.

We all slept in the same room. We took a narrow, hard bed which had been used by a servant. I slept in it, and my whole body ached. Inka and Vitek slept in a normal bed, and Julek and Marek were on straw mattresses on the floor space in between the two beds.

During the day the mattresses were placed on the beds, leaving us more room to move. The bedroom door was shut and only Inka came out to join me in the kitchen, where she performed miracles by preparing imaginative dishes. The men were smuggled in to chop the wood and pump the water.

'I have to congratulate you, my dear child', uncle Boyarski said one day, and kissed me. 'Your cooking has improved tremendously.'

'It wasn't me; it was Julek who did the cooking.'

'Mister Jozef, you mean? In that case, ask him to give me an injection — that nurse is never on time.'

'I am sure he wouldn't know how.'

'Nonsense. A man who can make such fluffy dumplings has a light hand. Do as I ask child, it is just a matter of putting a needle in.' Luckily, the nurse walked in. There was hardly any flesh left on his arms, and his skin was covered with bruises and needle marks.

On alternate days aunt Olga and I used to go to Warsaw, and Tania and mother would come over to bring provisions and library books.

Winter was approaching, autumn passing; rain, sleet and wind swayed the trees behind the always closed windows.

Vitek, Inka, Julek, and even Marek lived as though they belonged to a monastic order. They hardly moved, spoke only in whispers and only then when we were sure that the nurse wouldn't come again. We allowed ourselves to flush water in the toilet every second time. It was one of the many precautions we had taken, not wanting our neighbours to start asking questions.

In Warsaw all was quiet — from our selfish point of view. The policeman didn't return. There was only a phone call from a man who wanted to speak to Mister Jozef. Tania answered and told the man that he had moved out.

There was another phone call. My father's and Vitek's uncle Miron rang from the Ghetto while waiting for a transport to go East.

'Lydia, forgive me for ringing, but I wanted to hear a living voice', he said. He also must have lost trust in the German 'resettlement' plan. The whole Ghetto population must have known their true destination. My mother told him that Vitek and his family were with aunt Olga, and Miron was glad.

'Have you heard any news of my son? He was in the Russian zone too. I wish I knew what happened to him.'

'Don't you know? He was evacuated to Russia. Vitek

told us, I was sure you would have heard the news', mother improvised.

'Swear on your children's lives', demanded Miron.

'I swear; he is alive in Russia.'

Miron sobbed and mumbled. 'It will be so much easier to die. This is the happiest moment in my life. I am happy. Give my blessings to all.' Mother reported the conversation, which left us all speechless. I think I had never loved her more.

We were preparing for winter. We knew that everything would come to a standstill on the Front until the next spring. So we stayed put; we smeared eggs with vaseline and wrapped them in old newspaper, as we wanted to have a few for Marek. We ordered the coal, and nearly died when it was delivered in the middle of the night. They rang and rang at the gate; we were sure it was the Germans. Oh well, I thought, at least we tried.

We learned that the coal enterprise was highly unreliable; one never knew when the merchandise would be available, or when the train loaded with coal would stop in our vicinity. Usually, the driver and sentries were bribed to slow the train down. Our coal-man employed a few young boys to jump on to the wagons and throw off as much coal as was possible in the short time allowed. They were real experts in the field. Sometimes sentries would shoot at the boys just to make the job more exciting. Of course there were losses, but they were hardly worth mentioning. The boys were well paid. But if anyone was looking for a safer job, Jew-spotting was the game. Cattle-train after cattle-train was heading towards Treblinka. Sometimes, a few desperate people would jump from the train. They were easily captured, even without tracker dogs. The Germans were always ready to offer a reward — a bottle of vodka, sometimes money. Jew-boys were doomed anyway, so what was the difference. 'That's war for you', our coal-man said, 'so whenever you want some coal, Mrs. Boyarski, let me know in advance. It's my patriotic duty to keep as many houses as warm as possible. Always ready to oblige.'

The Boyarskis' cellar consisted of two rooms. In the first one they kept coal and wood; in the second, what was left of their wine, potatoes, carrots and beetroots.

We were determined to build a shelter. Vitek used his engineering skills and worked on plans. He was in favour of breaking through the cellar wall, making a bunker under the back terrace and eventually extending it to some spot in the garden.

'An escape-route, in case of fire', he called it.

One night the boy whom Boyarski had fed with soup came after curfew and rang at the gate, making two nervous uneven bell noises. He lapped his soup on the spot, then scratched himself all over. 'Lice', he explained in a matter-of-fact voice. He was covered with sores. He coughed and danced around in a crazy way.

'Couldn't we take him in? I would love to', I said. 'I want to wash him, to heal him, to shelter him from the rain, from death.'

My proposition was not very well received. Reasoning was lashed at me, and logical calculations.

Our chance of survival is not the greatest as it is. To take a boy like this would mean to reduce the chances even more. He has lost his mind as it is; he coughs, it might be tuberculosis for all we know.'

'Can you honestly imagine him here? Sitting all day in that room without uttering a sound? You should think, think before you put a proposition like this again. No, impossible. Categorically no.' I felt rotten, not because of what was said, but because there was no time for compassion.

I dreamed of the wizened, rotten, little boy with oozing sores and weeping eyes. So much for my fellow feeling.

He came for his soup four times more, then he stopped. I wanted to believe that someone better than us had

107

taken care of him, and therefore there was no need for him to come to us ever again. I wanted to believe it, but of course I couldn't. And I hated myself for having put Vitek in the position of being forced to say, 'No.'

We started on the bunker, Julek and I. To keep the noise to a bare minimum we used sharpened nails. We scraped the mortar around the bricks, and felt desperately in love. Every brick removed brought us closer to each other. Our hands were cut and bleeding; our progress, except on the personal level, was very slow.

We cut the first course of bricks only to come across another. Once the second was removed, a third blocked our way.

Boyarski had built his little citadel solidly.

We continued our travels between Zielonka and Warsaw. One day, when my mother had stayed with us overnight, I went to Warsaw on my own to exchange the books at the library which Jadwiga had recommended to us. The librarian never asked any questions and had even lent us a catalogue. She let us have twelve books per week, many of them banned by the Germans.

I rang Tania from the station to tell her all was well.

'You have to come to see me', she said.

'Not today, I promised to return as soon as possible.'

'You must come; you must', she urged.

'Has something happened?'

'Come and see.'

So, instead of returning to Zielonka, I went to see Tania, and was annoyed with her persistence. There was so much to be done. Marek always counted carefully the number of pages he allowed himself to read each day. When I left he had been on the last one.

The lift was out of order, or perhaps someone else had decided to steal away a few private moments as I used to do. I didn't need them any more; I had Julek and could say whatever I wished to him.

Breathless, either from climbing six stories, or thinking of Julek, I unlocked the door.

'Is it you?', Tania called.

'Yes. Where are you?'

'In the bedroom.'

The hall was in a mess. A coat was on the floor, the vase was overturned, and there was a mess in the dining room. Tania couldn't possibly have done it. I tripped over the upturned furniture and rushed to the bedroom.

She was in bed, her hair all matted, and her face, oh my God . . . her face was blue, swollen, distorted. Her eyes were puffy, hardly visible. I was not even sure it was her. My beautiful sister. What had happened, what was I to do, where was I to turn? And I had been ready to return to Zielonka without even seeing her.

'I can't even cry, the tears are salty and sting.' The voice was Tania's. 'It was Bronka's friend and a few more. They wanted money.'

What was I to do? Ring the doctor, the police — good joke!

To wash, to wash her tortured face and head. Yes, that was what I had to do. Bronka's friend, her best . . . Stop elaborating, first do something positive. Like what? Like asking Tania forgiveness, for it was all my fault. Wanting to take in a strange boy, giving our address to someone I couldn't possibly vouch for any more.

No, first to wash, to comfort; not to ask questions.

I boiled some water. There were feathers all over the place, and when I rushed through they flew around. The cupboards were empty and the contents on the floor — smashed glass, torn papers, books, everything. And I looked around and held my head in my hands instead of holding Tania's.

Tania, yes Tania, I had to think of her. To clean her hair, her face. To do it without hurting her even more.

Where were you, God?

I hated blood, and Tania's was clotted and stank like a

mouth after a tooth is pulled, but more. How could I do it, I had never done anything like this before. When I touched her face, she moaned, the brownish pieces broke away and the water turned red. I needed more water. Tania moved her swollen lips; they bled.

Forgive me, sister, for I have been irresponsible.

'There was someone ringing at the door, yesterday afternoon. "Who is it?" I asked. "State Electricity, inspecting the installation", someone answered. I opened the door. The young man came in, walked through the whole flat. I was thankful Vitek and the others were in Zielonka, safe from visits like this. "All seems in order." He went to the front door, opened it and let the others in. Bronka's friend, Stefan, you remember? . . . punched me first. It hurt and I cried. They covered me with an eiderdown. They kicked and from time to time would stop to check if I was breathing. "You rotten, good-for-nothing, bloody Jewish bastard. Where is the money?" They hit and hit. "We'll help you to remember." They punched and kicked till it didn't matter any more.'

Hush, my sister. Her mouth was bleeding and the words hurt her even more than they hurt me.

I washed her face, her head, her arms, her body, her legs — all bruised, clotted, wounded. I kissed her. 'Don't', she said.

'The door slammed. I stayed where they left me. I touched my head and was surprised to see blood, like when I got my first period. Thank God you came. I wondered if I would ever see any of you . . . The night was so long. I was thirsty, sore.'

'We can't stay here. They might decide to come back again. We'll go to Zielonka.'

'I can't, I can hardly walk. I look horrid. I can't move.'

'You'll have to move. We'll make it. Make an effort, get up, now.'

Tania got up; I helped her to dress. Once in a standing position her face sort of bulged and hung at the same time. She refused to eat, but she drank, in painful little gulps. I put a kerchief over her tormented head and a scarf around her neck, spreading it up to her eyes.

'Just as well it's winter; could you imagine being dressed like this in summer?'

I laughed; Tania cried and then I cried, too. We left shortly after, walking close to the buildings. It started to snow; the wind blew. People rushed past, bent over, cutting through the cold air — lonely ships in stormy waters. Nobody looked at us, and Tania said once that her whole inside hurt.

'Just a few more steps, just a few more.'

It was dark when we arrived at Boyarski's. Tania didn't want to come in.

'You go first, tell them what happened, and then I'll go inside.' She sat on a bench in the garden and shivered.

'What made you come so late? We were worried about you; you must be out of your mind. To stay away for the whole day, in times like this, when you promised to come straight back.' The family jumped all over me. If it hadn't been for Tania sitting there in the cold, I would've allowed them to go on at me for ever and ever.

'There was a reason.'

'What reason?'

'A very serious reason.'

'Not another piece of blackmail? Have you been followed? Oh no, where could we go from here?'

'Will you stop and listen? Tania is hurt.'

'Oh my God!' Mother covered her face. 'How?'

'Bronka's friend and his mates. They came for more money. They beat her up, pretty badly.'

'And you, you left her in Warsaw on her own; how could you?'

'No, mother dear. We came together. Tania was right not wanting to come inside before I told you. She needs quiet. No questioning. No inquisition. Please . . . She must be half frozen by now; you'd better bring her in.

111

She looks a mess; don't you dare notice it.'

I had had it. I went to the cellar, which was dark, cold, dank. I sat there until my hands were numb. They were revolting — cracked, rough and swollen; my feet too. I was using my father's skiing boots. 'You look like Micky Mouse', my mother had smiled when I put them on for the first time.

Micky Mouse, Disney, skiing, my father.

I wondered if they had left Tania in peace, and somehow couldn't pull myself together to face them all.

I couldn't get over the welcome they had given me. They should have been glad Tania was alive. My poor sister had fallen victim to unscrupulous blackmailers. Why her? She hardly knew Bronka. It should have been me.

Vitek, Inka, Marek and Julek, even my mother and I, we were lucky that we had stayed in Zielonka instead of Warsaw. I shuddered at the thought of what would have happened had the blackmailers discovered the whole family. None of us would have had a chance to get out alive. For they belonged to a new breed of men: they were brutal and ruthless, and their speciality was tracking Jews and using them as a target for extortion. Once their victim's funds were sapped dry, they would pass them into the capable hands of the Gestapo — which meant only one thing: extermination.

Bronka's friends had missed out on a big bonanza. A family which included three circumcised males would have been all the proof they wanted.

I wished my family upstairs could come to its senses and realise how lucky we all were. All except Tania.

I looked around. In one corner was a heap of coal, my silent company. I was just about ready to go up when mother called me, so I didn't. I licked my hands and tasted Tania's blood. I moved around, blinded by darkness, until I reached the entrance to our hiding place in the making. My fingers searched for a nail and found one. It pricked me. My hands moved over the wall and there it was, the roughness of our mortar. We must have that hiding place. My hands hurt. I licked them again. I tasted dried-up cement. Good. It should've been me who was beaten. Tania never gave our address to anyone; it wasn't fair. But what was fair? Maybe justice had existed once when the coal was a green forest, or when my father's boots were used for skiing.

——10——

Our situation had stabilised as everything does, given time. Winter had got hold of the world outside; food was scarce. There was no news from the Fronts, although people were full of expectations. 'Once spring comes . . . The Great War lasted for four years, conventional war mind you; the *Blitzkrieg* shouldn't last longer. Next spring . . .'

We waited for that next spring; Boyarski looked as though he would never live to see it. Tania's bruises, cuts and wounds were healing, on the surface anyway. Inka, Vitek, Marek and Julek spent most of their time in their room. The only exercise remained as before: cooking for Inka, pumping water for the men, and digging in the cellar for Julek and me. Aunt Olga stayed with uncle day and night. Mother and I kept on going to Warsaw and went to our flat once. We found it as I had left it with Tania. The general disarray was more extreme than my description, and mother reproached me once more for all the terrible things which had befallen us because of me. I knew she was right and in some way was ready, even relieved, to be reprimanded.

An everyday routine had been established. Inka, Vitek, Marek, Julek and I slept, as previously, in one room; mother, Tania, the parrots, the canary and Shel-minka slept in the lounge-dining room; aunt Olga shared her room with uncle.

I will never know if Boyarski ever suspected that the

114

whole family lived in his house. He never spoke about it, but he always made a lot of preparatory noises when he was about to visit the bathroom. Once, he asked how Mister Jozef was progressing with the hiding place, and told me to urge 'everyone' to finish it at the earliest date, 'before the whole house collapses'.

From time to time he asked for a parrot, or the canary.

'Come on, bird, sing me a song. I feel cold.'

But the bird sat passive on its perch and never sang.

'He feels death approaching. Take him away', he commanded.

'How could you say a thing like that? Winter is here, the sun goes down between three and three-thirty; the birds don't sing in this weather; they sleep, eat and moult.'

'You are talking nonsense, my dear. I know I won't last long. To some extent I am glad; once the Russians put their feet on Polish soil they will never leave. Britain, France, what do they care? They would sell us out again; it wouldn't be the first time, either.'

Our days would start with lighting the fires in the Dutch ovens. First, the inside had to be cleaned of ashes; then the paper, the kindling, and eventually the coal had to be placed in a pyramidal shape. Julek and I claimed to be experts in that field, and, without anyone objecting, the job was all ours. We often argued about whose method was better, but in reality we used that work as a front to fulfil our yearning to be on our own. We sat on the floor and watched first the paper, then the sticks starting to burn, break, collapse. The coal was still black and shiny at the top while it was already catching fire from the bottom. The crawling flames of yellow, orange and red made our faces glow; we felt warm. It was as good as sitting on the top of a mountain; as good as looking at some breath-taking view. It was good and quiet, and we were together.

Once the fire roared in all the ovens our idyll would

end. The whole house would be on the move. Inka would busily prepare breakfast, while others would wash, dress, clean the house, and whisper. Julek, with the most objective eye, was assigned to prepare the daily ration of butter. The honour of the chief slicer was bestowed on me. We always tried to smuggle a bit more for Marek who, with his spidery legs, was always hanging around. The whole family took part in that conspiracy, although we had to be more than careful. Once uncovered the consequences would have been irreversible.

Breakfast had to be finished and done with as early as possible; we were never sure when the nurse would choose to arrive. While we four ladies, sometimes three, sometimes two, often one, cleaned the dishes in order to cover up all the evidence for the prosecution, Vitek and the others were already shut in their room.

Another silent, still day would begin. Julek was teaching Marek, Vitek played solitaire, and Inka knitted. They all read books, talked only in whispers, looked at the dismal garden from behind the curtains, and waited for the War to end.

Tania day-dreamed, read, and kept to herself. Julek was teaching me, too, and I would often freeze in front of him because I wanted him to think me clever, quick, intelligent. His brain was geared to the sciences, mine more to the humanities. I used to spend many hours solving seemingly unsolvable maths problems; sometimes, to my great surprise, some light would descend upon me and I would finish my homework. And then Julek would write a comment: 'Very good; excellent. I take a great pride in my student. As a recognition of this student's potential a special award will be given tomorrow at the assembly in front of the fire.' A note like that made my day. My heart danced, my thoughts were kind and I looked forward to the next morning when my face and my jumper would be covered with charcoal marks.

A priest was called in and uncle received the Last Sacraments. He became less demanding and more passive. The nurse came as she pleased. Aunt Olga was at uncle's side almost all the time. She was brave, in a depressed way.

Sometimes mother would persuade her to leave uncle's room for an hour or more, and play bridge with Vitek, Inka and herself. Mother was a dedicated diplomat; she would beg Olga to sacrifice a little time to give Vitek and Inka a break in their long, never-ending days; she would press Vitek and Inka, pointing out that poor aunt Olga was in need of a rest from her predicament.

Bridge was played in Vitek's room. Marek was put on guard in front of the window, in case the nurse approached. Tania usually slept, or just rested on my bed while Julek and I watched over uncle from the lounge room. The first time, we sat on the settee listening to every sound coming from the sick room and reporting them promptly to aunt Olga. She would rush to his bed, say something in her soothing, melancholy voice, and then go back to the game.

As the bridge games became more frequent we got accustomed to the situation and learned when it was really necessary to disturb aunt Olga. We would ignore the little whimpering sounds, the ones which would last for a few seconds. Usually it was the prolonged silence which terrified us more. Like a professional nurse I would go and investigate, then return to Julek's open arms.

We whispered of love and life, we kissed and cuddled. The parrots would make noises, climbing all over the cages and making me feel uncomfortable by witnessing our timid intimacies.

These were my blissful moments. Uncle was dying in the next room. I was aware of it. But he was dying in his own bed, from his own disease. He was old and prepared for death. Everybody knew it.

117

'The other day someone greeted me, on the way to the station. Guess who it was?', I asked Julek.

'How could I?'

'A dashing young man — only he was the district funeral director.'

'They are like ravens, vultures.'

'He smiled and took his hat off, in that freezing cold. You know what was on his mind?'

'I'm not a mind reader.'

'Use your imagination! He was thinking: God willing, Boyarski will kick the bucket and we'll be able to put new curtains in our house.'

'Stop it.' Julek was angry.

'You don't believe me, do you? His wife must pester him, "Promise me, after the next funeral you'll buy me a new coat. Mine is out of fashion, which is a disgrace. Since the War started we have had good seasons, and you still guard the money as if business was bad."'

'Stop it!' Julek got hold of my arm, twisting it until it hurt. I cuddled up to him.

'Never say things like that; it's morbid.'

'But true.' I kissed Julek and then he kissed me. Uncle sang one of his songs.

'I'd better call aunt.'

'Wait, we'll see.'

We kissed again, and by the time we'd finished uncle had stopped singing and dozed off.

Once Vitek opened the front door thinking it was my mother returning from Warsaw, and let in the nurse. It worried us, because she didn't ask who he was. Aunt Olga chose to offer an explanation: 'The gentleman who opened the door for you is a lawyer friend of ours. He came to discuss certain matters; he will go home tomorrow.'

'Why do you tell me all this? It's no concern of mine.'

Her answer hung over our heads like threatening, black clouds, like a bad omen.

The days became longer; the snow started to melt and the birds were nesting all over the garden.

Boyarski suffered; he even gave his consent to plant vegetables.

'You must do it in an aesthetic way', he urged. 'None of that vegetable patch nonsense. You can use the centre lawn, the back one naturally. But remember, plant the seedlings tastefully, in squares, the way some people plant flowers. For example: one row of carrots, one of beetroots to add a bit of colour, one of dill, one of tomatoes, then beans, peas. By now you should understand what I mean.'

All that talk exhausted him and he slept for over an hour; his breathing was heavy and he wheezed.

Mother and I went to clean the Warsaw flat; Jadwiga reassured us that it would be safe. Soon after, a couple of pre-war friends with 'butter on their heads', whose previous dwelling had become 'too hot', moved in, though they were told that our address was known to a Polish policeman and Bronka's friend. They simply couldn't find anything else.

Our hiding place was progressing well. Once the weather had improved it was easier to work in the cellar.

The original plan proved too complicated, so we ended up with an opening four bricks by five, three deep. We made a narrow passage leading from the cellar wall to a trench running under the lounge room. There was sand from under the house to be disposed of, and we carried bucketful after bucketful, mostly at night. We scattered it throughout the garden so that no one would ask where all the sand came from. One was never sure if a neighbour, or a passer-by wouldn't denounce the unusual to the Germans. Aunt Olga was always telling us of people denounced, of hide-outs being unmasked. Once hidden people were found out, there was only one outcome: death.

We were more than eager to finish the shelter. We

119

worked on it with desperation. Using the shelves which once proudly carried Boyarski's wines and conserves, Julek built two-tiered cages, four in all. The bottom ones were backed with wooden panels, part of which covered up an entrance to the hide-out. The trapdoor stood open all the time.

In case of a German raid, Vitek and the others were to hide behind the cages. We planned to populate the cages with rabbits; we'd heard that the Germans used tracker dogs while searching for Jews. We reasoned that if the dogs were to lead the Germans to the cellar, the rabbits should be a reasonable decoy. We argued and discussed the matter of safety over and over again, and we desperately hoped that once the hide-out was completed our chances of survival would improve.

On the day we completed the shelter Julek and I were too exhausted to rejoice with the rest of the family, but we all felt safer once the job was finished.

Boyarski sang all night through; the doctor came in the morning.

'He might last a few days, a week; hard to say. How many morphia injections have you left?' He examined aunt Olga's reserve. 'I strongly advise you to get more.'

Aunt Olga rushed to Warsaw and came back with a few ampules. She couldn't secure any more. Her supplier informed her that his stock had run out and he certainly wasn't prepared to risk his head in search of new contacts; one of his mates had lost all his stock, and his life.

Two days later, after consulting aunt Olga, the doctor administered the remaining morphia in one fatal dose. Boyarski went to sleep and died peacefully.

Aunt Olga cried painfully, silently.

The priest arrived, paid his respects and then touched on the delicate subject of the funeral. Would we require all the lights in the church . . . carpet, choir, organs?

'Sorry for bringing all these practical aspects up. Your

120

late husband, may he rest in peace, is in a better place now. As a true gentleman he deserves a proper funeral. Just let me know what your wishes are. God be with you, my daughter.'

The news of uncle's death spread throughout Zielonka. The nurse came and helped aunt Olga to arrange the body in a coffin.

As was customary, uncle's body was to be on view until the funeral.

At the very moment when the nurse was leaving Vitek popped his head from their room.

'God Almighty', shrieked the nurse. 'Mrs. Boyarski, your place's haunted. I saw a ghost, so help me God. Mr. Boyarski, with his face all white — couldn't see the rest of him, just the burning eyes. And then he disappeared and the door shut itself, without any noise.' She crossed herself.

'It can't be; let's inspect the room.' Aunt Olga was at the door. The nurse shook her head. 'No, no. God have mercy on us all', she said, and she ran away.

For a change it was Vitek who was accused of endangering our lives. He thought someone had tapped on the door. What else could he have done?

To prove there was nobody but us four women living in the house, we took the opportunity to open it to whoever wanted to see uncle's body. All the rooms were thrown open. Our outcasts took refuge in the hide-out. Tens and tens of people walked through: people who had never spoken to Boyarski, people whom he had despised. They must have felt they were entitled to see him dead. They went through the house with hushed voices and curious eyes. The funeral director assisted people in and out, and at one stage arranged a queue. He was efficient and felt very much at home. I wondered if he was really planning a new coat for his wife.

I summoned all my courage and went to see uncle, to say 'Good-bye', as aunt Olga put it. He was dressed in

121

his new suit, as he had wished. And he was peaceful, at peace at last. People whispered and some pressed a handkerchief to their eyes.

Had he died in peace-time I would have cried; I had been really fond of him. I knew I would miss him. I stood for a while, then left the room. I wished people would stop coming.

Our family in the cellar must have been hungry.

After Boyarski's funeral, life for our fugitives became more tolerable. They were free to move throughout the house; the nurse returned the key and it was much easier to live. Aunt Olga worked a lot in the garden among the 'vegetable arrangement'. We all had our meals in the dining room and nobody cared who sat at the table first.

If someone rang at the gate we would check through the window who it was; Vitek and the others would go to their room and stay behind the shut doors until the coast was clear again.

Everything seemed to work all right. We had ordered iron bars to secure the indoor shutters; and once they were delivered we gained an additional sense of security, especially in the evenings when they were placed across the windows, isolating us completely from the outside world.

——11——

Aunt Olga was approached by the Underground organisation through a Polish ex-army officer, called Janowski, who lived in the neighbourhood. One day he presented himself at our gate. Aunt Olga called, 'Hold on a second', and Vitek and the others disappeared behind their door. There was no sign of them when Mr Janowski crossed the threshold of Boyarski's household. He marched inside in a truly military fashion: left-right, left-right, one-two, one-two.

'My sister, my nieces', introduced aunt Olga.

After the initial handshakes and niceties we all sat around the table. The parrots shouted and Shelminka growled from her cushion.

'I represent the local branch of the Polish underground, security section. Our boys have been observing your place for some time now . . .'

Mother, aunt Olga, Tania and I exchanged looks.

'To be precise, since the passing away of your husband.' He jumped to his feet. 'My most sincere condolences', he said, and kissed aunt Olga's hand.

'Thank you.'

'Not at all!' He took his position back at the table. 'Where was I? . . . Oh yes . . . Your house, Mrs. Boyarski, is solidly constructed; the whole property is surrounded by high hedges. Even now, in early spring when the leaves are still young, one can hardly see the house from the outside. The only inhabitants, four women.'

We breathed more easily.

'To sum it up, you have here an ideal place for our purpose.'

Aunt Olga took the glasses out and poured vodka; we all raised our glasses.

'To a free Poland', toasted Janowski. 'What we propose to do is to run a radio transmitter from here, to send daily reports to England. The procedure is very simple . . . To Victory!' He emptied another glass.

'To Victory!', we echoed, and Tania hiccoughed.

'Sorry.'

'As I said, your place is ideal for our objective. Everyone should make a little sacrifice; it's your patriotic duty. If you ask me, the whole nation should be involved. Don't be alarmed; don't get me wrong; I'm not putting pressure on you. The fact is, you see, Germany is on the brink of collapse. Think it over. Our victory is not far away. All Poland should be united. I remember when the Great War ended. I was a little kid then, no higher than this. You should've seen our Germans then; a little nothing like me would say, "Hände hoch", and the officer, all shaky, would allow himself to be disarmed. Now I'm waiting to relive those days again, to strip them of their ranks, of their arms, of their haughty arrogance. Down with the Huns!' He emptied yet another glass of vodka.

Mother and aunt Olga looked at Janowski; starry-eyed, nodding, smiling, agreeing. Tania pressed the palm of her hand against her mouth and hiccoughed.

'Your work must be very dangerous', my mother remarked timidly.

'It has its moments. You probably heard of the army transport that never made it to the Front. All blown up.'

'You mean the explosion two weeks ago?'

Janowski smiled, nonchalant, satisfied.

'Two weeks ago, last week, three weeks ago. Not everything is reported; we do it all the time . . . To you ladies! To our co-operation!' Another vodka disappeared.

Tania alternately hiccoughed and begged pardon.

'May I offer you some advice? Take a glass of water, hold your breath and then drink it in one go. This always helps when used by my subordinates!' Tania left the room and immediately returned with some water.

'Hold your breath', commanded Janowski. 'Now! One, two, three. Drink, don't breathe.'

She drank. Finished. We all waited, full of suspense.

'Hic.'

'Obviously didn't work in that case . . . To your hiccoughs!'

We laughed.

'Tell us more about your work', I asked Janowski.

'It covers a great range . . . Sabotage is the main task but we must also maintain contact with our Government in England and eliminate communists and other subversive elements from our ranks. As far as the Jewish question is concerned the Germans are executing their plans in a methodical fashion, thus allowing us to concentrate on more vital issues.

'There is a constant shortage of couriers, go-betweens; somehow they manage to fall into the hands of the Huns. Not that they could do much damage to our Movement. Usually they know very little; a couple of addresses, that's about all. But of course our main aim is to build a strong, free Poland with a vision of her greatness in mind. We work day and night. Fortunately, the Germans are fools. No imagination. To give an example, guess how we smuggled a pile of important documents into Cracow?'

'How could I? It's not a guessing game', I said.

'You are right, my child. Mind you, the documents were received directly from London. Definitely not a guessing game. To our successful missions, now and in the future!'

I noticed that aunt Olga was obviously uplifted by both the vodka and the inspiring visit; and mother, given the order, would have leaped into an open fire.

Shelminka slept, the parrots manicured their claws; Tania was all red in the face, frightened to breathe; and I, as usual, remained sceptical and suspicious. Patriotic duties were all very well, but what were the consequences? Lists of hostages were displayed throughout the whole of occupied Poland and contained more names each day. Every act of sabotage was followed by executions, by people being deported to concentration camps. The Germans were not fools as Janowski implied; they were plain dangerous.

I looked hard at Janowski; he must have sensed my attitude. He lifted his glass high: 'To those who fell in the fight for justice!' He replaced his glass on the table. Shelminka lifted her head and growled

'Be quiet', warned aunt Olga.

'As our history has proven, retaliation will never arrest our patriotism. We have always held Poland above all other interests, only then is life worth living . . . To our beloved country!'

There was not much vodka left when he eventually got up from the table. But he stood steady, upright.

'With your permission, I'll get in touch with you tomorrow. Think of the importance of our cause, of your duty. Once you decide, you'll be sworn in and be given code-names. Our people work on a voluntary basis for obvious reasons; the little money which reaches us from England is better spent on armaments, bribes and such.

'No need to explain; it is perfectly clear!', mother and Aunt Olga exclaimed almost at the same time.

'You shouldn't be too critical.' Janowski put his heavy hand on my head. 'It's not right for a young lady like you. Believe me, for an old trooper like me, no sacrifice is big enough, nor sweeter than the one we make for our Motherland.' He turned his eyes on Tania. 'I'm glad your hiccough has stopped.'

126

'Thank you for your advice; it really helped.'

'It was nice to meet you all. I'm looking forward to our successful association.'

Shelminka first stretched, then barked.

'Don't worry, Mrs. Boyarski. She'll get used to me once she knows me better; I'm certain. What beautiful parrots you have. I've heard a lot about them; never believed they really existed. Magnificent.'

He kissed mother's and aunt Olga's hands. Overwhelmed by his irresistible charm, they walked him to the gate. Just then Tania hiccoughed and we both rushed to the room to set our prisoners free. But when we opened the door nobody moved; instead all four sat still holding round-bottomed containers. It was stuffy inside.

'What on earth have you got there?'

'Shshshshshsh!', whispered Inka. 'He is still in the garden.' With her head she pointed to the ceiling.

The lamp was stripped of its lampshades.

They had been locked in for ages, without having had a chance to go to the toilet first. So while we were drinking vodka and solving all the problems connected with the future of Poland, their bladders were just about bursting.

I have never seen lampshades put to better use.

Tania and I emptied them one by one while Vitek, Inka, Julek and Marek apologised and then stretched their numb limbs until mother and aunt Olga returned.

'What happened to the lamp?', aunt Olga asked.

'Sorry, Olga. Marek was the first; he couldn't hold on any longer. We didn't know what to do and then Julek noticed the lampshades and brought one down. We ended up sitting here, each of us holding a lampshade till the visit ended. Sorry.'

'The damned things had to be rounded at the bottom,' Julek stretched and smiled.

'Be thankful they have a bottom.'

'Oh I am, I am.'

127

'I never liked the lamp', said mother. 'I always wondered why my brother-in-law, who had such an exclusive tastes, had to put up that atrocious lamp. It was the worst in the whole house, with those four hideous shades. Now I know. It was meant to be here so that, in case of emergency, my husband's family would be able to use the shades as chamber pots. It was meant to be, I tell you. Like all the other things. Boyarski had to leave his family estate and settle in Zielonka. He had to be very superior and not associate with the people around. He had to build a little fort of a house with a locked gate, surrounded by unheard-of high hedges. He had to marry Olga, who happened to have a sister who married a Jew, a Polish Jew, who had happened to land in Moscow during the Revolution. You must admit, this house was specially designed for us to survive. To top it all, Janowski has come and offered us an opportunity to be useful.'

Vitek kept on bending up and down. Inka lay on the bed. Marek ran on the spot, Julek went to pump the water and Tania hiccoughed. Shelminka jumped on my bed, although she had never done it before. Aunt Olga laughed.

Our Kazia would have called it 'a real nut-house'. I missed her and her straightforward common sense.

Aunt Olga and mother were very excited by the idea of being involved with the Underground. We learned that Janowski worked for the Armia Krajowa, the Home Army, the organisation which was fighting the Nazis under the direction of the Polish government-in-exile, whose temporary location was London. There were other underground organisations ranging from the extreme left to the extreme right. Those on the left were affiliated with the Communist Party and Russia; the others were more involved with fighting communists and Jews than the Germans, whose ideology must have been very appealing to them.

The Home Army was the most active and the best known of the underground organisations. Among its ranks were people from all political persuasions, united by their loyalty and trust for the Western democracies and their contempt for the Soviet Union. On their home ground they hit at the Germans whenever possible. We heard of transports of political prisoners being ambushed, of munition trains being blown up, of accommodation and financial assistance being offered to people in trouble.

Somehow Janowski didn't seem to fit into the picture. His proposal was not as simple as he implied. As Vitek explained to us, radio transmitters were easy game for the trained army technicians who patrolled the district in specially equipped spotter-cars. Once they picked up a broadcast, they manoeuvred their antennae in the direction of the best reception and pinpointed the location of an illegal station. By that time the whole region could be swarming with Germans directed by the radio. But aunt Olga and mother didn't give in easily. Only when the vodka evaporated did reality become more acceptable to them.

On the following day aunt Olga went to Janowski and declined to give permission to use her house as an illegal transmitting station, using mother's recent nervous breakdown as an excuse. Instead, she and mother offered to work for the Underground. She also mentioned her readiness to hide documents, guns and ammunition at our place.

'I have a very good, small hiding place where I could hide all these things,' aunt Olga said.

'I would be a liar if I pretended I was not disappointed by your decision', Janowski replied. 'During the transmissions your place would have been surrounded by our best boys, all armed, well trained, ready to rescue you if spotter-cars were noticed. Our boys know what to do; they usually execute their missions satisfactorily.

'Nevertheless, the final decision is yours.

'There is still a shortage of couriers, so if you and your sister are willing I'd be more than pleased to use your services. If it's not too much for your sister . . .'

'Oh, she will be fine; you will see!'

'Very well then. I also intend to take up your offer and use your place for our local arsenal. I'm not too happy with its present location; there are too many people around. I'll let you know when and where you'll be sworn in.'

Olga returned home quite exhausted but full of expectations.

Once our ladies were accepted by the Underground, Janowski visited us frequently. He came only at night, as arranged. His entrance was preceded by three lots of two rings at the gate. He usually stayed for hours with aunt Olga and mother, while Tania and I waited with our prisoners for the visit to end.

The arsenal was building up: two revolvers, one automatic gun, one ordinary gun and three World War One hand grenades. It wasn't sufficient to declare war on the Third Reich, but it was enough for us to feel more secure; for we knew that if the situation arose we would never surrender to the Germans.

Janowski kept on bringing masses of documents which were mainly bulletins published by the numerous political parties. We became well informed about the political situation and the progress of the War; we also had detailed reports on the activities of the Underground.The most objective information was offered by the *Bulletin*, the official voice of the Home Army.

But when we learned of the existence of the 'Black Book', in which the names of people helping Jews and communists were listed, the whole ideology of the organisation took on a different complexion. Among the condemned were individuals who were supplying arms to the Ghetto.

Janowski told us that our neighbours from across the meadow, a widow with four sons had organised a 'rescue' scheme for Jews. They would take in a person of their choice with all his belongings, and a few days later they would kill their victim and bury him in a nearby sand dune.

'It surprises me that you've never heard of it; it's well known throughout our district. The sons are very active in a right-wing underground organisation. Brave, daring soldiers they are, always volunteering, often for dangerous operations. Why d'you question it? They have been reprimanded and I think their scheme has come to a stop. Strange things occur during war. Good, well disciplined soldiers must be preserved; there's not many of them around.'

I couldn't go to sleep at night; I waited for human voices, for some movement outside. It was quiet, except for dogs barking.

We kept to ourselves the news regarding the widow and her daring sons. In situations like this I felt very close to mother, aunt Olga and Tania.

Our vegetable 'flower-bed' looked magnificent; the septic tank got blocked, or simply overflowed, feeding our vegetables well.

Aunt Olga couldn't call the septic tank service because for so many years the tank had never been cleaned more often than once a year. Obviously, eight people produced more excrement than two. Vitek expressed concern that, if not emptied, the tank might feed back into the cellar. There was no other way; we had to do it ourselves. Aunt Olga showed us the location of the tank and we uncovered it. It ran under the main path in the back part of the garden.

Jasmine, roses and lilac were in full bloom, but their fragrance could not dull the ever-present, penetrating stench. We fastened a bucket to a gardening fork and used it as an emptying device. The bucket slipped several times and sent geysers of muck high into the air, spraying us all over.

There was little poetry in that task; shit just stinks like shit.

The only consolation was the fact that it was a family matter.

——12——

'Ja, ja, Ich weiss du bist eine Jüden.'

I sat very still in my soft seat and looked through the window. The voice next to me kept on repeating, 'You are Jewish, yes, I know'. It was a soft voice, murmurous, continuous, like the sound of the train. I tried to ignore it and wished it would stop, but it didn't.

We were on the way to Warsaw, mother and I. The trains were getting more and more overcrowded. On this occasion we had thought we would never make it on board. The gendarmes had to pull away the people plastered to the train; we were waiting on the platform and wondering what to do when a young German soldier opened the door of the 'Only for Germans' compartment and let some people in, including mother and me. We were offered seats. I landed between a soldier and a civilian; mother sat opposite me, but the people who were standing up screened her from me.

The soldiers returning from the Russian front were all young and noisy, on the way home for two whole weeks.

'I am a pilot', said one. 'The best of all the services; the most rewarding. You fly high, nothing above, the city below. You press the button, get rid of your load. In a matter of minutes the city is gone. Wonderful!'

My immediate neighbour pushed some worn-out photos in front of me. 'My mother, my brother.' I couldn't help seeing. A mother like any mother, a brother like so many others.

Everything was going all right, with the singing, the

laughter, the excitement, and then that voice started. First slowly, quietly, then quicker, louder as if gaining speed. 'I know, I know, you are Jewish. I know.' And then he said it even louder; the whole compartment became hushed and the voice became rhythmical and precise. I looked at him. He could have been a friend of the family. Not a cruel face, just ordinary. The eyes were quiet, the voice rather melodious. 'Ich weiss, ich weiss . . .'

I turned my head towards the window. The soldier who had showed me the photos watched me with amazement and, I thought, pity and then he turned his head away and sat very still too. The photos were still in his hands.

'What's going on?', asked my mother.

'She is Jewish, I know.'

'She is my daughter; you must be crazy.'

'You are crazy yourself. A lot of Jews jump trains on this line. Take my advice dear lady; don't try to save that Jewess. I know she is Jewish. I know.'

They argued, the train gained speed, the trees, the houses rushed by and I was feeling a terrible guilt. I didn't have enough guts to stand up and say, 'Yes my man, you are right, I am Jewish'. He would have pulled a gun and that would have been the end of me. I had seen it done. He would have killed me, not because I had picked flowers I didn't really need; not because I had wasted food so many times; not because I had led a selfish life and turned away from the little boy who had cried for help; not because of all the things I had done wrong; but because of something that nobody could have ever changed.

So this was how it felt. I promised myself not to cry. Mother was sitting next to me; she must have changed seats with the soldier. I felt as if I wasn't me but some impartial observer. I wondered how one went to death and how long it took to die.

134

'Jude, Jude, Jude.'

Would they ask me where I came from, where I slept last night? Would I be strong enough to withhold aunt Olga's address? They might torture me. What if they chose to threaten my mother; would I keep my mouth shut? I didn't know. I knew I wanted to live and remembered what Irma had said in her letter: *The less right we have to live, the more we want to survive.*

'Give me your Kennkarte', mother said, and then took it out from my bag herself and handed it to the man.

'Of course! Born in Litzmannstadt. So was I. I know she is Jewish, I never forget a face'. His voice was as full of satisfaction as the fields were rich in colours, as my whole inside was full of panic and pain.

Litzmannstadt/Lodz; he knew. He must have seen me somewhere and remembered.

Where, when?

On the day Irma and I had gone to the swimming pool and had watched a girl our age jump from a diving board? There was a crowd around and the day was oppressively hot. A girl climbed to the highest point, lifted her arms up, glided through the air and with a splash cut the water open. One of the boys next to us said: 'I bet you one zloty, no Jewish girl would ever dare to jump from such a height.' I climbed up and up and, when I reached the highest point, I shut my eyes and jumped, landing on my belly. It happened quickly. My body hurt. Dripping with water I had gone to the boy. 'Hey you! You lost your bet. I just jumped from the top diving board and I'm Jewish.' The boy had looked puzzled. Irma and I had laughed and were very proud to have defended Jewish honour.

It was ages ago, probably when we were eleven, twelve; had the man who 'knew' been there?

Or was he the one who had sat in the park when a whole group of us thirteen-year-olds had walked through and pretended we were leading a dog on a

135

leash? Irma barked, Bronka giggled and someone said, 'Disgusting, the young people of today. Especially the Jews.' We had copied the whole stupid routine from some crazy American movie. That was what we were doing, nothing else. We had meant no harm.

Had he been there?

No, it must have been on a train. That train mother and I had travelled on, when I was eight, for our skiing holiday. The train had been packed; mother had led me in front of her, following the porter who at long last had found seats for us. He dropped our luggage in the centre of the compartment and disappeared. Immediately, two very chivalrous men jumped to their feet and, by the time they finished their discourse on the laziness and lack of responsibility of servants in general and the railway staff in particular, our very heavy suitcases were stowed securely on the luggage rack.

Mother thanked them.

'It's my pleasure', one of them said, while the other offered us a weekly magazine. Just then my father walked in to say good-bye to us.

'Take care and write.' He kissed me.

'I will walk with your father to the door. I won't be long', mother said. I was left on my own, and then the man who had helped us burst out in a loud, dry voice, 'To think I offered my assistance to a Jewess; she looked quite normal to me. One can never tell with them.'

When mother returned I had put my head behind her back and cried. She had asked why, but I hadn't told her.

Was the man who 'knew' on that train?

Or had he seen me during the War, on the way to my school, or when we were going to my father's funeral, or leaving Lodz, or where? I didn't know.

We left the meadows and the villages behind. The train was passing through the suburbs of Warsaw. The streets were already in view, and I could see the people. The passengers collected their belongings. The man who 'knew' stood at the open window and, for a moment, I thought he would let us go. After all, my mother had been brave, which wasn't difficult with her 'good looks'.

The train jerked to a stop. My man let all the passengers out.

I thought the soldier who had shown me his family photos winked at me. The station was crowded, full of people and full of smoke. The engine was still puffing. We were at East Warsaw station.

'Notify the gendarmes', the man instructed my soldier.

'Heil Hitler.'

Six gendarmes marched in, filling the compartment. They inspected my papers and mother pushed hers into their hands, too.

'Seems all right', one of them said.

'I know she's Jewish,' said the man. 'She must have jumped the transport. They usually have good papers. The name, look at the name. Typical Jewish name.'

'Or a German name', mother added, but was ignored.

'I'm well known for my punctuality', the man said, pointing to his watch. 'I have to be at my post by 8.55; therefore I'm entrusting this matter to you. Take her to the Gestapo. The older one doesn't have to go unless she wants to stick her neck out for that Jewess. Heil Hitler.' He threw his hand forward and left us under arrest.

'Heil Hitler', the six voices responded as one.

They stood all around us, with shining oval number plates on their chests and helmets reaching their eyes, setting their faces in severe, rectangular frames.

It took ten minutes to reach central Warsaw from the East Warsaw station. My mother said something like, 'She is my daughter. It must be a mistake', and one of them said something like, 'Trust the Gestapo; there's nothing to fear'. I wanted to live.

I wanted to see the end of the War and then go into the

streets and say, 'I am Jewish', and hear someone say, 'So what? Big deal. Go home in peace'.

I remembered a man who had worked for my father, a kind of messenger and a jack of all trades. One day, when I was walking with my father, we met him. He was carrying a roll of fabric on his shoulders. He stopped, lifted his foot up, looked at the sole for a while, and then continued on his way. He and father had exchanged greetings, but I had not. My father asked me why I had not done so. 'Because he works for us', was my explanation. He picked me up. 'Listen. Listen very carefully. Mr. Dzialowski has a wife and children. He is worried that his shoes need to be repaired. You didn't say hello to the man. Greeting is a sign of respect. Run to him, say hello, apologise.' I did as I was told. The man was puzzled, he smiled and then walked away quicker than before.

I wanted to live so that one day I would learn how to respect people.

The train stopped. Four of the SS men left the carriage first, forming a semicircle in front of us. We stepped down, followed by the remaining two. They marched us towards the Gestapo. I felt very small. Mother wanted to hold my hand, but I didn't let her. Two gendarmes walked in front of us, two at the back and one on each side of us.

I wasn't ready to die. We should have bribed them. Now it was too late. I took my mother's arm and she smiled.

'Shouldn't we . . .'

'Shut up', snapped one of our escorts.

We marched. I knew how to march; I was good at it at school. I knew how to dance. Rhythm: that's what marching and dancing were all about. School functions with girls blue and pink and white, shuffling and gliding: one to the left, one to the right, them forming pairs; one pair to the left, one pair to the right, then forming fours, and then eights. And the music told you exactly what to do; good, joyous music . . . For a moment, just for a moment, I thought the SS men would go two to the left, two to the right and leave us to ourselves.

I thought of an American film I had seen, in which people became invisible. It was like a fairy-tale, about a boy and his magic hat. Whenever he put it on his head, nobody in the whole wide world knew he existed. Absolutely nobody.

The crowd parted at our approach. There was constant noise. We marched. Panic rose within me; my heart beat loud, fast. I had heard that, sometimes, before people die, their whole life comes back to them; that was how I felt. Faces and episodes crowded my mind. I resolved not to disclose Aunt Olga's address but felt a disturbing, frightening doubt whether I would prove myself strong enough not to.

The Gestapo quarters were upstairs; I thought they should have been in a downstairs dungeon. The stairs shone; the long corridor shone. There were doors on both sides, with signs in Gothic script. Someone screamed and the sound bounced from wall to wall, from floor to ceiling, from ear to ear.

Someone opened a door. We walked in. The room had a shiny floor and a desk, as in any office. There were no windows. We were confronted by three Gestapo men in black uniforms with the skull and cross-bones insignia, and a huge portrait of Hitler on the shining wall. Our escorts lifted their hands up in a precise, squarish way.

'Heil Hitler.'

'Heil Hitler', responded the others and one asked, 'What have we got here?'

'A Jewess denounced by the district employment man.'

'Kennkarte?'

Mother handed him mine and hers, and I hoped it was only me who noticed that her hand trembled. The man, a perfect specimen of the Nordic type, looked at me.

Let me be strong, oh God. Please, let me be strong. I have to be strong.

Could a man like that be cruel?

He spoke with his assistant. He placed my Kennkarte on a glass plate and shone a light on it, first from the bottom, then from the top.

Give me strength. Don't let me betray the people I love. Forgive me for withholding my identity, for I want to live. Let me live for all that my life is worth.

And then the Gestapo man laughed. He threw his head back and laughed.

'Good joke?', he addressed his men, 'isn't it? Observe her: blonde hair, blue eyes, light complexion, papers in order. Mother and daughter. What an amusing beginning to a day, I haven't had such fun for a long time'.

He handed our papers back. 'Good joke; good joke indeed. You are free to go. Heil Hitler.'

We walked back through the corridor and his laughter carried from wall to wall, from floor to ceiling; but the shrill cry was stronger and was still present in me for long after we left the Gestapo.

Good joke.

I kept glancing back and mother told me not to. We walked down and stepped among the crowd. I couldn't believe I was really free. Mother smiled and hugged me, 'You see?'. I couldn't keep my head still, it turned in every direction. I could feel eyes watching me, although the hustling, busy street looked normal enough.

'I want to go home now, immediately.' There were too many faces, too many eyes; all of them looked at me, detecting my Jewishness.

'We'd better stay in Warsaw, so we can change our books and buy bread,' mother said, but I was sure it wasn't what she thought. She must also have been worried that someone might follow us and must have wanted to be sure they were not before she was prepared to return home. She told me I was imagining things, that it was all over and that I shouldn't think about it any more. I didn't believe her. Oh yes, she was brave. No wonder; with her look she could afford it.

She was a beautiful woman, but at that moment I almost hated her non-Jewish face. It was easy for her to save me. No-one, not even the Gestapo, could have suspected her of being Jewish. Mrs. Kohn couldn't save her daughter, not because she was less brave, not because she didn't care for her child. She couldn't save her because she looked and was Jewish; my mother belonged to the Super Aryan race and this was the only reason why she was able to save me. I resented her; I hated myself and the whole world. I almost wished I had been killed and then I felt ashamed. I couldn't be honest with myself.

We went to the library. There was a man scanning through a book and, as we entered, he looked at me and my heart missed a beat. He left when we did. Things were not that rosy yet, I knew; I felt it in my bones. He turned in a different direction.

'See?' Mother was convinced, but not I.

We bought some bread from a corner vendor. A youth was standing there, smoking a cigarette. I was positive he looked at me, and then he spoke to another man.

'Let's go, quick!'

'We will walk as always, slowly, normally.'

My clever, daring mother — her face, her pass to life.

The books were heavy; the bread warmed my arms; women were selling small bunches of spring flowers; a police van wailed and sped past; the church bell rang; my feet hurt; my hands felt numb; my shifting mind moved in a crazy labyrinth; we walked and walked; and above all, people stared, looked.

The magic hat; I wished I had one.

We arrived at the station in the late afternoon; the bread had cooled off and felt heavier than stones. Our train was already in. They must have put it there specially to trap us. Mother pushed me in; we found seats. I looked out the window and saw the man who 'knew' walking from one carriage to another, searching for me. He was 'punctual', he had said in the morning.

'Mother, he's looking for me.'

She scanned the platform. 'He is nowhere to be seen. You are imagining things. All is well. Don't worry. Go to sleep, I will guard you.'

I covered my face with a scarf. The train was still stationary. My mother kept her protective wings over me.

What about the other mothers whose hair was dark, whose eyes were dark? How did they protect their children?

The train puffed, the steam hissed, the compartment filled up with people and bundles. First the whistle, then the wheels turned, and I could have sworn that the man was running from one carriage to another and had pressed his face to the window of our compartment.

The train was already gaining speed, and mother advised me to uncover my face because the carriage was stuffy. Maybe I was having a nightmare; I wasn't sure.

When we reached Zielonka the sun was setting and everything and everybody was tinted glowing red. We crossed the railway line; we crossed the main road; the shadows were long, grotesque. There was only a large clearing between us and aunt Olga's home . . . and there was a man planted there, holding a bicycle. He was waiting for us to open the gate, and then he would jump on his bike and catch up with us just when we were about to open the door to the house; he would discover our 'illegal' family. So this was the reason the Gestapo had set us free. This time I didn't allow my mother to dim my foreboding. Instead I dragged her to Boyarski's nurse's house.

She was surprised to see us.

'How are you? Is Mrs. Boyarski all right?'

'My sister is as well as can be expected.' Mother chatted while, from a strategic point behind the curtains, I kept watch on the man with the bike. He was still there waiting for us.

'Mr. Boyarski was a fine gentleman'. The nurse sighed. 'Is he still visiting you?'

'Every evening towards dark we see his face, always smiling.'

'You should do something about it, maybe ask the priest to offer prayers for the eternal peace of his soul.'

'Yes, we must do it.'

Mother joined me at the window. 'What a nice view you have from here.'

The man with the bike moved. A skinny shadow was coming closer. A woman appeared. He sat her on the frame and pedalled away. Mother looked at me with a mixture of impatience and contempt; no words were needed. I was a fool but I couldn't help it.

'We'd better get going before the curfew. It was nice to see you again. Thanks once more for everything you've done for my brother-in-law.'

'It was my Christian duty; don't mention it. And how are the parrots? Have they adjusted to their loss?'

'They miss him, as you can imagine.'

'If Mrs. Boyarski would agree, I know of someone who would be only too happy to look after them. The change of environment would do them a lot of good. Not to mention all those apples, biscuits; it must be difficult for you.'

'We manage, but I will tell my sister; it's up to her. Thank you just the same.'

The sun, full of dying flames, shone over the roofs and treetops. The swallows circled in mid-air, the frogs croaked. Light sand shifted on the dunes.

We were back home.

It had been decided that I should be exempted from the Warsaw 'missions'. I put up a feeble protest, just to be contrary, but in reality I was glad and relieved. So it rested with mother and aunt Olga; they kept going to Warsaw three or four times a week, fulfilling both their patriotic obligations and keeping us all from starvation at the same time.

By a majority vote they were released from all the everyday tasks, which in turn were assigned to the rest of us. Inka was the Chief; she had the ability to organise work and was most capable in her task. The rest of us poor Injuns were ever-ready to assist, although we weren't always successful. While Inka swept the floor her men lifted the pieces of furniture, one by one. At the end of the line Julek would be crouching, holding the dust-pan, ready to sweep the dirt away.

Inka cooked; I helped her with the preparations; Julek chopped the wood. We did the dishes in turns. Our task force was as well organised as circumstances allowed. Tania caused certain problems by her 'housework phobia'. As she put it, she was 'not meant to do that kind of work'. An excuse like that freed shallowly suppressed indignation.

I spent a lot of time weeding and watering the vegetables. As aunt Olga did after uncle's death, I used it as an excuse to be alone, to question things, to think. My recent experience was still very much present, while things that had happened earlier, including even Tania getting beaten up, had become obscure, remote.

Integrity, willpower, honesty, loyalty had become shaky concepts. Oh yes, I knew I had been spared this time, but not because I had done something daring or heroic. It had ended well because a Gestapo man had taken the whole episode as a joke, and because I had been with my mother, whose typical Slavic features had been like a protective shield. For other Jewish mothers all prayers, screams, curses; all kicking, spitting, fighting were completely useless.

The 'Final Solution' was in full swing. I read of a nameless girl who threw herself, bare-handed, on an escort in Treblinka and was shot on the spot. I wished and then convinced myself that it had been Irma.

——13——

By early spring 1943, the population of the Warsaw Ghetto had shrivelled from the original 450 000 to 30 000 or 40 000 people.

I often thought of Dr. Janusz Korczak who, in the August of 1942, went voluntarily to his death because he would not part with his two hundred orphans who had been condemned by the Germans. Throughout my childhood and youth I had been constantly under his influence and spell. I had read all his children's books and some of his psychological works. He wrote:

> You claim you lived?
> How many loaves of bread have you baked, for how many people? How many trees have you planted, how many dwellings do you intend to build before you go? How many buttons have you sewn, how many patches? To whom and how much warmth have you given? What were the main stages of your journey? It's irrelevant if bright neon lights, or a kerosene lamp shone on your road. But have you helped when help was needed, have you given assistance, have you shown the way — today, yesterday, some time ago, without waiting for gratitude and thanks, without asking for reward?

I worked in the garden, I ate, I slept; I was moody, frustrated; I was in love. I existed.

What had I ever done in my life?

We were infested with fleas. The first victim was Shelminka, who had forsaken her daily grooming and

146

seemed to be scratching all day long. Next, Inka got up one morning covered in sores, then Tania. The rest of us developed little pink circles, each with a tiny red spot in the centre.

The newspapers announced yet another German victory and a plague of fleas.

That cunning bug would jump on to his victim, suck his blood and then jump off.

We scrubbed Shelminka and searched through her thick coat. The best result was obtained when her hair was still damp. With experience we learned that fleas didn't like wet surfaces; their legs became tangled up and they couldn't jump in their usual springy way.

Shelminka was patient and allowed us to groom her with little fuss. We humans were quite impossible; we complained, scratched, hunted for the tiny tormentors day and night. Our eyes became sharper, our flesh super-sensitive. As soon as a little dot was noticed we wet our index finger with saliva and placed it firmly on the flea. Then the thumb would come into operation as the flea had to be placed in between. While subjecting a flea to rolling torture we would either flush it with running water, or squeeze it between two fingernails.

But no matter how successful we were in the extermination, the fleas, the master breeders, kept on multiplying in record numbers.

We never went to bed without making sure that our legs, clothes and bedding were flea-free. Alas, as soon as we tried to sleep, either Inka or Tania would jump off the bed and start the nocturnal search.

Someone advised us to place dishes full of water all over the house, using them as traps. As soon as we'd put them in place, their surface would fill with tiny corpses, but even the suicidal tendency of fleas didn't solve our problem. Among their ranks there were always the experienced, more conservative ones who preferred human flesh to adventure.

Someone else recommended vinegar, which achieved only one result — our house stank like a vinegar factory.

In the end we declared a full-scale war with organised battles taking place day in, day out. To prepare the ground we would flood the floors with boiling water and offer our bare legs as an alternative escape route. We ran, then walked all over the place, ready to be used. Panic must have reigned among the flea-ranks; they were ready to take the risk only to meet their tragic end; our very experienced thumbs and fingers were on the alert at all times.

We kept up our campaign; we were determined to eliminate the enemy; we were determined to liberate our territories and thus return freedom to all our people. Victory was ours; we won.

Our life fell into an everyday routine once again, monotonous, full of boredom. Apart from eating, sleeping and attending to our daily needs, we read. Vitek played patience over and over again. Sometimes he would stop in the middle of a game and stare out through the window. I was sure he was dreaming of designing bridges and railways again, for almost all of his constructions had been bombed at the beginning of the War. They must have been considered strategic objects.

After a while Vitek would go back to his game. From time to time we would catch him cheating. He would smile, embarrassed, and explain that it was absolutely necessary because he had promised himself that we would all survive if the game ended successfully.

I thought about how unfair life was. Vitek was a brilliant man who had much to offer in his professional capacity. He had missed a chance to migrate to Australia before the War because he hadn't wanted to part from the rest of his family. And now he was wasting his talents on playing patience. It must have been terrible for him, but he never complained.

Inka and I knitted a lot, recycling old worn-out garments. Marek spent most of his time reading, preparing his lessons and being constantly reminded to lower his voice and not to walk too close to the window.

That spring of 1943 Marek was almost twelve, tall, skinny and very even-tempered. Aunt Olga gave him one of the kitchen stools which he used as a desk, to do his lessons. Later, Julek made a couple of shelves under the top of the stool and Marek arranged all his wordly possessions with fussy precision. Every note, every piece of paper had its rightful place and all the pens and pencils were placed in regimented rows. We tried to draw him into light-hearted conversation to which he would respond enthusiastically, just in time to be reminded not to laugh too loudly.

The trouble with us all was that we had stewed in each other's company for too long. Our temperaments, tempers and problems were coming to the surface all the time.

Tania kept to herself, participating little, if at all, in the necessary chores. Mother and aunt Olga travelled to Warsaw almost daily and were very much involved in their Underground work. I seldom ventured out; only when it was necessary. I hated going out and, if I was sent shopping, preferred it when the weather was really bad. If the weather was good I felt like a traitor walking under the trees, breathing in the fresh air, feeling the warmth of the sun and being conscious of the fact that my family, especially Marek, was denied that right.

I constantly argued with my mother, who urged me to spend more time outdoors. What hurt me most was her lack of consideration towards our family.

'Please mother, leave me alone', I begged her one day when we were alone. 'I don't want to sit in the sun, I can't, with Marek and the rest cooped up inside. One day, when the War is over, we'll all go outside together.'

'Vitek, Inka, come quick', mother called them and then, with tears in her eyes, told them of my 'heart of

149

gold'. I felt utterly humiliated and refused to speak to her.

'Don't be too harsh. The fresh air will do you a lot of good', intervened Vitek. 'There is no point in you staying inside; it doesn't help us; it doesn't change our situation. Your mother means well.'

I didn't answer; I was in one of my moods. I couldn't even tell him that whenever I went shopping I hated the spring air and the flowers bursting open. I hated the harmony of colours, I even hated the freshly opened branch of the lilac. The more perfect the weather, the deeper my feelings.

That spring was a great disappointment to us all. The German army was still deep in Russian territory. The end of the War was as far away as the end of our people was close and imminent. What was the point? I often wondered. We had sentenced ourselves to house arrest in the name of some very dubious prospects for the future. It was us versus the mighty Reich. I often thought that maybe we should all go out: walk through the meadows, under the trees, over the sand dunes, to the river, through the forests and cities and villages until we reached the frontier. And then what? There was no freedom on the other side, either. Wherever one looked, wherever one turned, every place, small or large, was under German domination.

My morbid mood was easily affected. I looked for signs around me: 'If this bird lands on that tree we will survive'.

I looked for omens, numbers of pickets in fences, numbers of carriages in a train: 'Will we, will we not?' Clouds in the sky: 'If it covers the sun we are doomed'. Fortune telling through birds and clouds was too risky; I tried to stick to numbers — at least they offered us a fifty-fifty chance.

I was more tolerant as far as Vitek, Inka, Julek and Marek were concerned. I was bitchy towards my mother,

Tania, even aunt Olga. Tania irritated me because she seldom helped, being mainly preoccupied with herself. Mother and aunt Olga complained that the War robbed them of what was left of their lives. 'Marek and you, you will have plenty of time to catch up with whatever you missed because of the War. But as for us, our best years are gone, never to come back.'

When we had lived in Warsaw the laundry hadn't presented any problems. We knew a washing woman who did the job efficiently and well, and who asked few unnecessary questions. If she did, it could be dealt with on the spot, in a matter-of-fact way.

'Got yourself a husband, miss?', was her logical reaction when she discovered men's clothes in our very feminine bundle.

'No.'

'I see.'

'What d'you see?'

'Don't worry, miss. I wasn't born yesterday. Young blood's strong. I know life. You'd be surprised how much one learns by handling dirty linen.'

'It's our friend's clothes.'

'Call him what you like . . .' She shifted our soiled clothes separating whites from colours, her hands and face driftwood dry. 'Sure, sure' she mumbled to herself. 'No worries. It will be ready for you in a week's time.'

And it always was.

Warsaw was a big city where one could find all kinds of services and remain anonymous, but Zielonka was inhabited by people who were always hungry for exciting events, such as news about who washed whose clothes and what the dirty bundle consisted of.

None of us had ever done any washing, except for a few personal things. In the pre-war situation all our washing had been done by a laundry woman who lived in the attic of our block of flats and catered for all the tenants. I never saw the woman at work. She spent all her working hours in the laundry situated next to her dwelling. But when she worked for us, she had her meals in our kitchen, so I knew her. She ate yards of sausage, tons of bread and drank litres of coffee. She never refused a glass of vodka; which made her upturned nose red and her hair, tied in a pathetic bun, shake on the top of her frightfully thin head. She ate slowly, as if with piety, and always apologised when she asked for some more coffee.

'The water drains you down a lot; I'm always thirsty.'

'Drink, drink. The more the better', Kazia would urge. 'The water makes you dry. No need to apologise; everyone knows.'

The woman had fascinated me. Her knuckles were thick and twisted, her hands red. They were like flails, ready to be put into motion at any time.

She never said much. I didn't even know her family name. When we left Lodz we had persuaded her to take my father's books and keep them in her tiny room during the War.

'Look after them, Antosia', we had said.

At Zielonka, when our dirty linen started to mount, we were confronted with a problem. For the first time in our lives we had to wash our own clothes. My mother, aunt Olga and Tania made such a fuss that Inka and I volunteered to wash. We did it well, to the amazement of us all. We scrubbed the linen over the tub, then boiled, rinsed and soaked it. The whole operation used to take three days. We were lucky that aunt Olga had a washboard, a tub, a copper and a hand-wringer.

Julek used to assist both Inka and I in our tasks and became the chief clothes-wringer. Whenever we left the washing overnight, it was he who would conceal the men's linen among the other articles; so that in case of a raid, the presence of our men wouldn't be disclosed.

The time I always looked forward to was the hanging-up of the clothes to dry. Julek and I would go to the attic and, between hanging one thing and another, Julek would kiss my red, rough hands all over and I would kiss his. For us it was a rare moment. It was quiet. We talked and cuddled; time seemed to slow down. I would open all four attic windows and air, saturated with spring, would rush in from four directions.

'What's taking you so long?' Inka would call. If it wasn't Inka, it would be Tania, or my mother. Once summoned we had to go down.

But I remember the occasion when we decided to present our case to my mother, to ask her to let us sleep together.

Mother sat at the the table reading.

'We want to sleep together, Julek and I . . . Mother?'

'I heard you. There is no need to be vulgar.' She didn't even lift her eyes from the book.

'Keep your lecture on vulgarity for another occasion, please. All right, mother? We are serious.'

Mother looked at me, her pain transparent.

'I understand. You're childish and that's that. You should wait till the end of the War and decide then. You are only eighteen. This situation is not fair to yourself or to Julek.'

'Brilliant advice, mother. Are you sure the War will end for us? And if it does, what then? You doubt me. You doubt my feelings. You married father when you were eighteen.'

'It was during the Revolution.'

'The War is not much different.'

'You have an answer for everything. How little you know.'

'You doubt me.'

'I don't. I know your feelings. I am trying to find a solution, it's not easy.'

How old-fashioned, how pompous, how hypocritical

153

my mother seemed. To us, the situation was more than simple. We were in love, in need of each other, at a time when the future had become an abstract idea. If there was a chance to make each other happier then why not take it? Thinking of the future was as destructive as thinking of the past.

And mother wasn't a puritan, either. When Mr. Kohn came along she had grabbed those short-lived moments of happiness, or whatever, disregarding the feelings of others. At least I didn't think I was hurting others and, if I was, it was because of their own stupidity and lack of understanding. I was more than sure of my feelings. I wanted Julek — not because there was nobody else around, not because he was the only male available — because I loved him. I promised myself that, if by some freak chance we were to survive, I would let him go free should he choose to do so.

Mother avoided me as a liar avoids the truth. I was sure my request had been discussed with everybody in our household except Julek and me. The whole atmosphere was saturated with the unspoken.

——14——

A few days later we had just finished our lunch. The 'old generation' had gone to play bridge, or maybe to talk about us. Tania had deserted me, going outside to warm herself in the sun and leaving me with the dirty dishes. Marek, under Julek's guidance, was getting familiar with another aspect of knowledge.

So I washed the dishes. The branches of the huge maple tree swayed. Shelminka begged to be let out, for she was in love with the mongrel next door. Both in love, she and I. If only uncle could have known.

'Wait a second. I'll let you out as soon as I finish.'

There was an urgent knock on the door. Trust my sister. 'Let me dry the dishes, you can surely wait. Can't you?'

But Tania knocked and called and knocked again. When I went to the door mother and aunt Olga came to see what was happening and the rest of the family watched from a distance. Tania was still shouting, and when we let her in she waved her hands, pointing to the garden.

'Germans. Hide, quickly. Germans.'

Aunt Olga slammed the door. 'What do you mean?'

We all rushed to the window. A group of Germans was running towards our place, guns in hand.

'Denunciation.' I didn't know who said it. Vitek grabbed Marek's hand and ran towards the cellar, followed by Inka and Julek. Nobody said a word, apart from an occasional 'Oh, my God'. Shelminka barked. My breath was uneven; I was panting.

'I'm going down to shut the trapdoor.'

Before I managed to reach the cellar the Germans were banging on the door, and Shelminka started to bark louder than ever. Inka was half way into the shelter, with only her legs sticking out.

'Hurry up, hurry up', Vitek whispered.

'She's changed her mind, she doesn't like it here any more.' Julek smiled.

'Hurry up, mother', panted Marek.

Inka reappeared, dripping sand. From above came the sounds of cursing, banging, and Shelminka's vicious yapping.

'Push me from behind, the sand's caved in.' Inka's head was back in the tunnel. We pushed her in, at last. Then it was Marek's turn. Inka pulled him from within and we helped from the outside, knowing that the Germans were already inside the house.

'I won't be able to do it', Vitek said simply.

'I'll go in first. All will be well.' Julek touched my hand.

We heard footsteps and sharp voices above. Julek and Vitek went through a wiggling motion before they disappeared. The trap door was secured. Shelminka growled, doors banged.

I waited for a moment of quiet and then returned to the kitchen where I started pumping water. We had no rabbits in the cages. Who could have denounced us?

Shelminka pressed hard against my legs and licked them. Good old Shelminka. Thanks for barking. I patted her while she shivered. They re-entered the kitchen, four soldiers in green uniforms, with shiny boots and guns.

I pumped. Let us not die at their hands.

The voices, what language was it? I pumped. Mother's face was all flushed. Russian? Was it possible? Russians in German uniforms?

'Where is the cellar?', one of them asked, and it was

said in the language of Tolstoy but with an intonation worthy of the German uniform.

'Cellar, cellar . . .', mother mouthed the word as if trying to comprehend. 'Oh, cellar', she exclaimed, and led the men to the attic.

'Phew', I thought, and pumped.

They stayed up there for a while, talking and moving around loudly, then they came down. They left the house and there was silence, except for my pumping, and then it also came to a stop.

I put my arm around Tania. Mother embraced both of us and we watched from behind the curtains. Aunt Olga unlocked the gate. The soldiers left, and we heard them laughing. We ran down to the cellar with Shelminka constantly in our way; she was wagging her tail and trembling at the same time.

We let our prisoners out.

We all looked at Tania.

'I was sunbaking . . .' she began.

'Thank God you were outside', said mother.

'There were some noises. I didn't pay much attention, the sun was so warm. The noise roused me from my lovely, peaceful state. I opened my eyes. Germans were running towards our house, shouting, with guns in their hands.'

Tania was visibly excited. I wondered what would have happened if she had been a well disciplined member of our small community and had scrubbed the floor as she was supposed to do, instead of sitting in the sun. Vitek lit a cigarette and Inka pointed out that he shouldn't.

'I banged at the door. I thought you would never open it. What took you so long? By the time you let me in they were already jumping the fence!'

'Was it denunciation?' Vitek's eyes were circled with dark, feverish rings.

'No, nothing of the sort. They were looking for the

157

body of some high official disposed of by the Underground, so they told us. Imagine, Russians in German uniforms! Members of the Russian Liberation Army, under German command.'

'The sand caved in.' Inka stood on the side and talked as if to herself. 'Sand was all over the place and it was impossible to get in. Only when they started pushing me from behind could I manage to swim through the sand and make a passage for the others.'

'Let's go up; this calls for a celebration. The hideout has passed the test.' Aunt Olga was as relieved as the rest of us. We went upstairs and, while the women were taking the glasses out and chatting, Marek told me that the tunnel was very dark and dank. They had spent some time firming the sand to prevent any further slides, and it had reminded him of the time he used to play on the beach, building sand castles and high walls.

'Rabbits', said Inka. 'We still haven't got any rabbits. What will happen if they come with dogs next time?'

'There won't be a next time', said mother. Just then the banging on the door started all over again. Shelminka barked viciously and we were on the run again. Aunt Olga called, 'Ein Moment'. We all breathed hard, and Shelminka, our funny little terrified dog, created a lot of noise, the life-saving noise which drowned out our breathing, our heart-beats.

This time the whole operation was executed faultlessly. I was back at the pump in no time, even before they had entered the house. This time they were real Germans.

They looked into every corner, under beds, in the cupboards. They asked many questions and their voices produced a temporary paralysis, in me anyway. They were thorough and demanding.

'What's that?'

'My late husband's clippers.'

'So you don't need them any more?'

'Not really. If you can put them to good use, take them.'

'If you insist.' The man put the clippers in his pocket and, soon after, they all left. Again aunt Olga took them to the gate and let them out.

It all seemed like a bad dream; with wave after wave of soldiers jumping over the fence; Vitek, Inka, Marek and Julek rushing to the cellar; and the search going through the house while Shelminka either barked or shivered. The constant interrogations brought confusion and left us with feelings of uncertainity. We hardly had time to tell Vitek that all was well before we heard once more the banging at the door, and the hysterical barking of Shelminka.

'Rabbits; get some rabbits', urged Vitek. So, while mother said, 'One moment', Olga and I sneaked out through the back door. As the last of the soldiers went inside, we left through the gate.

We walked briskly towards the main road, wishing and hoping that all would be well on our return. Aunt Olga was praying.

'Rabbits are important. Let me think . . . The Pavlak family; I remember, someone mentioned that they breed rabbits.'

The weather was perfect and it made me wonder why, whenever there was a crisis in my life, the sun shone; as it had when my father died; as it did now.

There were groups of Germans entering and leaving the houses. Dogs barked, soldiers shouted. Sometimes someone cried. The shadows were getting longer; it must have been late afternoon. I was hungry. I thought of Marek and the others, sitting in the dark and firming the sand; they must have been hungry, too.

The Pavlaks' house was small with a crooked gate leaning against the side. Clay pots were turned upside-down on the fence, potted geraniums sat in the win-

159

dows, and along the narrow path flowers crowded in on both sides. Someone inside was crying.

'Mrs. Pavlak? I am Mrs. Boyarski. This is my niece. We were wondering if you could spare us two rabbits. I promised my niece I would buy her some.'

'Holy Mother! You must be out of your mind; forgive me for saying it. Those Russian devils stole my daughter's watch — a present from her boyfriend; it has broken her heart. Rabbits today? Out of the question. No, definitely not. Come back some other day.'

'As we are already here. Please Mrs. Pavlak, it won't take long. You see, I promised.'

'What's the matter with you people?' Mrs. Pavlak was openly annoyed. 'People have been robbed, a girl across the road was raped. Can't you think of others? Oh, what a world!' She reknotted her kerchief tighter under her firm chin and turned her back on us.

We left.

'The whole family must be mad', we heard her saying. 'My rabbits aren't for sale', she called after us. 'Not today, not tomorrow. You . . . you . . .' she shouted, while her daughter cried.

'Look.' Aunt Olga squeezed my arm.

In front of us, some distance away, marched a patrol of six Germans leading two Alsatians. We knew that the rabbits were essential. We had to have them, even if the whole village pronounced us crazy.

But, on that day of all days, people were not interested in selling rabbits. We walked miles, we knocked at many doors, we pleaded with many people and, as always happens, when we had just about given up the whole idea, a dry-looking peasant woman said, 'Sure'. We left her place carrying one little rabbit each. Mine was soft, warm and white. It had a funny, never-still, pink nose.

We hurried home.

The gate was wide open; there was yet another group of Germans rummaging through the house. Mother

160

seemed calm, but of course she wasn't. Tania had found herself a rightful place in the kitchen, cutting or rather reducing potatoes into small useless pieces. Shelminka was nowhere to be seen. I went outside and let my rabbits nibble at the grass. Only when the search ended did we put the bunnies into the cages. Mother informed us that there had been six more raids while we lucky ones were away. Vitek decided not to leave the hiding place and mother said, 'Rightly so'; and, before she had time to add something else, Shelminka started to bark again. She was quite hoarse by then, almost as hoarse as some of the searchers.

They came in variations of the same pattern, shouting, abusing, making us feel small, reducing us to nervous wrecks.

Darkness fell and we turned on the lights. Shelminka re-emerged from under the darkest corner, all ruffled and shaking. Once the shutters were closed we felt some illusory security. We were not sure if the raids had ended and, after consultation, it was agreed that our prisoners should stay behind the rabbits in safety.

I buried my face in Shelminka's moppy hair and we both shivered. The Germans could spring on us again at any moment. We had become wise to the fact that they didn't always ring at the gate as we had imagined at first. Once they came, they came. There was no time left to hide, or very little time. There was no time to call from the window, 'One moment please'; there was no time to think, to organise, to be reasonable. There was only time for basic reflexes: the barking and yapping of Shelminka, the quickened beating of the heart, the sweating and blind fear, and nothing else; nothing.

We hardly ate and avoided looking into each other's eyes. We four sat around the table; we could stretch our legs if we wanted to. We didn't have to worry about luxuries such as getting up and sitting down, or going from one room to another, or going to the toilet, or washing away the sticky fear from our faces and bodies. So I refused to go to bed and, when the others went to sleep, I lay on the floor directly over the hideout. I must have dozed off, because suddenly it was morning and I felt cold, although the whole room was spiked with sun-beams which squeezed their way through cracks in the shutters.

We let Vitek and the others out. They struggled through the small opening, one by one, physically and spiritually crushed.

'Was it really necessary?', questioned Inka. 'For the whole night?' Her voice was dark like her eyes.

Nobody answered.

Marek picked up one of the bunnies. He rubbed it against his face. Rabbits. Yes, rabbits, fluffy, warm and uncomplicated, were better than words. Mother told of how many search parties had gone through the house. Aunt Olga explained how, 'At the very last minute', we managed to buy the rabbits.

'The Russians said that they are coming to visit us next Friday. What shall we do?', said Tania, and she told us how she cut the potatoes so that nobody would suspect she was nervous.

'Don't call them Russians. They are Vlasov's men — Moslems from Asia — not Russians; that's why they have Fridays off', Mother insisted. 'We have to find some way out.'

'We will think about it later. The mind can take in only so much.' Vitek shuffled upstairs, followed by the rest of us.

While the four of them washed, the four of us prepared a meal. We were ever so eager; it was our 'conscience' meal. The division we never allowed ourselves to acknowledge had became visible in all its ugliness.

I stayed in their room when they went to bed. I listened to their slow breathing and watched their still faces. Outside the window the branches had new leaves, and pink, puffy clouds floated in the spring sky. My people, my family. I loved them all so much. I looked at Julek and wanted to touch him, to cuddle up to him. I moved to the window and scanned the meadow in front; there was nobody in view. The buttercups, which must have been trampled down the day before, lifted their yellow crowns to the sun again, yellow and green. 'You should never use those colours together; they clash; like egg and spring onion', my art teacher had once instructed me. But she was wrong. To me, now, they were soothing, as soothing as those sleeping faces. I caressed my loved ones and kissed them with my eyes. I wished them good dreams at a time when there was no room for dreams.

The local butcher's shop was ugly. There was a drab serving counter and a chopping block. Huge hooks hung from the ceiling. There were always people waiting to be served. And there was the butcher.

'Have you heard yet what happened?' He chopped and carved the chunks of meat while he talked. His humble customers listened.

'Never been a secret to me that the Germans are better than the Russians. Civilised, that's what they are. Once you bribe them, you're all right. They close their eyes, that's what they do. They stick to their business; I stick to mine. As you know I keep the whole district in meat, doing my patriotic duty.'

He handed a woman a scrap of meat. 'Thanks.' She paid him. He looked at the bank-note against the light. 'Have to be extra careful, there's a lot of dud money around', he said, and put it in his bulging pocket. He wiped his hands on his apron, spotted with blood and dirt. 'So, as I was saying, those Russkis invited themselves to a wedding. Got drunk, then raped the bride after killing the groom and his parents. They squealed all right, my God, more than pigs. One kilogram is all you'll get. If you don't like it, don't worry. Someone else will be only too grateful to get it.

'Look at the Germans. They would never do a thing like that; not in front of others. They brought in the Russians and now the Russkis give them a bad name. And the reason they brought them in was to perform certain not-very-pleasant duties. Because they're cultured people, a messy job is too much for them.'

His knife sliced through the meat. 'Who wants a liver?' He tossed the piece of offal up and down, and the shoppers followed his movements as if hypnotized.

I was glad when I was given a small cut of meat which would last us until the following week.

I walked away quickly, not even counting the holes in the fences, thinking about Vlasov and his men. There was a mention of him in the Underground press, but until the recent raid we had never come in contact with his men. Vlasov was a Russian general who had defected from the Russian army after the fall of Kiev. He placed himself and his men under the German command and organised the so-called Russian Liberation Army. He drew on conscripts from the prisoner-of-war camps. The conditions in those camps were beyond description; it was as if the Germans had never heard of the Geneva Convention.

Once my mother and I came across a camp of Russian prisoners-of-war when the train to Warsaw was channelled to a remote track to let a military transport go through. The prisoners were kept under the open sky. They were all in rags, without boots, and they had a haunted look. They were heavily guarded and the whole area was surrounded by barbed wire. The men must have been starving; there was not even one blade of grass left within the reach of an outstretched hand. They were doomed and silent. We couldn't see much more; the guards were vicious and ordered us away from the train's windows. Good old General Vlasov drew his recruits from the men he had deserted. The men were given the choice of exchanging the camps and death for food and life. It was a matter of conscience and of life at any cost.

At the cross-roads I looked at the little wooden wayside chapel. The Holy Virgin looked down, her wooden eyes painted bright blue. Freshly cut flowers lay in front, as always; a sign of love, respect, hope. She had been standing there for a long time, patient, indifferent, painted blue and white and gold.

When Friday came we secured the shutters and pretended the house was deserted. From the attic we watched over the whole area. The Russians arrived in the afternoon. This time they rang at the gate and waited patiently for it to be opened. They waited for a while and then left, cursing to the sky above. Shelminka wriggled in my arms and squeaked in a tiny voice.

Jadwiga visited us shortly afterwards. She brought lilac, and her goodness.

'One can really see the end of the Germans in sight. The American and British invasion should take place at any time now. The Eastern front is just about to collapse. You have to believe, now more than ever.'

I told her of my love and of mother's attitude to our proposal.

'I will speak to her', she promised. 'I will come again before long.' She gave Marek her old, maiden diary with a security lock, the one she had never had the time or desire to use.

'Perhaps you will put it to a good purpose?'

We kept watch for a few weeks until we learned that the garrison of Vlasov's men had been moved to Warsaw. We worried for Warsaw, but at the same time were immensely relieved that they had left our district.

——15——

We were man and wife, Julek and I. We were lovers, sinners, married, unmarried, or whatever the correct term was.

Naturally, Julek was obliged to propose to my mother — which was slightly idiotic. The proposal took place in the attic. Mother's attitude had swayed in my favour by then, the winning argument apparently being that the Russians were committing rape wherever they went. So mother must have decided in her wisdom that Julek would be a better person to introduce her daughter to sex. After all, one had to compromise all the time; war was war.

So one day, when I was on attic duty with her, she turned her head and said: 'Have it your own way'. She avoided my eyes, she was so shy. So was I, and her following words of advice bounced off me, while my heart performed uncontrollable acrobatics. Spring was everywhere, even in the attic, where the dust particles danced within the narrow lines of sunbeams. 'That's what I should do, dance, yes dance in a confined space', I thought.

'Send Julek over.' Mother's voice was funny in its seriousness. 'At least he should announce his intentions properly.' She was leaning on the wall.

'Please mother, I don't want any fuss. No questions. Tell everyone not to make any fuss.'

'How little you know.' Her voice sounded uneven, as

though she were covering and uncovering her mouth while speaking.

'You somehow always manage to hurt me, regardless of what I do.'

'It wasn't my intention, now at least.'

'Yes, yes.'

I went down and when I told Julek of my mother's request he looked puzzled and bewildered. He climbed up to the attic and I stayed in the kitchen for ten long minutes. I couldn't catch a word of what they were saying; they must have talked in a whisper. So I went to Inka and put my arms around her. She was pleased.

'Trust me. I really love Julek. I'll try to be good to him.' She kissed me.

'I know, my child. I know.' She sounded happy, warm-happy and very emotional. She must have thought of Julek's parents at that moment as I did.

I went back to the kitchen to pump water, and thought that even a water-pump could come in handy. Tania appeared from nowhere.

'It has been decided. Julek and you, I mean.'

'What has been decided?'

'Julek and you will sleep in the lounge room. How do you feel about it? I am your sister. Tell me?'

'I've nothing to say.' I pumped and pumped.

In the end Julek came down.

'So now we're engaged!' He still had that stupid, bewildered expression on his face.

There was a triumphant cry: 'I knew it; I knew it!' Marek ran to us on his long spidery legs and hugged first me, then Julek.

'Don't shout', Vitek tried to reprimand him. But he was happy too, and kissed us. And then it was Tania's turn, then aunt Olga's and then Inka's again; we were tossed from one pair of arms to another. Even Shelminka jumped around and barked in a happy way.

The family assembly had decided that Julek and I were

to be exempted from kitchen duties until the end of the day — an engagement present. They ushered us into the lounge room and left us on our own. We could hear their voices, shushing and excited. We stayed apart all the time, apart and uneasy, until they called us in, in an artificially indifferent way. Then they looked at us calculatingly, all of them except Marek.

'My fiance has told me about our engagement, mother; how long do you propose our engagement to last?'

'You are impossible. You will never learn, will you?', said mother.

Julek reached for my hand. 'Never mind, never mind', he said.

I left the room and went to pump some more water, carrying with me Marek's hurt expression.

Four days later, after aunt Olga and mother had returned from their latest visit to Warsaw, we sat for our evening meal, and a bottle of vodka was produced.

'To our young couple.' Mother proposed the toast, to which we all drank.

Vitek stood up.

'There is an old Jewish custom — provision, I mean. Under special circumstances, if there is no rabbi available, the elder of the family can perform a wedding ceremony. I don't exactly know what to do, except perhaps to wish you survival and good luck. Remember, we are always behind you.

'From tonight on you will use this room. We shouldn't really have more than four beds visible. So, as before, Inka and I will sleep in one bed, Tania in another and Marek on the floor in between. Olga and your mother will sleep in Olga's bed and you two can have the settee. In an emergency Marek's mattress will be placed on Tania's bed.' He stopped for a while and I wanted to tell him how much I loved him, but of course I didn't.

'We also must, the four of us, have all our clothes made into a bundle every night. So that, if the situation arises, we will be able to grab our things and run to the hideout without losing any time, while you four will take your rightful positions with as little fuss as possible.'

'O.K. We should also leave the trapdoor open at all times and leave the passage clear of chairs and things', Julek added.

'Good idea . . . I feel very tired; it must have been that vodka!' Vitek smiled. 'Another thing which came to my mind; we should never use more than four plates at the one time, four settings only of everything . . . Come, Julek, I want to ask you something.' They left the room together, the elder of my clan and my husband-to-be.

We cleared the table, and everyone started yawning and complaining about how tired they were. Aunt Olga showed me how to set up the settee for the night, and mother and Tania pushed the little corner table next to it. While I was preparing the bed aunt Olga placed a bedside lamp on the table, and then brought in a few twigs of jasmine which filled the whole room with its perfume. The fragrant, white miracle of spring.

Everything became quiet. Shelminka curled up on her cushion, the cages were covered for the night, the parrots went to sleep and Julek and I were left to ourselves. Light came in from aunt Olga's room, diffused light, which allowed us to see each other. We breathed stupid little words into each other's ears; we wrote messages on each other's bodies; but, above all, we loved. Our feelings, bottled up over a long time, exploded. We gave, we took, we became one. There was pain and serenity . . . willingness . . . consideration. And love.

The room was dark by then but every time we moved, the bedside lamp switched itself on. The stupid lamp didn't have a proper switch. Our impatient fingers unscrewed the globe. We fell back into each other's arms, rolling, tossing. Suddenly, we were stopped again by the shining light and by the parrots screaming, objecting to being woken in the middle of the night. On that of all nights!

Electricity at night spelled trouble. We knew it meant that a search was being conducted in the district. That thought filled the room until Julek took the globe right out . . . and then came only darkness, warmth, closeness, and feelings of happiness, fulfilment and laziness until my sudden awakening in the early morning greyness in the arms of my husband.

Three days later there was smoke over Warsaw. Planes were bombing non-stop and shells were exploding over one square mile of Jewish territory: there was an uprising in the Warsaw Ghetto. My people. Easter 1943.

'No, no', they said. 'Don't. It's sheer lunacy.'

But I went to Warsaw anyway. I had to see. I had to. On the train people behaved as if nothing had happened. In the streets they hurried, smiled, talked. Next to the Ghetto the Germans had placed guns; they were firing bullets.

There was a fun-fair there, with merry-go-rounds and shooting galleries, ready for the holiday crowd. People seemed to be enjoying the sunshine, even if it was dimmed by smoke. Around and around went the fun rides, zooming up, up, and coming down with an unreal sound of laughter. Balloons, red and blue, yellow and green, floated above the crowd.

'Look. Look there!'

'Where?'

'Over there! Can't you see? Jewish bugs jumping from the window.'

Over there. People, their clothes on fire, cut the smoked-filled air. There was a thumping, final sound and the merry-go-round whirled on. Around it went to its gay music. There were so many happy faces.

'The best houses in Warsaw are burning down.'

'See, I came here to give my kids a bit of fun. Nothing wrong with fun, is there? Look at him, instead of enjoying himself he rubs his eyes. "Too much smoke", he says. All that fun and he frets, wants to go home. "Too noisy", he says. A boy shouldn't be afraid of guns, not my son. The trouble is . . . '

Guns and colourful balloons . . . burning houses and merry-go-rounds . . . laughter and the final death cry . . . dry, sonorous detonations and gay music.

Sharp shooters were everywhere, standing, kneeling and firing every so often. The holiday crowds stood in front of their shooting gallery, aiming at their targets. One received a medal, another a clay figurine.

I stood war-shocked, angry, numb, impotent, until someone took my arm. 'Better go home, miss. Not the safest place to be.'

They were selling lilac on the streets and the boys waved newspapers. 'Latest from the Jewish fro-ont. Ta-anks, heavy artillery in actio-on'. It was Easter. One thousand nine hundred and forty three years before, one innocent man went to death; He came to bring peace to the earth. Or so they claimed.

That night I went to the attic and looked at Warsaw: a glare on the horizon with a clear, starry sky above. The best houses in Warsaw were burning, the locals were saying — the houses I knew, the people I knew, the people I had deserted.

So much for my honeymoon.

The Ghetto was burning, defending itself longer than Poland, France and the rest of the Continent.

The Ghetto was burning and Vitek was suffering with a toothache. He followed Julek, pliers in hand, face swollen.

'All you have to do is to pull it out. It shouldn't be too difficult.'

'No. I really can't. How could I?'

'Just grab the tooth and pull.'

171

'No, not me.'

Our rabbits were blessed with six offspring. So they were not two males as we had thought. They ate like horses and produced an enormous amount of excrement. If their cages were left unattended for a couple of days, the air became vile, their white coats changed to a dirty brown and the straw dripped. So I cleaned their cages . . . while the Ghetto burned.

Vitek poured gallons of cold water over his face. 'It helps', he claimed. I didn't think that toothache could be infectious, but all of a sudden both Inka and Julek joined Vitek and complained that their teeth were giving them trouble too — although not as much as Vitek's.

Who but Jadwiga could come to the rescue? Her sister happened to be a dentist, which meant she was trustworthy from both a dental and security point of view. She agreed to come with Jadwiga at short notice, in four days' time.

So, in the meantime, Vitek kept on pouring water over his cheek, while the rest of the family explored their teeth with their tongues, or simply looked at them in the mirror, counting holes.

While the Ghetto struggled.

We never touched on the subject. One is not supposed to speak of death in front of a dying patient. It was an unspoken agreement. But we caught each other looking in the direction of Warsaw, where the black smoke hung and drifted.

Vitek came out with another story, this time of a poor family who lived in one overcrowded, miserable room. They were desperate; they couldn't stand their life any more and, as a last resort, decided to seek the advice of their learned rabbi. To their amazement, the rabbi ordered them to take a goat to live in the room with them for a whole week. They did as they were told. Naturally, they cursed their life and poverty, and they cursed the goat. After a week the rabbi gave them permission to remove the goat and told them to report to him again. When they saw the rabbi a few days later they kissed his hand, blessing him for his wisdom and goodness.

They told him how happy they were, for their dwelling had proved to be just right for them all, once the goat had gone. By allowing them to get rid of the goat, he had given them back their freedom.

When Vitek finished I wasn't sure if he was referring to his tooth, or to our situation in general.

'Once my tooth goes, I'll be at peace again. Please, Julek. Pull it out. Give it a go. What about it?', he pleaded.

I remembered how my father had once defined Jewish pleasure to me. 'Try it', he urged. 'When you are well tucked-up in a warm bed, stick your foot out and keep it there till it freezes. Then pull it back inside your cosy bed. Only then will you understand what pleasure really means.'

Jewish philosophy: the philosophy of a goat and a cold foot.

The Ghetto uprising entered its fifth week. Its days were numbered, but the German press was still reporting from the Jewish front. How much longer could it last? The whole of Poland had been conquered within a month; the whole Continent hadn't lasted any longer.

Jadwiga and her sister Vanda arrived. She carried a little bag full of shiny, cold instruments which she arranged in order on a small table. She said she would have something to eat and a cup of whatever was going, but not immediately. Duty called and she wanted to finish her job first.

Vitek was already sitting in an armchair, his mouth wide open. Vanda examined his teeth. 'I see', she said. 'Someone please hold his head.' I held his head; it was a strange sensation. It seemed cool, firm, pulsating, throbbing. All his thoughts were born there, it was the storehouse of his childhood recollections, goat stories, philosophy . . .

Vitek sighed while Vanda probed around his teeth.

'I'll fix it all up. There's no need to worry, so please don't.' She paused for a cigarette. Her fingers were like her instruments, sharp and pointed. 'I want you to know that I don't have to prove my professional competence, so please don't fear.' She blew out little cotton-wool puffs of smoke. 'I will do my very best, as I always do.' She stubbed her cigarette as if she was packing the tooth.

She was attractive, much more beautiful than Jadwiga, but too clinical. Jadwiga spoke with her eyes. She had an ugly chin and her mousey-coloured hair fell all over, but she winked at you; she made people feel good.

'Will you please sit down again.'

Once Vitek was seated, Vanda caught my eye.

'Hold your uncle's head firmer, will you please. It will make my impossible task a bit easier. That's better. Now to work. I will try . . . to fill a couple of those ghastly . . . cavities . . . Then I will prepare you for the extraction; don't be alarmed; I will give you an injection.'

Click went the steely instruments. She leaned over Vitek with not even one hair out of place. She packed Vitek's mouth with cotton wool and, after a while, asked him to leave the chair. He sat on the bed with his mouth wide open; Inka piled some cushions behind his back. The corner of Vitek's mouth jumped up and his eyes sort of bulged.

'Next please.' Vanda wiped her hands while Julek took a seat.

'Firm grip, remember.'

She didn't even bother to look in my direction when she said it.

'Well, what do we have here? We will have to extract . . . this one for sure. Shouldn't be too . . . difficult.' She gave him an injection and sent him to the waiting queue.

174

Inka and Marek were easy.

'You have to understand that it is impossible to prepare a tooth without previously cleaning the area properly. It can't be done without drilling as you must appreciate. All I can do is a patch-up job. No guarantee.'

'We are more than grateful', said Inka.

'Don't mention it. Jadwiga wanted me to do it, so here I am and, believe me, I am doing my best.'

'We appreciate it very much.'

'Back to your seat, young man', Vanda instructed Julek. 'We will give the other gentleman a while longer, his tooth is more complicated than yours. Time never stands still; we have to finish the job we started.'

I held Julek's head, with Vanda's face next to it.

'A-a-ah', moaned Julek.

'Keep still', commanded Vanda. 'Unfortunately, not all injections work; some are stale and useless.' She pulled something out, her hands smeared with blood. 'One out. I had to pull a healthy tooth to gain a better access to the decayed one.'

Julek's forehead was covered by tiny, cold droplets; his eyes rolled. I wiped the perspiration off.

'You are useless, aren't you? You were assigned to hold his head, not to nurse him.'

I felt faint. Aunt Olga took my place and I sat next to Vitek, utterly ashamed. Vitek watched the whole procedure, his skin tight, his eyes popping out. Vanda struggled, Julek cried, aunt Olga held on, minutes ticked by. Vanda came up with another tooth.

'Now for the right one. Shouldn't be too long.' Her cheeks were flushed. Julek's face was white. Aunt Olga shut her eyes and held his head really tight. Vitek placed his hand over his face.

Outside, thick smoke hung over Warsaw.

'He is all yours', said Vanda.

All mine! So pale, with his cold hands and suffering eyes. I led Julek out of the room. He lay down on our

175

couch, turning his head from side to side and wiping the corner of his mouth. Blood.

Life seemed unreal to me. Where should I have drawn a dividing line? What was suffering? There was Julek and his endlessly bleeding, butchered gums. Should I have felt sorry for him, or should I have dismissed all his hurt because of what was going on in the Ghetto?

Shelminka had given birth to two pups. I named them Inva, from Invasion, which was to occur any day; and Paxa, from the Latin *Pax* meaning peace. Both were pretty sickly. At night they snored and whimpered endlessly; Shelminka seemed frightened and cried. I carried them in my arms.

In those mad times, was there room for compassion?

Was there room for Shelminka's tragedy?

Was there a place for our situation, for our self-arrest, for the ever-present death sentences.

Was there room for parents whose sons had been killed or injured?

What about the military tragedies, the civilian tragedies?

How could one ever sort it out?

The whole situation frightened and confused me. Should I have felt only for my own people and hardened myself to the point where there was no room for a normal reaction to the suffering of others?

Should I have disregarded the miracle of a spring day because darkness was descending over us all?

Inva and Paxa died.

No more symbols and symbolic associations for me.

——16——

Spring changed into summer. There was no more smoke on the horizon, and Warsaw was officially declared to be a city free of Jews.

The walls tumbled down and a lot of people worked at demolishing what was left of the Ghetto houses — their ulterior motive being to search for legendary Jewish treasures.

I planned to go there but put it aside as one does with a visit to a cemetery.

I can't say much about that summer of 1943 except, perhaps, that all of us became quiet.

There was some movement on the Russian front. The African campaign had ended in the Allies' victory, which allowed their armies to land on Italian soil. So things were looking better, brighter. I knew it, as we all did, but I also feared that the Germans would dispose of us before liberation came. And, if by some miracle we did survive, we wouldn't be whole people any more; we would be just shadows.

Our vegetables grew. On hot days Vitek, Inka, Julek and Marek would lie down on the floor in front of an open window, to catch a bit of fresh air.

Shelminka recovered after her loss and became her old self again.

Sometimes I would sneak out to the garden and put my ear to the ground. Mother told me that in this way one could detect the distant artillery shelling, long before one could hear it, listening normally. But the earth didn't tremble; I heard nothing. Still, it felt good to rest one's face on fresh, warm ground and breathe in its musky fragrance.

Before autumn arrived we went through a lethargic stage. We functioned but were dispirited, except for aunt Olga and mother who were involved in the Underground. They were in constant touch with Janowski and kept on bringing home unbelieveable stories of Polish courage and German stupidity. According to our ladies, things were great; the Germans were doomed; it wouldn't be long. Mother was hurt by our indifference. She came to the conclusion that we were all depressed and badly in need of entertainment. What about Popov? With his songs he would bring a little bit of life and sunshine into our prison.

Vitek said, 'No'.

We should have known my mother better. She brought Popov with his guitar one day, and was hurt when Vitek refused to show up and hid in the shelter together with Inka and the others.

We, 'über alles', sat at the table, just above the cellar. We sat down to vodka and sausage while our family below waited, amidst the sand, the darkness and maybe, rats.

Popov sang in a strange, melancholy, quiet way, caressing rather than strumming his guitar. He must have been hurt and saddened by Vitek's mistrust, but he didn't mention it at all.

Aunt Olga went to the kitchen to prepare ersatz tea, while I went to the cellar and opened the trapdoor.

'Please come up. Popov knows, anyway, so why won't you? Mother meant well.' I spoke to their legs; it was all I could see; and then Vitek's face tilted into view, red and angry.

'I am surprised at you. If we were to join them now,

this kind of surprise would never stop. Can't you under-stand? If your mother, no matter how good her inten-tions, were just once to get our co-operation, she would bring over all her true and trusted friends. Eventually, one of them would denounce us.'

Vitek's head was in semi-darkness. He whispered to me; there was wounded pride in his voice, in his face. I was on all fours and so was he. The rabbits jumped about in the cages above.

'And one more thing. You must tell Popov that we are not here. Say that your mother is not very well again — the old nervous trouble — and say she's got her facts mixed up and that, actually, none of you know where we live.'

'At least get out of there', I said. 'After all, it's not a raid. I'll bring you something to eat.'

Vitek said, 'No'. Inka said, 'Yes'; Marek said, 'Yes'; and Julek was the first out. They all looked crumpled stiff, and I felt awful because my legs didn't hurt, because my back was all right, because I had to leave them in the damp cellar again.

Popov sang for his supper and then he ate. His wife was fine and so was Chechachov, bless his heart. He sent his regards to all of us along with a message never to give in. The War was just about to end, anyway.

'If you don't mind, I think I'd better be going. It wasn't a very successful visit.'

On the contrary, we insisted, it was great, really great, and so good of him to come all that way and bring his guitar and even to give us a private concert. 'And please give our love to your wife, and to Chechachoff.'

And then we took him to the gate. When mother said, 'I want you to take some flowers for your wife. Wait a minute', and left us, I said:

'Of course, you realise my father's family is not here. Mother's nerves are not the best; her imagination plays havoc sometimes, as you know . . . '

Tania looked at me with contempt. 'I'd better help my mother,' she said. 'She might pick the wrong flowers, with nerves you never know.'

Popov said, 'Of course. I understand'.

My little speech hadn't been easy to make, and when our guest left and we assembled together I couldn't look either my mother or Vitek in the eye. I wondered what loyalty meant.

I went to Warsaw and on the way saw row after row of military trains heading for the Russian front.

In the public toilet some poet had left his mark in the form of graffiti.

> On Bismarck's silver cask,
> On Hitler's proud forehead
> And on all Germans in the world.
> . . . But not on the toilet seat!

Warsaw hadn't changed. It was as vibrant and laughing as ever. A noisy crowd surged forward as if ignoring the presence of uniformed Germans. Trams were plastered with people, and the freshly pasted lists of hostages were a gloomy reminder of German supremacy and our helplessness. As always, there were people staring at those placards in silent submission.

The acts of sabotage were growing in number. High-ranking German officials, especially those connected with implementing repressive measures, were often ambushed and killed. In turn, the Germans would slaughter hostages, putting a high levy on the whole population of the Generalgouvernement and becoming even more vicious towards us all.

But life continued. On the pavement the smugglers were selling their forbidden bread. The crowd was pushing past, disregarding the withered spray of flowers which showed that the location had been used as a place of execution.

I reached the Ghetto's fallen territory. The ruins were being pulled down, even though the walls must have been still warm from the fires. The place was swarming with people. The less damaged dwellings were being reconstructed and, in some instances, a new pot-plant stood in the window and new curtains swayed in the summer breeze.

Mrs. Stein's place wasn't damaged much — obviously it had been located too close to the Aryan side. I started to go to our room. The smell of rotten potatoes had vanished, and someone passed me, dragging a table down. The door to Mrs. Stein's place stood wide open. A woman was busy cleaning our room and the Kohns' room.

'May I come in?'

'Why not? But we've already taken it.'

'I don't want the room. Just curious. I wanted to see how they lived.'

'Nothing to see. You came too late, like us miss. There are no more valuable things left. If you want to see something, go farther up. Not even a house left; ruins as far as one can see. The Germans told us they'll build new houses there. What d'you think?'

'I don't know.'

'I reckon it would be too long to wait. This flat is not so bad. Needs cleaning; you know how the Jews are.'

'Yes, I know.'

The woman kept on talking and a sparrow flew to the window; so Irma must have kept on feeding our birds. The wall bordering the Aryan side was gone. Our chair was standing in the room. I searched for a sign of the people who had lived there, but there was none. All that was left were some spots on the wall and some nails sticking out in the places where we had hung our clothes.

I left and searched for a solution in the crowded streets. People, traffic flashed by. Nobody knew me and I didn't know anyone — all my people were gone. Even if we were to survive there would be no-one to share the liberation with. Jadwiga: yes, there was Jadwiga, I thought, and I walked quicker. Her street was less noisy, full of half-hidden villas and gardens where people were toiling with bent backs, and birds were flying from one tree to another. I rushed straight into Jadwiga's open arms.

'I went to our old place.'

'Quiet, quiet.'

She gave me something to drink, something cool and tangy.

'You have to keep on believing. Some people managed to escape; some joined the partisans.'

'The War is not over yet.'

'It will be. If not this year . . . '

'And what then?'

'Peace and rebuilding, rejuvenation and freedom.'

'On the graveyard?'

'Quiet, quiet.' She stroked my hair and pressed my head to her side. She gave me a small package before I left.

'It's for Vitek.'

'What is it?'

'Capsules.'

'What capsules?'

'You ask too many questions. Capsules. More as a security measure than anything else; sleeping tablets of one kind or another . . . In case you are discovered.'

I placed the tiny box in my hand.

'Thanks.' My fingers tightened around it like tentacles. Good, I thought.

I went to the park and sat under an old tree, far from the crowd. I watched the branches closing over me and looked at the sky. I wondered how many capsules were needed — one, two, three, all? And what then? My mind would cease to function. Everything would stop. No

182

more war. And pain would be wiped away. Peace. Nothing. Lights out.

It seemed so easy, so inviting, so logical, so very selfish.

'More of a security measure', Jadwiga had said. She had arranged it for us, who knew at what risk.

I thought of Vitek, and then I knew I would not take the capsules on my own. I envisaged Vitek standing in front of the Germans. And Marek, my skinny Marek; who wasn't allowed to go outside and play in the sun or walk in the rain and wind; who had to keep his voice down all the time; who, when he laughed, found all of us hissing at him because someone might have heard him.

So, if they were to come, they would drag out all my loved ones; they would hit and kill and, before they killed, they would abuse. And Vitek wouldn't have any capsules to share with the others before it happened, because I had lacked courage and had been ready to take the easier way out.

I got up and went to the library. Loaded with books, I returned to Zielonka. Vitek was glad of the capsules, and his fingers embraced the tiny box in the same urgent manner as mine had done before.

However, I had borrowed a little book for Marek entitled, *What Every Boy Should Know*, and now all hell broke loose.

'I don't want Marek to read it', said Vitek.

'Why?'

'I have my reasons. It's not necessary.'

'How could you possibly think it's not necessary?', I stormed. 'If we survive, as we hope we will, Marek will go to school. His chums will find a way to teach him the facts of life, be sure of it. Why shouldn't he be familiar with the subject beforehand? The book doesn't offer much more than information about bees and flowers.'

'Nobody instructed us and somehow we managed. The discussion is closed.' And Vitek took the book away.

A day later, while our card players indulged in bridge, Marek read the book, with my encouragement. Vitek and Inka were furious. The whole drama ended in tears. Marek fled to the cellar, where he sat on a heap of brown coal. He refused to come up to tea, so I smuggled some food to him. I was pleased that 'the damage had been done', but tempers were high for many days to come. And then it was forgotten.

Our tomatoes ripened; the shadows became longer and the days shorter. It was time to prepare for another winter. The Russian front was coming to a standstill and the Germans had more time to fulfil their racial programme. A few villages were raided and all the small children who looked Nordic were transported to Germany to be brought up as true Germans.

'Nov they have finished with the Jews. We are the next on the list', people prophesied.

Disturbing news reached us. The Germans were evacuating the whole civilian population in the path of the advancing front.

So this would be their last revenge. On the very eve of Liberation they would take us all somewhere deep into Germany.

Vitek was more than concerned.

'In the event of evacuation I suggest you take Marek and Julek with you. Inka and I will stay where we are; we have discussed the matter already.'

'I won't go without you.' How dark Marek's eyes were; how large and sad.

'Of course you will go, son. With you gone our chances of survival will be greater. But now, because the possibility is closing in on us, we should be more concerned with the way we look. First of all, hair. Our hair has to be trimmed regularly.'

It was hard to keep our men's hair in order. Vitek's was the easiest. He was bald, except for a reef of hair at the very bottom of his skull. I often wondered, and once asked, how he could wash his face, how he knew the demarcation line between his forehead and head.

Julek's hair was thick — the main reason, I was sure, why Vitek gave him an Amazon Indian-style cut. The result was devastating so I took over, not trusting Vitek any more.

Marek's hair was more like springs which were thin and winding, impossible to keep down, jumping out in unexpected places. Since the Germans had taken away our clippers I had to use scissors. This led to a side effect, a persistent itch caused by tiny splinters of hair which withstood the shower, scrubbing, even brushing.

I wasn't really cut out to be a hairdresser but even I had to admit that I showed more promise than Vitek.

Lethargy hung over us. We hardly mentioned the future; in desperation, we clung to topics like food or weather.

Marek's solitary existence was well organised. He divided the library books into daily reading quotas, never allowing himself to abuse the routine he had set for himself. He studied a lot, and was the only one who firmly believed in our survival.

Aunt Olga and mother still worked for Janowski. I don't think he had ever dreamed of more loyal subordinates. They blindly accepted everything he said. The fibs he told them were neither malicious nor dangerous, but they were fibs nevertheless. He was a man of imagination who could never tell where reality ended; he was very good at extending the truth.

Vitek was very quiet and, often when I watched him, his eyes bothered me. I saw in them a mixture of lost hope, regret, concern and deep darkness; or perhaps it was just the reflection of my own mood.

As soon as he felt my eyes on him, his expression would change.

'All will be well. You will see', he would say, and then he would put his arm around me.

185

My bald uncle.

I wrote him a letter. 'What was my father really like?', and, 'Could you reply because I hardly knew my father?', I asked.

'Let's have a little chat', Vitek came to me. 'It's better than letter writing.

'And by the way, now that I've thought about it, I have to thank you for bringing that little book for Marek. I grew up in a proper family; I had an older brother, so this kind of instruction wasn't necessary. Of course, the present situation is different. So thank you for thinking of it.'

We went to the attic, and he told me that my father had been all right. He said that people often make a mistake when they lose someone dear by creating a myth hardly resembling the real person, and this should not be done, because the most exciting characteristic of a human being is his ability to be unpredictable.

He began to tell me stories about my father and himself when both were boys.

'May I call the others to join us?', I asked.

'Go ahead', he said.

I called Marek, Tania and Julek. I wanted to share that rare moment with them.

Vitek continued, this time with a tale of my father during his adolescence, when he demonstrated much more concern for romance than for brotherly love.

These recollections had a strange, soothing effect on us all. The world which used to be, which had disappeared, had been brought to life in a few brief moments when our morale was low.

How right Vitek was. Instead of remembering my father as he had been all I had been doing was idealising him.

I wanted to live; to learn more; to hear more.

I wished for the time when Julek and I would be able to go for a walk together, without arm-bands, without risking our lives. To be free seemed the greatest happiness; not to be branded, not to be condemned.

My family had been hiding for a year and a half. The breeze, the rain, the wind had been denied them. Their skins were like parchment in colour and texture; Marek's legs were like sticks with no muscles.

At night I often wondered about life — an arrangment; a happening; an illusion? If we were to die, I often told myself, 'Let it happen suddenly by a bomb, even by our own hands; but spare us, oh God, an end executed by our oppressors.'

I started writing a diary.

The wind howled outside. The grass clung to the ground and the trees swayed. The puffed-up birds assembled on the telegraph lines ready to migrate.

And, shortly after, everything was covered by snow. The trees lowered their branches. Shelminka went out reluctantly and left little holes in the places where she walked on her stilted legs. And, in the spot where she urinated, the snow melted, it steamed, and was tinted yellowish-brown, until it snowed again.

Mother was going to Warsaw early one morning. It was cold, so when she said, 'Till tonight', we turned over, determined to go back to sleep.

But she was back, immediately, panting, red in the face, catching her breath.

'Get ready, get dressed; for God's sake be quick, hide.'

Everyone got up; we all ran to-and-fro while mother told us what had happened.

'The military police, thousands of them with guns, are surrounding house after house. I didn't know what to do; you were all asleep; they might have been here within minutes. So, when I drew level with them, I clicked my fingers and said loudly, "Blast". And when one of them asked what was wrong, I told him I had left my library book at home and that I was going to Warsaw. He advised me to fetch the book, and I said I was frightened I'd miss my train. "So hurry up, run!" he said. And here I am; I have to run back. A book; give me a book and hurry; hide! See you. I wish I could stay, but I have to go.'

She left holding the book under her arm.

In no time at all our fugitives were hidden and all signs of our criminal activities were covered up. There were only four beds left and only four used cups left in the sink.

I went to the attic and watched. House after house was being surrounded, as mother had told us. People, mostly men, were being dragged out. They were herded into tight groups, which were still, except for gendarmes who paced around. The sun was coming up and the snow-covered fields glittered.

In front of another house, a man was joining the hostages and a woman was standing in the doorway watching.

There were freshly made birdish footprints in the snow; icicles were hanging from the roofs; and the square helmets glinted on the gendarmes' heads. The guns were pointing, ever present.

I couldn't understand the reason for this raid. Was it just a routine check-up? They were rounding up men and sometimes women, too, although not too many. It must have been routine. They searched every house; they would come to ours, too. But this time we felt no fear. We were ready for them. The coast was clear. We were on the same footing as all the others. They would come, not because of a denunciation, but simply as they did to any house in the district. We were safe. They were taking men, and our men were well hidden; officially, there were none. I watched. Perhaps other people watched too, from their attics, from behind their curtains. Perhaps a woman looked at the group of men and

188

recognised her own among them . . . What about them over there, stomping from foot to foot, pulling their heads in? All was quiet. All is quiet when observed from far away. What about those men? And the people in bombed-out towns; on the front lines; in camps; sick; hungry; being interrogated? What about the wounded; what about the ones who were frightened and heroic enough to face brutality?

How I had hardened! Yes, I was thinking of others, but it was really side-tracking. I was glad mother had warned us. We were prepared like good scouts should be.

Certainly I felt sorry for the men who were rounded up, but only just. The reassurance that there were no men to be found at our place dominated my feelings.

And I shivered. If I were to live, would I ever again be capable of a normal human reaction? I wondered and I shivered.

The search went smoothly, as anticipated.

Janowski and his men carried out a heroic raid on a food co-operative. They were very successful, too. They took away tons of sugar, which they later distributed among themselves. The fact that the sugar was meant as a bonus for Polish peasants didn't bother them much.

'My conscience is clear. The bastards shouldn't supply the Germans with food anyway', was the answer.

It didn't enter their thick skulls that the peasants were forced to supply monthly quotas under the threat of the death penalty, or they just chose to disregard it. My mother, my own mother, defended Janowski's stand with passionate vigour.

That winter we quarrelled a lot, often over stupid, petty issues. I came up with an idea that I should go to work and start earning some money. Vitek and Inka were dead against it. They needed me, they argued.

'I have had enough of my parasitic existence.'

'Be reasonable.'

'I am. It's degrading for a married couple not to be independent financially.'

'There is a time for everything under the sun', Vitek said gravely. 'To be dependent, to be wise; to be independent and to be stupid'.

Inka complained that her underwear was all in shreds. She even accused Vitek of not advising her to prepare herself better for solitary confinement.

While Inka and Vitek aired their differences, we others were glad to discuss both of them.

'Inka has never appreciated poor Vitek, being as spoiled as she always was.' Mothers eyes were shining. 'Vitek is too good to be true. As for her, she is the most egocentric person I have ever met.' Mother said whatever she wished, and then joined aunt Olga in their room where the two most altruistic women in the world munched crisp, fresh apples. We couldn't help hearing.

Julek noticed, and pointed out that my mother was being really selfish.

'Your mother hides like a little girl and stuffs herself with vitamins while her own daughters, not to mention Marek, who looks dreadful and is a growing child after all, go without.'

'Thanks a lot', I replied. 'You say, "Not to mention", and then you ramble on and on . . .'

'In the first place . . .'

I replied that my mother was my mother and it was not a crime to eat an apple, 'One miserable apple', and that we should remember that she was endangering her life for us all.

Julek replied that he couldn't possibly draw a parallel between an apple and a mother's courage, and that he was surprised at my complete disregard for logic and clear thinking.

'Do you intend to keep on reminding me that your

mother and Olga risk their lives in order to save me?', he said. 'If so, I'm not certain I want to survive.'

I knew he was right but couldn't possibly admit it, so I told him that this was exactly why I wanted to go to work: 'So nobody can begrudge my mother one miserable apple'.

And then Tania joined in, saying that she missed fruit very much, too.

'Do you indeed? So why don't you do something positive about it?'

'Like what?'

'Like finding yourself work; earning some money for a change.'

'What kind of work? I wasn't meant for manual toil.'

'Indeed you were not! Only Inka and I were born and destined to slave for you all.'

'Correction', interrupted Julek. 'As you have to admit, even if you don't want to, it is I who chop the wood and am in charge of the stove.'

'How noble of you! It's the easiest thing to do, anyway.'

'You are so preoccupied with yourself, you don't even realise how tired I feel.' Tania's face started to twitch. 'I haven't even recovered properly from the assault your friends . . . '

'Are you going to blame me for that incident all my life?'

'It might have been an incident to you; not to me.'

'Are you implying I'm heartless?'

'Stop it', shouted Marek. 'What are you trying to do? You are mad, all of you.'

His was the voice of reason; so we stopped and there was an uneasy silence — until the next time.

——17——

Our financial situation was deteriorating. There was not much money left from Vitek's resources. Ours had all gone. Who could forsee how much longer the War was going to last? For all we knew it might go on for ever; even in the best estimation it could still last some years. It was supposed to be a *Blitzkrieg,* and yet it dragged on and on. If the Germans didn't kill us we would surely die from starvation.

We had to eat. Someone suggested some of our rabbits.

'No, we couldn't.'

We couldn't possibly eat our rabbits.

Who was going to be brave and kill them?

Not me.

Not me, not me.

'The local butcher might. He would know how. There is a special technique, a painless way. After all, rabbit is meat.'

Mother and aunt Olga left the house carrying a basket. I didn't question them, but I knew a rabbit was in it. They came back half an hour later, slightly under the weather.

Aunt Olga put the basket in the kitchen.

'Now all that has to be done is to clean and skin him. He did it very quickly. Just shook him by the ears; a very quick method.'

While aunt Olga looked around our dead rabbit lifted his head and jumped out of the basket. He stopped for a while, moving his ears and nose in a most unconcerned way.

Someone screamed. Aunt Olga picked up the rabbit and proposed taking him back to our friendly butcher.

'You'd better leave him there; we'll never eat him anyway', cried Inka, and for a change we all agreed.

I suppose we were not really starving; we were still at a stage where we preferred not to face the simple truth that, to eat meat, one has to slaughter.

Aunt Olga and mother came up with an idea. While waiting for the rabbit to be, 'Hmm, hmm . . . prepared', they had met a man. He was a friend of the butcher, a man well known in the district. Well respected and trusted, he had made a fortune by producing vodka. His was of the highest quality: well distilled, much better than the one produced by the government monopoly. They had sampled it, so they knew. The man had been extremely friendly and had mentioned his willingness to help 'the poor widow' of the late Mr. Boyarski, whom he had admired very much, although he had never had the good fortune to meet him. It just happened that he knew a fellow, a chemist who supplied chemical essences which were used in the production of liqueurs. The operation was a very simple one. He also happened to know a glass merchant who would be willing to supply any amount of bottles. He also knew of a fellow who was prepared to make a seal according to one's design and whose friend could offer, for a minimal price, sealing wax as well as labels.

'So, as you see, it's all very simple', aunt Olga concluded. 'There is plenty of big money around, if one knows where to look. The good God has us all in his mercy. Even if the War goes on we will have plenty to eat. All our problems are solved.'

'I don't like the idea', said Vitek.

'Whether you like it or not I am going to do it', said aunt Olga. 'The man is prepared to wait for the money till

193

the liqueurs are sold, so there is no risk involved. Given our situation, I was more than sure you would welcome the idea.'

'You can do as you wish; it's your house. But don't you think it's dangerous? It is illegal, as you must know.'

'Hiding you is illegal, too.'

'You couldn't put it more bluntly.'

'I didn't mean to; you forced me. Let's give it a try. The man is ready to give me all the necessary ingredients on credit, as I mentioned before, till we sell the first batch. It should cover all our expenses, leaving us with enough capital to continue.'

First the spirit arrived in gallon bottles at night time. We sampled it. It was good. Then Janowski was kind enough to arrange the sugar delivery, at night. Then came labels, seals, wax and, in the end, the essences.

Cacao Choix, Curacao, Cherry Brandy, Creme-de-Menthe . . . Wow!

Once the production started the whole house smelled like a brewery. Shelminka was slightly intoxicated, as were the parrots — but none so much as we.

We cooked the sugar and the essence together, then blended the mixture with alcohol.

'A bit more essence?'

'Definitely not; too artificial as it is. Add more spirit.'

'How is it now?'

'Let me taste . . . Much better, isn't it?'

'Too strong for my taste. More water?'

'Oh no, the liqueur should burn your throat.'

'I can't breathe as it is.'

'Try again . . . Any better?'

'Not quite sure.'

'Let's try again.'

The production line was prepared — the bottles washed, the labels, wax and seals arranged. But first we had to sample the product. Hmmm . . . Which one would sell best?

194

By the time the bottles were filled we had spilled quite a lot; somehow, our hands were not too steady. Everyone participated except for Vitek, who stubbornly refused to join in. We worked until late. Nobody felt hungry. So, in the end, to celebrate our mutual effort, we opened one bottle and drank to our success: to Hitler's downfall and to our survival. Then we opened another bottle, and aunt Olga proposed inviting a Russian Orthodox priest to wed Julek and me, because it wasn't really proper for a young girl with a traditional background to live in sin.

So I started to cry; the parrots screeched; Shelminka barked; aunt Olga cried; mother cried. Tania asked, 'What happened?' and Vitek opened the window to let the vapour out.

The cool, wintry air rushed in, and soon afterwards we all went to bed. Julek tried to comfort me and begged me not to cry, because it wasn't aunt Olga who spoke, but the alcohol. But I howled and cried into the night, until mother came to me and told me not to worry. 'To love is not a sin, only to sin is a sin.'

So when she left we made love.

Aunt Olga organised the sale of the first production run. The profit was incredible and so were the promotional expenses.

'One shouldn't worry. Once people accept the high quality of our product, sampling won't be needed any more.'

The success of the first transaction called for a celebration. Aunt Olga brought home sausage and smoked fish. She opened a couple of bottles, filled the glasses, and we ate and drank and drank. We toasted to our future success, to victory and to Hitler's downfall. Vitek stayed in his room. We reached the conclusion that he was really mean and took pleasure in spoiling these brief moments

of harmless fun, 'given to us by God', as mother concluded. To which I said, 'Not by God but by liqueur.' So
the conversation turned to a higher level, and we discussed the existence of God.

When we went to bed, and it was with some difficulty,
because our beds seemed to be far away, my mother
sobbed openly. She was worried that I would never be
allowed to enter Heaven, so that once she died she
would never see me again.

During the day aunt Olga and mother were busy
organising promotional samplings of their products to
which prospective buyers were invited. The result was
inevitable: our ladies were perpetually drunk — a half-
happy state which would change to tears or anger at the
slightest provocation, or even without any.

Little by little, aunt Olga and mother were left to
themselves. We stopped celebrating the sale of every
single bottle by drinking at least two.

These 'promotional parties' worried me more than
anything else. Some men of dubious background would
drink at our place, wandering through the house while
our prisoners waited frightened, first behind locked
doors and then in the cellar, where it was cold and damp.
It was beyond me to explain to mother that the whole
exercise should end. She enjoyed her financial freedom
and used to return home loaded with all kinds of deli-
cacies which only Vitek was strong enough to resist.

I was even more disappointed in aunt Olga than in my
mother. She was always the one who had been so level
headed, always the one we could depend on. But this
time she was totally engrossed in the venture. She was
like one possessed. She even sold the parrots to one of
her moonshine dealers who bought them for his mis-
tress. But on the following day she was so utterly miserable that we all felt sorry for her. She reproached herself
for her treachery. She had deceived 'the enchanted
birds', and God would never forgive her for it. We tried

to comfort her, pointing out the good fortune of the birds: she had placed them in a good home where biscuits and fruit were plentiful. But we didn't really believe what we were saying. As far as the birds were concerned, they couldn't have had a better place than Boyarski's.

We also missed the parrots: everyone did, in his own way. The place became quieter, the floor cleaner. We didn't have to sort seeds any more, or to change water, or to clean cages. The dining room became more spacious. Why we missed them was hard to explain. Even Shelminka looked where the cages used to be; Hippolit chirped and sang without interruption. Then, one day, he sat at the bottom of his cage all fluffed up, and the next moment he was dead and so very small.

I cried when we buried him. The snow was deep, the soil was frozen, and even to dig a small grave for a tiny bird was hard. I cried; and remembered that I had never cried for my father, or for Irma, or for all the people who had been killed. It seemed so stupid to cry because little Hippolit had died from old age, or overeating, or loneliness. So I cried even more and couldn't stop.

We were awakened in the middle of the night by Vitek.

'Shshsh', he whispered, 'get up'.

Julek grabbed his bundled clothes and was ready to run.

'Thieves', explained Vitek. 'I think I frightened them away.' We were all up by then, shivering. Cautiously, we walked from room to room. Cold air hit us when we entered the kitchen. The back door stood open. Aunt Olga and I went outside and followed the freshly made footprints which led us to the front fence. The snow was knee deep and there were large imprints on the other side: whoever it was must have left in a hurry. It started to snow again, so we went back inside. Inka and the others were counting the losses, while Vitek tried to reconstruct what had happened. The back door had been forced open and so had the kichen door. The thieves had emptied the pantry. And my books; my books were all gone. I had brought them with me from Lodz; I had left them with aunt Olga for safe keeping while we were in the Ghetto. My few miserable books — gone.

The drawers of the small buffet were open but the cutlery was still there.

'This must have been the moment when I was woken', said Vitek. 'I heard footsteps. I thought that someone must have gone to the kitchen for a drink, but then I saw a flickering light. I heard cautious steps, and saw light flashing on the walls. On and off, on and off again. I froze and called out: "Who is it?" The steps quickened, it became dark, the cold air hit me. And then I realised they were gone, so I woke you up.'

'My favourite cooking pot has gone, and so has the mincer', lamented aunt Olga.

'All our winter provisions', sighed Inka.

'My books, my books.'

'The blanket', moaned Tania. 'Why did I leave it in the nook? Our pre-war blanket.'

'Did he look into your room?' Mother was serious, quiet.

'I don't think so but I can't be sure.' Vitek was also serious.

'My silver spoon.' Aunt Olga rummaged through her cutlery.

'How can you worry about what's missing?' Mother was annoyed. 'Someone was here. Did he stay in the kitchen or did he look inside? Because, if he did, we are in trouble. He heard Vitek's voice. He heard a man's voice in a place where there shouldn't have been any men.'

Mother, as always, was superb in danger; her mind was clear, logical, quick.

'I don't think they would have bothered with books

198

and crockery had they discovered us. We'd have been a much more profitable catch than a mincer.' Inka was right, or so it seemed.

'That's true', reflected mother.

'I think that, tomorrow, aunt should go to the shops and tell everybody about the thieves and how she frightened them by calling out in a very deep, masculine voice.' That was Tania's idea. Good, very good. My sister had come up with a solution; and I was in the habit of running her down.

Shelminka yawned and stretched. She hadn't even barked. Aunt Olga defended her dog's honour by arguing that sleeping drugs must have been given to poor Shelminka, because normally she was always so good.

'I don't really mind thieves like those.' Mother smiled. 'They come by night, take what they want, try not to wake anybody, and are frightened to be discovered. What a refreshing change from pilfering Germans.'

Mother was right.

We all went to bed but nobody slept. We constantly turned and tossed. Had they seen us or not? And was there any connection between our liqueur production and the robbery?

I didn't sleep at all and I raised the question at breakfast time. It wasn't well received by aunt Olga and mother, but was applauded by the rest of the family.

We went to the local shops and aunt Olga spread the news about the theft. She gave a very convincing performance; her imitation of a man's voice was faultless. But on the way home she nervously kept expressing the hope that the people who had listened to her so attentively would believe what she said.

Our ladies now drank less. The liqueur production still went on; and we had to admit that, thanks to it, we managed to replace the stolen goods, including even the mincer and the blanket. Only my books were never replaced. I had to agree that the War was not a time for

199

crying over books. Nevertheless, I missed them very much.

Towards the end of winter the spirit supplier was shot dead. He was a victim of denunciation, or of a greedy gendarme who hadn't been satisfied with the bribe offered. The fact remained that the man was dead, and nobody was sure whether his customers' records had fallen into German hands or not. What was known was that all his spirits had been confiscated and his wife had managed to run away.

Aunt Olga and mother, without any persuasion, disposed of all the labels, essences and sealing wax. The bottles ended up under the house. The remaining alcohol didn't last long, and aunt Olga left one bottle of each flavour, 'For after the War'.

18

Spring came. People said they had never experienced a spring like it before. It came with a strong, warm wind. The snow and the ice melted, and the trees bent as if in a welcoming gesture. The rivers flooded, and before we knew it the flowers burst into a splendid riot of colours.

People said they had never heard so many birds singing, seen so many birds flying so high.

The Underground press carried news of German defeats on all Fronts. Even in the official rag one could find carefully camouflaged references to German failures. It was called, 'Strategic breaking away from the enemy', 'Strategic withdrawal', and 'Redeployment'.

What a joy it was to read.

The Army was on the move. The civilian train time-table had almost ceased to exist; military transports were given priority.

Army detachments often went past in one direction and then returned. Something was in the air.

Janowski prophesied a quick victory for the Allies, but we nevertheless decided to plant vegetables again. The septic tank needed to be emptied, anyway, and not to use it would have been an unpardonable waste of good manure. We planted a great number of tomatoes and cucumbers, as well as other vegetables. Aided by good weather, our crops grew rapidly.

Then one day the warm wind played havoc. It lifted skirts, banged doors and windows, tore off flowers and leaves, messed people's hair, threw dust in their eyes, and carried voices far and high. 'On a day like this someone must have hanged himself', a woman said to me. I was on the way to the shop. The clouds were gathering, dark and threatening, but they never had a chance to stay still. The wind frisked them in a confusing way until they sailed through the sky at record speed, all torn to pieces, fragmented. The wind sang an eerie, fiendish tune. Somebody said that Hitler must have hanged himself; someone else confirmed that he had heard the announcement of Hitler's suicide.

On my way back home, big birds flew over the meadow low over my head. Their wings were black one second, silver the next. The clouds sailed past, uncovering layer after layer of heavenly confusion. The air was fresh, I felt alive, but couldn't get rid of a creeping feeling of uneasiness.

'Hitler's hanged himself, or that's what they're saying!' I delivered the pronouncement together with a loaf of bread.

'What are you talking about?'

'The whole of Zielonka is talking about it. They say it was bound to happen on a day like this.'

'It doesn't make sense', was the general reaction.

The wind dropped suddenly and the clouds trampled one into the other and covered the whole sky with greyness. The air became still as if holding its breath in expectation of what might happen next.

Big, splashy drops fell first, followed by a penetrating downpour. I stood by the window and watched a newly formed puddle, where circular ripples extended towards the edge, chasing each other.

Janowski came around in the evening. He had heard 'from the Chief of Staff of the Polish Underground', of a revolt among Hitler's generals in which Hitler had been killed. Mother and aunt Olga cried and hugged Janowski for bringing the good news. Janowski saluted as he left, 'Won't be long, my faithful soldiers', he said.

On the following day there was a small announcement in the official press reporting an unsuccessful attempt on Hitler's life.

We hadn't really believed in Janowski's story, but still we felt cheated. We wondered if Hitler's death would have shortened the War, anyway.

They marched us away and I wasn't even sure why they were taking us.

In the morning they had rung at the gate, Shelminka had barked and our fugitives had run to the hideout. It had all seemed like a recurring nightmare; one you dream often, knowing what will come next but being unable to prevent it.

When aunt Olga opened the gate, the soldiers ran inside, guns at the alert, and demanded that everyone aged between fifteen and thirty go with them.

'Please leave them with me', pleaded mother. 'I lost my husband in the War; all I have are my two daughters.'

'No-one is going to hurt them. They will be back home before dark. A day's work in the open won't do your girls any harm. Hurry, hurry', they urged us, and I was glad that there was no time for kisses and good-byes.

They marched us, Tania and I, and while we proceeded other groups of escorted teenagers joined us.

In the still air not even a leaf moved. The road was empty, and only women stood in front of their houses staring. Sometimes a dog ran alongside us. Birds drew circles in the tall sky. Flies travelled on people's backs and, once disturbed, buzzed while performing hieroglyphic aerobatics in the air. It lasted a moment or two, till they settled on somebody's back again.

We reached the village square; the shops were all

shut. The church stood there quietly, forlorn. It was a tiny church, all white with a slender steeple. A few very white, puffy clouds hung above, as if planted by the hand of a pedantic artist to complete the idyllic picture.

We were allowed to sit down.

'Where are you going to take us?', someone dared to ask.

'You'll learn soon enough.' The soldier who answered was as young as us, but he carried a gun and he looked at us with contempt and power.

'We were crazy to go with them', I whispered into Tania's ear. 'Next time we'll hide.'

'Do . . . d'you think they will kill us?' Tania's breath was hot; her thoughts were freezing.

'Don't be stupid', I hissed.

'Look', Tania said aloud and heads turned to the main road.

A small detachment of Germans headed towards the square and, before they entered, burst into song. 'Heil-li, Heil-lo,' The goose-step was splendid in a barbaric way. Some from our group stood up, and were immediately pushed to a sitting position again.

The officer barked a command in a Wagnerian voice; his soldiers marched on the spot before they came to an abrupt halt.

The officer stood in front of us as if he were a tripod. *'Achtung!'*

We were now completely surrounded. They watched us and recorded our every movement, their boots flashing and clicking all the time.

'We have assembled you here today . . . The situation demands it', the officer started, and I was angry with myself and wondered why we hadn't tried to escape when there had been only a few soldiers.

There was one civilian standing with the official party.

'As you must know from the press, some communists

have detached themselves from the Russian army and are on the run. They might reach your homes. I don't have to tell you what this means. It means pilfering; it means rape; it means death to your loved ones. Therefore, in order to protect you, we have to build a stronger defence line; it's more in your own interests than in ours. The final victory will be with us before long. Our army is at the gates of Moscow, at the gates of the oil fields of the Caucasus. Before long, as I said, we'll join with them to crush the shaky Communist army once and for all, when their morale is at its lowest and their incentive to fight is nil. We want your co-operation. Let me remind you of Katyn; let me remind you of the Russian atrocities. We are a civilised people; we are ready to defend your homes, your ageing mothers, your young brothers and sisters. Long live Germany. Heil Hitler.'

The civilian translated the officer's address into Polish, adding a few words here and there, instilling fear and underlining the need for us to be loyal to the 'cultural, western democracy of German people', and to guard against the 'primitive Russians, renowned for their cruelty'. He stressed that, once the War was over, he was more than certain that the Germans would establish a new Polish State, free of Jews and other subversive elements, which at present they couldn't do because they were too involved in fighting for freedom and defending democracy. Therefore, it was our sacred duty towards Poland and our families to build a functional defence line.

Someone commanded us to get up; so we did. We formed an orderly column, were handed shovels and picks, and were ordered to march.

Tania ended up a few rows in front of me. I wanted to join her but was stopped. We marched carrying the tools over our shoulders, heavily guarded by our friends and saviours. They prompted us to sing; some did and others joined in only after being persuaded by our benefactors. We walked, our faces wet and lips dry. My pick seemed heavier with every step, as everybody's must have done.

They turned us from the main road, right into the scrub. We trampled over heather, spiky turf and little branches. We were not permitted to break ranks, and I felt as though I was surrounded by bayonets. We pushed and swayed; some fell to the ground. The Germans yelled and shouted; they laughed. In the end they allowed us to break our ranks. The air was saturated with the fragrance of firs and young pines. I felt hungry. We struggled through the thickest part of the scrub. It was so dense there was no breeze at all. In the clearings the undergrowth looked soft and tempting. Everyone must have known the feel of such surroundings; everyone must have rested in such a place on such a day, in days of freedom. The path twisted and turned, and I thought that all our folkdances and tunes must have been born in spots like this.

There were rabbit-droppings galore. Tania and I had collected them as kids, thinking they were nuts. One day when we were playing hide-and-seek we discovered a secret hide-away. Its walls were lined with young firs, giving perfect isolation from the outside world. The entrance was so well hidden that we always had to force an entry through the thick branches. Our legs and arms were constantly covered with scratches; so much so that, once, mother thought we had the measles or some other dreadful disease. Then she accepted our version and pleaded with us to be more careful while collecting blackberries. We were pleased that we had not disclosed what we were doing, and kept on returning to that place for the duration of our holiday. It was our very own place which nobody else ever knew about. Its floor was made of moss and heather, the walls were made of fir branches, and the sky was our ceiling. The area was restricted, but large enough for us two. We loved to stretch on the ground, watch the clouds, and tell each other stories full of horror and magic. Only our beloved dog, Lord, was welcome to stay with us. Then, one day when we arrived, we saw a big turd right in the centre of our paradise. The air was vile; thick maggots crawled all over it; and huge flies buzzed in the air. We almost cried for our paradise lost. We never returned to that place. We stopped telling each other stories and, besides, it was much more fun to play cops and robbers.

How many years ago had it been: fifteen, fourteen? Good old hiding place, I thought as I marched. Then someone shouted a command and we stopped. A few soldiers ran past; the earth thumped and quivered; there was a lot of running and commotion; orders were given, and then we heard a salvo, so very near and so very dry; and then there was a cry spiked with agony, another shot, a hubbub of agitated voices and someone's laughter. It was a thick, insolent laugh and was followed by the words, 'Hurry, hurry'.

The thicket resolved itself into an uneven clearing where the trenches zig-zagged and the freshly dug soil lay in mounds. They ordered us to dig. The young man next to me said that his mate had hidden in the thicket because he wanted to run away and, what did I think? Maybe it was him they had shot. He cried, 'So what d'you think, is he dead or what?'

'I don't know.'

'D'you think I should ask them?'

'I don't know.'

We sweated; my eyes were prickling. My back, my arms, my legs, my whole body hurt. Oh, how it hurt; but we dug and dug and dug, hardly ever being allowed to stretch. And I remembered how on the eve of the War we had worked on trenches and had been so enthusiastic, how we had sung songs and had been sure of instant

207

victory. I thought of all my friends who never lived to see the end of all that madness.

A young man had now met his death in that thicket; he had wanted to return home, a desire which had now become an unforgivable crime.

I wondered how long they were going to keep us there. My stomach was all tight, my throat dry, and the day was so unbelievably beautiful that it hurt.

And then they allowed us to stop. They gave us water to drink, divided us according to sexes, and I found myself with Tania again. The air trembled and was filled with distant explosions and I trembled too. So the Front was approaching.

'Quick, quick', our masters shouted, 'Hurry up. That section must be completed before the thunderstorm.'

They were nervous and, as a result, became more efficient. I wondered how they felt, what went through their minds, and whether they trembled, too.

The mounting soil shaded the trenches; so it was cooler to dig, although we had to throw the soil higher. A soldier stopped just above us; he was fat and sloppy, if there ever was a sloppy man in the German army. His face was all lined and quite stern.

'You don't have to kill yourselves. Take it easy. It's useless, anyway.' His face was very severe and I wasn't sure if the voice belonged to him. And then he shouted, 'Quickly, quickly . . . Useless I'm telling you. Half of Russia is dug up, half of Poland . . . Quickly, quickly . . .' and he moved awey.

We took his advice and slowed down. I listened, hoping to hear more explosions, but there were none. The only sounds I heard were human — voices of power and sounds of fear.

We worked until the horizon turned orange-red. They commanded us to form ranks and the fat soldier collected all the tools. We were to leave them behind under his guard, so that they would be ready for us when we resumed our work the next morning. We were instructed to assemble at the square at 7 a.m. sharp, and reminded that from the next day on we were expected to work faster and better. Otherwise they would be forced to make us more productive.

We arrived home late in the evening. We were very tired, but before we went inside we put our heads to the ground to listen. The earth was absolutely still; only the frogs croaked nearby. Tania went inside, but I stayed out a bit longer. The faces of the people I worked with were with me and the voice of that young man. 'You don't think th-e-e-e-ey killed h-h-h-im?' I wondered what he would tell his mate's family and if they would go there at night to look for the body.

We hardly ate, Tania and I. We talked of what our slob had told us and of the explosions we had heard. Everybody became excited, and Marek and Julek copied the map of Poland. They marked Zielonka as a centre and drew circles every fifty kilometres, speculating upon how long it would take the Russians to liberate us.

Before we went to sleep it was decided that neither Tania nor I would present ourselves for digging trenches ever again. We should have been hidden in the first place, anyway. I couldn't have agreed more.

Julek woke me up at night when I screamed and cried.

I dreamed I was a child again. I was on the way to our hide-out, knowing that something terrible was going to happen. I couldn't go back because there was only one path leading to it, and when I looked back there was nothing. The body of a young man was lying in my hide-out, covered with maggots and blow-flies. And another young man stood there and kept on asking, 'Do you-u-u think he is dea-ea-ea-ead?' I bent down to see; he had my father's face, which changed to Irma's.

And then Julek woke me up. He wiped my face and held me close until I stopped shivering. The windows trembled again and again. The Front was approaching.

Next day Tania and I stayed at home and nobody came to look for us. Later in the day aunt Olga came, with news that a German had been slain near the trenches. It must have been our slob; but why him? The answer was simple: there was no justice or logic in time of war.

19

It was no longer necessary to put one's ear to the ground to hear the bombardment. It was constant. Whenever it stopped we feared the Russians had been pushed back again, and we waited anxiously for the renewal of war activities.

From our observation post in the attic we could see units of the German army marching to the West, loaded with heavy military equipment, obviously in retreat before the advancing Russians. Sometimes they would reverse their route and march back towards the East; and our jubilant mood would disappear. We feared that, in their desperation, they had decided to launch a new attack against the Russians.

We stood guard day and night. Everyone held on to a secret hope that, during his own turn on duty, the Russians would break through the front line and liberate us.

The weather was hot and dry, and dust particles danced in front of my eyes, suggesting distant roads full of sunshine. The newspapers, both German and Underground, reported the names of cities recaptured by the Russians — Polish cities which we knew. The Germans informed us of Russian atrocities, and urged the whole population to undertake voluntary evacuation in the event of the Russians' temporary advance in our area. The German army has always been victorious, and once the new offensive started the barbarian communists

211

would be pushed back where they belonged, never to harass the Polish countryside again.

The Underground Press listed German bestialities. The recent liberation of the Majdanek concentration camp brought the incredible efficiency of the Third Reich into the open. All the rumours about German atrocities against the 'inferior' races had become a reality in these sordid and brutal revelations. The Polish underground advised us of the German scheme to evacuate the entire population from the front-line zone. They urged people to stay put, to avoid being moved away from the approaching Russian army. We felt that the end of the German occupation was near. They were retreating across the whole Eastern front. Their civilian population was being subjected to constant, heavy bombardment. We read of daily raids on Berlin, Hanover, Hamburg. With a certain dose of satisfaction we learned of the low morale of the German people, both among the civilians and the armed forces.

The news was good, but I still feared for our future. We knew the Germans: there was no limit to their inventiveness. It was impossible to foresee what diabolic measures they had in store. In their last fury they were quite capable of razing the whole of Poland and killing her entire population. The full dimensions of Germany's perfidy and 'efficiency' had come to our notice when we had been issued small cakes of soap as part of the monthly ration. First we heard a rumour, then we read in the Underground press that human fat was used in the manufacture of soap, as a by-product of the process of mass extermination. The soap cakes had the letters R.I.F. stamped on them, and it was widely accepted that the letters stood for Pure Jewish Fat. Even for us, who knew the Germans so well, it was hard to accept. We were stunned; and then we buried those small cakes of soap, the remains of our people, in the garden.

Jadwiga visited us. She told us that Warsaw was full of

expectation and excitement. The Germans seemed uncertain. They seldom walked on their own, preferring to
move about in groups. Russian planes were flying over
the city: they were dropping mainly pamphlets, calling
on the Poles to keep calm, to resist evacuation, and to
increase sabotage activities.

It was good to see Jadwiga again. As usual, she
brought freshness into our stale existence.

'Have you heard of the Germans' new arms?' she
smiled like a little urchin.

'No.'

'You know they are desperate. They came to the
conclusion that their only chance of winning the War was
to invade England. They called a meeting, and it was
decided to place the entire German army alongside the
English Channel. On the command, "One, two, three",
every single soldier had to take a mouthful of water and
drink it. The plan was ingenious. All they had to do was
to drink the Channel dry in order to simplify the crossing. The great German army would occupy England,
which would capitulate in a matter of a week or two.

'The plan was put to the test. The soldiers drank and
gulped, drank and gulped. The Chief of Staff was surprised that the level of water remained the same. So he
ordered a reconnaisance plane to investigate. The plane
flew over, and discovered that the entire English army
was lined up on the other side of the Channel. On their
officer's command, "One, two, three", they were pissing
into the Channel.'

That was Warsaw: that resilient city, whose people
kept on joking regardless. And that was Jadwiga who
collected or invented all those stories, from one visit to
the next, to boost our morale.

'See you all after the War. I don't think there will be
enough time left for me to see you again while the War
goes on', she said while leaving. She advised us to store
personal things away, 'in case of a sudden evacuation'; to

213

prepare as much food as possible; and to keep on believing, 'In case you survive'. She kissed us all, and when she left we stayed very quiet.

Food became scarcer. It wasn't a matter of money any more; food had simply disappeared. The shopkeepers had lost their trust in German money and shut their shops. A new way of trading was born — the barter of goods. Our tomatoes and cucumbers came in handy, as they were the best crop in the district. So our friendly butcher and others were ready to give us a pound of meat here, a loaf of bread there.

Janowski came one night. He was more flamboyant than ever.

'Jerry's days are numbered.' He looked at me. 'You don't believe me, do you?'

'How come you know when nobody else is certain?'

'I'm not going to disclose all our military secrets to you just to prove my point. It should be sufficient when I say I know.'

'You shouldn't mind her; all youngsters are alike. The War has made them cynical.'

I wasn't sure whether mother was defending or condemning me.

'Never mind.' Janowski was smiling. 'I understand. As a matter of fact, I would like to store a few of our things with you; with your permission, of course. Your house has the best chance of withstanding the shelling.'

"Bring over as many things as you wish', aunt Olga and mother cried in unison. 'You shouldn't have asked. You know you are welcome.'

In the afternoon, while Vitek and the others stayed in the cellar, Janowski brought over his stuff. There were cases and suitcases and huge milk containers full of sugar, evidently stolen during the raid on the peasant's co-operative some weeks before.

We saw a lot of him, either when he was bringing an additional bundle or some incredible news. One day he

214

introduced us to Zofia, the wife of a friend of his. She was small, plain and hardly uttered a word. Zofia had come to spend a week in the country; Warsaw was very hot at this time of year. So even a few days in the open would be beneficial. Janowski was making faces to mother and aunt Olga, to their delight.

On the following day the temperature reached the high twenties. Vitek and the others kept close to the window, as fish which are starving for oxygen keep close to the surface of the water. Even towards evening the house was intolerable; and then Janowski arrived, noisy and excited, and sent our prisoners back to their room.

'Bring the glasses. The occasion calls for a toast.'

Our ladies produced the glasses and vodka in no time. Janowski raised his glass.

'The uprising has started. Warsaw, of course. All according to schedule. Zofia's visit wasn't a coincidence; she was sent to us. Her husband, who is the Commander-in chief, wanted her far from danger.'

We drank to victory while our captives fried in their stuffy room, while all the windows trembled, while the air was filled with the echoes of the barrage.

'As you must appreciate, we are fighting the Germans now, so the Russians won't be able to claim that they liberated Warsaw. Warsaw is our business.'

'How far away are the Russians?'

'Can't you hear, young lady? Close enough. They should be here any day.'

For the next few days the smoke over Warsaw grew thicker. We watched German planes coming and going. We watched the Army being transported. There was an air of expectancy. We were awaiting release. The sky was dark, the horizon turbulent; it had to resolve itself in a storm with thunder and lightning to clear the air, to clear the entire country and its people, to clear the entire world.

Janowski kept us informed. Warsaw was almost free;

our boys were terrific, and the Germans were behaving like the rats they always were. In a few more days Poland would be free and, once Warsaw was liberated by 'our army', General Anders would fly directly from London and enter the city on a white horse. Army equipment and highly skilled paratroop forces would follow, and then both the Germans and the Russians would be sent flying back to their territories.

Mother and aunt Olga believed it all, but the rest of us took Janowski's news with a certain dose of scepticism. His optimism seemed, if nothing else, slightly premature. Army detachment after army detachment marched towards Warsaw. Once more the night sky glowed as it had during the Ghetto uprising, or even more. We weren't sure any more if we were in the middle of a thunderstorm, or a bombardment, for the weather changed frequently, with electrical storms and downpours unlike any we had experienced before. Not being certain, we spent more time in the cellar. The rabbits seemed indifferent but Shelminka cuddled in my arms and shivered.

Once again we discussed the possibility of evacuation and what steps we should take if it were to occur. Vitek confided in me the difficulty of deciding whether to go out and risk denunciation or to stay. The house might easily be bombed or burned down. I couldn't truthfully say what step was better to take. Nobody could have.

And while we weighed the pros and cons Warsaw burned and the air was filled with smoke. Shelminka was constantly frightened: when she wasn't in the cellar, she shivered under the kitchen stool, refusing to go out; so we had to carry her, and she would relieve herself only if we stood next to her, or, even better, patted her.

The days became hot again. People kept to their dwellings. Nobody wanted to come in contact with the Germans, either in military form or what was even worse, semi-military form like the gendarmes and the Gestapo. We heard of many arrests and executions. 'A mad dog becomes especially vicious just before he dies.'

And then Janowski arrived one morning accompanied by six of his friends; men we had never seen before.

'The Russkis are here', he announced. 'We have come to take our weapons. We are on the way to Warsaw, to help with the uprising before the War ends.'

'Mr. Janowski, correct me if I'm wrong, but d'you intend to take your guns now, in broad daylight?', I said.

'Certainly. We need them now.'

'I wish you would wait till night; it would be much more sensible.' Janowski and his merry men were busy putting on red and white arm-bands and saluting each other.

'A time has arrived which demands self-control, Irena. How could a daughter be so different from her mother, a mother whose bravery will be known long after the War ends? Stop panicking and kindly return our arms to us.'

'Is that a command or a threat?'

'Both, if you're asking for an honest answer.'

'Where are the Russians?'

'Here. Go out and see for yourself. The Germans are all gone. I spoke to General Rokossowski just a couple of hours ago. Now we have to concentrate on Warsaw before the Polish-English landing takes place.'

So I did as I was told and went to collect Janowski's arsenal, and wondered how it could help in liberating Warsaw: two hand machine-guns, four hand-grenades, five revolvers. I kept one back and hoped Janowski wouldn't notice. I was more frightened by the thought of being left without any weapons than by Janowski's possible outburst.

I heard mother apologising to Janowski for 'Irena's unpardonable behaviour'.

Janowski distributed the weapons, called his men to attention, and marched them in military fashion. Left, right; left, right; left, right. They paraded for the whole of Zielonka to see, for every blasted blackmailer, denouncer, collaborator.

I just could not understand how Janowski's mind functioned. One thing was clear: he still believed that Poland was to be liberated by the West, that Polish-English paratroopers would make a landing and install the pre-war Polish government in Warsaw. This was a commonly accepted view, not only by the Underground but also by the community at large. At least Boyarski had been more realistic in accepting the fact that England w.s too far away, too much pre-occupied with her own war, to come to Poland's rescue. He feared that the Russians would never leave Poland once they had liberated her. I understood all that; but, in my selfish way, I counted the days, waiting for the Russians to come.

Contrary to mother's suggestion, Vitek did not want to leave the house; he wanted us to investigate first. So aunt Olga and I, the famous scouting team, set out on the assignment.

Zielonka was deserted. We walked through the meadow first; and then crossed the road. Only the flies bothered us. Again there was that feeling of quiet before a storm. The birds flew low and we talked in a whisper. The guns were silent.

We reached the main road leading to Warsaw. And there they were: four Russian tanks. Eight crew members sat or stretched out on the side of the road under large poplar trees. Not even a leaf moved. A few people were grouped nearby, watching.

We greeted the Russians. They exposed their gums and smiled. How young they were, younger than me; sixteen, seventeen perhaps.

218

'What is the situation?' asked aunt Olga.

'Good', answered the one who looked oriental. He was chewing on a bit of grass.

'Where is the Army?' I was puzzled. There were only four tanks.

'Nothing to worry about; they'll come. It just so happened we went forward, ahead of them, didn't we?'

They stretched; they smiled.

'Sure we did.'

'The rest will come. So there is nothing else for us to do but to have a bit of a rest now. We deserve it, don't we, kids?'

'Sure we do.' The other soldier made the same sluggish movements, used the same intonations.

'Are you hungry?' asked aunt Olga.

'No, not really. Tomorrow or the day after, we'll be reunited with our comrades and there'll be plenty to eat.'

'One day or two? Are you sure?'

'One day, two, three. I told you we went forward . . . We were fast.'

'Sure we were.'

'How far is the Army?'

The youngest, the blonde one, jumped to his feet.

'If we knew how far, d'you think we would be sitting here?'

'Steva, leave it.'

Steva swayed. 'I'm tired; bloody tired. All these shitty questions. We need a bloody rest.'

'Steva', the oriental-looking one said. He tried to catch Steva's hand but couldn't. 'He's sleepy. Don't pay any attention to him.'

We went back home. It was still so unbelievably quiet, it almost hurt. Dark smoke had built up over Warsaw. Janowski and his men marched by; they saluted us.

At home, we all discussed the situation. Mother was

219

convinced that the War had ended for us; Vitek was more cautious and of the opinion that we should stay as we were. Four tanks and eight crew wasn't a big enough force to build our hopes on. We all became silent. The stillness was depressing. Inka suggested that we should cook something while we could. Julek went to pump the water while we cooked stale millet with some apples which we had gathered in a nearby deserted house. I went to the attic, opened one of Janowski's milk containers, and scooped out a whole cup of sugar. So I started on a new career as a thief. But I gave myself absolution; Janowski himself had stolen the sugar from the peasants' co-operative where it was waiting to be distributed among its members. We hadn't tasted sugar for years. I smuggled it downstairs and, while Inka was out of the kitchen, I stirred it into our stale goo. God would forgive me, I thought. He would, but my family wouldn't. So, on Inka's return, I told her that I had added saccharin already. She tasted it and remarked that, 'Today, the grits taste really great; most probably because we haven't eaten any warm food for days and days. And of course the apples make all the difference'. I wholeheartedly agreed.

We ate and hardly spoke. Our senses were sharpened, listening to every sound. We jumped up at the smallest provocation; inwardly, if not openly.

We bathed and went to bed, a luxury we had been denied for weeks. Shelminka went to sleep on her cushion but she slept lightly, moving her ears and squealing.

The next day started hot, but the clouds were building up and the birds were silent. We took some of our rusks, eight to be precise, and offered them to the Russians. We found them in the same spot as on the previous day.

Yes, they had slept well. They would have slept better if it had not been for the blasted mosquitoes. The worms in our rusks didn't bother them, and Steva laughed and remarked that he'd rather eat them, than them eat him. They made cigarettes out of dark tobacco rolled in torn pieces of old newspaper. Two girls sat with them, and one called out, 'Steva, oh you, Steva'. He let her draw on his cigarette. She coughed and they all laughed.

Before we left they assured us that it wouldn't be long before the Army came. They had got themselves separated from their unit three days before, so 'tomorrow should be the day, for sure.'

For the first time in weeks, Shelminka went outside by herself. She frolicked in the garden, barking at her lover over the fence. I wondered if the girls were going to stay with the Russians; if they were going to offer them food or their bodies.

The clouds were getting denser but the smoke over Warsaw was denser still. At night it thundered — or was it a barrage? We were not sure, although it rained. We all got up, speculated about what was happening, and Shelminka hid under our cover and wouldn't budge.

Someone rang at the gate, impatiently, urgently. Who? We worried and ran from one room to another. Should we open up, or not? We had learned from experience that the fence wasn't much protection. Our fugitives descended to the cellar, Shelminka barked, and mother volunteered to open the gate; she came back with Janowski armed to the teeth, his arms full of the weapons he had taken from us two days before. He appeared minus his arm-band, and minus his merry men.

'I though you were in Warsaw, helping to overthrow the Germans?' I couldn't help but say it.

'No time for sarcasm, Irena', he responded seriously. 'There's been a counter-offensive. The Hermann Goering division is attacking along the front line. Hide the guns.'

'And where is General Rokossowski?'

He didn't answer. Mother carried the arms out and I

picked up what she couldn't manage. We placed Janowski's arsenal in the hands of Julek and told everyone the latest news. A ferocious bombardment began. Vitek was stunned.

'What can we do?'

'Let's go to the Russians. They might take us back through the German lines', was my suggestion.

'If there was any way out they would have taken it already. They are doomed and so are we.' Inka was sad, so very sad, and so very right. Boom, boom. Ra-ta-ta-ta-ra. Boooom.

'If we stay here we'll be denounced to the Germans; everyone has seen the arms being taken from our place. General Rokossowski! Janowski is mad. Perhaps the Hermann Goering division is another of his fantasies?'

'I doubt it very much!' Vitek suddenly shivered. 'There is no other way. You'll have to tell Janowski of our existence. Maybe there is a chance of joining the Russians, no matter how slim it is. Anything would be better than . . .'

'Shall we all go up?', I asked.

'Better wait here till I call you.' Mother was already on the way up.

'You go too', Inka urged me.

Ra-ta-ta-ta-boom-baroom.

It wasn't easy to leave. Shelminka trembled in my arms; Marek clung to my side. I couldn't carry him, so I carried Shelminka instead. Maybe it was safer in the cellar by then anyway.

The exchange of fire was constant; even our shutters didn't prevent the flashes from lighting up the rooms. Janowski declared that the shell which whizzed over our heads was, without any doubt, a 186 millimetre. Apart from that he seemed quieter than usual. Mother asked him to sit down.

'I'm waiting for that noise to stop; I have to go home.

Really, Lydia, I don't think the time for celebration has arrived.'

'I am not proposing any celebration. I have some important matters to discuss with you. Will you please sit down?'

He sat, and just then another shell burst nearby. This time it was a 96 millimetre; not so large as the one before.

'I have to tell you something, but before I do I want you to take an oath that you will never use the information against us.'

'What is this, a military tribunal? I admit I was wrong when I took the guns from you the way I did. But that has happened already. I know what you want to tell me. I have had my suspicions for some time now. Obviously you are hiding a high Polish official; that explains the gate, and the fact that we are now sitting upstairs, instead of in the cellar. It doesn't bother me; I am accustomed to all this racket, but you? Tell me who he is; I would love to meet him, and then I will definitely explain the whole situation.'

There was an eager look in his naive, childish eyes. For he was and always would be a boy who loved white horses and banners.

'Take the oath', mother said. 'Repeat after me. I swear . . .'

'I swear'

'On my wife . . .'

'On my wife'.

'On my children . . .'

'On my children'.

'On independent Poland . . .'

'On independent Poland'.

'I swear to secrecy . . .'

'I swear to secrecy.'

'So help me God . . .'

'So help me God.'

223

All this, to the deafening booming, trembling of the earth, to the shells in calibres 172, 96 and 112, whizzing through the air.

'You are quite perceptive. Yes, we are hiding people here, but it has nothing to do with the Underground. We are hiding my brother-in-law, his wife, their son and Irena's husband.'

'What have they done; why do they have to hide?'

'You see, my husband was a Jew.'

Janowski got up. 'He was what?' He looked at me. 'So she is half Jewish. And her'. He pointed at Tania. 'Oh, my God!'

'Spare us your reaction. We need your advice.'

'Advice?'

'Yes, advice.' Mother raised her voice to make herself heard, for the attack was in full swing. It was a never-ending cannonade of mortars and shellbursts. 'We don't know what to do now. Which would be better: to stay here or try to join the Russians? In a single word, is there any possibility of breaking through the front line?'

'No; absolutely, categorically, no. Don't you realise we are in the midst of it all? There is no way. I had better be going. My wife, my children must be wondering what has happened to me.'

'Don't you want to meet my family?' Mother was superb.

'Too late now. Tomorrow, perhaps. May God keep you all in his mercy!'

Janowski left. The sky was flickering, the air vibrated, the barrage roared. We were all glad to be in the cellar.

So there was no way out. We had to stay as we were, at the mercy of whoever had seen the arms being taken from our place.

——20——

It was a long night, pregnant with silent speculations and badly concealed fears. Vitek sat with Marek in the corner and told him another story from his never-failing resources.

This one concerned a time when he was six years old; when he and his younger brother were given new, tailor-made coats. The coats were very smart, so the boys went outside to show off. Suddenly, they were approached by a man who introduced himself as the tailor's assistant; he asked the boys to hand the coats back, for they were in need of a small alteration. The boys did as they were told. They waited for hours for the assistant to come back with the coats, and only then realised that they had been swindled by a con-man. They went home cold and humiliated.

We listened to the story, but I didn't think Vitek succeeded in taking our minds away from reality. We couldn't sleep, not even Marek. Suddenly, everything became quiet. The bombing stopped abruptly. We waited for one hour, two hours, and when it didn't resume Inka decided to have a bath and stretch out on her own bed. We all went upstairs; and, while Inka bathed, I stole more of Janowski's sugar, cooked more gruel, and promised myself to return it to Janowski if we survived. And if not, there was nothing to worry about. Who cared?

Somehow, we must have slept. When we awoke there was a German tank in front of our place. An officer was

225

sitting on it, scanning the house through field glasses. This is the end, I thought, and wondered what to do: whether we should hide, or get the guns and wait for them upstairs; or maybe, even better, go to the attic and start shooting at them from the top. The tank started with a roar of the engine, and overturned the fence. For a moment I thought he would hit the house — he was going straight at us — but then he turned to one side and came to a standstill on the path.

Vitek and the others fled to the shelter. Scores of soldiers ran towards the house. And I thought again, this is the end; and wondered what we should do. Maybe it would be better not to shoot, but rather to take Jadwiga's tablets. I wanted to go to Vitek and ask him to give us the poison, and then I heard a command and saw the soldiers digging a ditch. And I thought, was it for us? How come they knew how many of us, and how big a ditch to dig? Then one of the soldiers broke a whole branch of the tree and put it on the tank, then another and another, until the whole tank was covered up and from high above must have looked like a huge tree. The soldiers laughed and dug, and I saw that the ditch was getting too large for us and that, unless they were to kill the whole of Zielonka, it must have been for another purpose.

I wanted to go to the cellar and tell Vitek what I had seen, but there was a knock on the door; it was quite a civil knock. Aunt Olga went to open the door. A young officer was standing there. He excused himself for disturbing us, and asked to use our bathroom. He had hardly slept for two nights. We shouldn't fear any more, he said. The German attack had ended in total victory; they had eliminated scores of enemy soldiers and destroyed countless numbers of tanks. He apologized for overturning the fence. 'What a shame; your beautiful garden, your solid fences. War. What a shame.' He bathed while his soldiers prepared the dug-out for the tank.

226

So far, so good. I pumped water, and thought of Steva and his comrades and wished they were alive.

From then on Vitek and the others seldom left the cellar. Only during the exchange of fire, which would start every afternoon, would we be together. The Germans, as a rule, remained invisible during the raid. It was an excellent opportunity for our fugitives to come upstairs, wash, use the toilet, change their clothes and stretch their legs.

During the lulls our house was constantly used by soldiers and military police. They came and went all the time, mainly to use the bathroom. So we concentrated all our efforts on acting in a normal way; from time to time we even cooked. We reached the conclusion that, as the War was nearly over, no-one would dare to denounce us.

A shell landed in our attic without exploding. Aunt Olga asked Janowski to dispose of it. He followed us up, very serious, and examined the shell from some distance. 'Ninety-eight mill', he said. 'Could easily blow the whole house to pieces.' He picked it up with one hand. We froze. He opened the window, crossed himself, 'In the Name of the Father, the Son and the Holy Ghost', and threw the shell out. It landed in the meadow without exploding.

My thanks went to those slave-workers in German ammunition factories who sabotaged so many missiles.

Janowski eventually met the Viteks. He was quite charming to them, but one day couldn't help himself and remarked that my cynicism was very un-Christian and had always puzzled him. I must have inherited that streak of character from my father. It was very unfortunate, but this was how things stood.

We lost our very dubious sense of security by having either a tank or a big army truck parked and guarded in our garden. There was little food left and, as usual, Marek refused to eat more than his share.

The meadow in front of the house was transformed into a defence line. We watched trenches being dug, and all kind of military equipment being placed there. Before long, the whole area was surrounded by barbed wire and, as was suggested by Janowski, mines. With all my inherited cynicism, I believed him. We were trapped, and lost faith in the possibility of survival.

August was hot. We were all depressed; nobody even pretended any more. The daily exchange of fire often extended late into the evening.

We were visited by a gendarme. He inspected the house, said 'Jawohl', and placed a requisition order on the front door: 'Reserved for the commander and his aide-de-camp'. It was all sealed, swastika and all. That was all we lacked in our situation — a *Kommandant mit Adjutant* was badly needed to share the house with us.

I wrote in my diary, 'Vitek's story of the goat; but where is the rabbi?' I constantly thought of death, and kept on wishing that, if we were destined to perish, it might be as a result of war operations and not at the hands of the Nazis.

Janowski advised us to remove the hand-grenades from under the house. 'If a shell lands on them you will be blown to pieces', he said.

His logic never ceased to amaze me. And what amazed me even more was the fact that mother and aunt Olga still followed Janowski's command as gospel.

Our *Kommandant mit Adjutant* had not arrived.

In the morning we took the three grenades, the floor runner and a carpet beater, and aunt Olga and I went to the back boundary of Boyarski's garden. We were going to clean the runner, if someone asked. We had to clean the runner; it didn't really matter that it was drizzling and it didn't really matter that we were under bombardment. We had to clean the runner. Aunt Olga shook the runner very gently, because the grenades were hidden in it, and I dug the hole. The garden was devastated. The shrubs were either cut or run over by our very own tank. One of the guards looked at us, so I sat on the hole. Aunt Olga froze.

'What are you doing there?', he asked.

'My carpet was getting filthy. I had to air it a bit.'

'I like good housewives. You are a clean woman. Go ahead.' He turned away.

Aunt Olga performed some magic tricks. She waved the runner and beat it and shook it up until, presto! The grenades disappeared. To finished our act we performed a tap dance over the freshly dug ground. We sprinkled it with leaves and twigs.

Mission accomplished.

The *Kommandant mit Adjutant* still hadn't arrived. But the requisition notice proved to be of great value. The soldiers and the lower ranking officers stopped using our bathroom. Our morale improved again, although nobody could explain why.

We were quite experienced in guarding and patrolling our territory. The safest time for our prisoners to venture upstairs was during the shelling. We couldn't see the Germans anywhere. Somehow we were not frightened of the bombing. I even found morbid satisfaction in the thought that bombs and shrapnel treated all people alike, so there was no reason we should have been frightened of them.

My thieving didn't bother me any more. My only regret was that Janowski had possessed nothing of value except sugar and flour.

I even got used to the presence of the Herman Goering division. The young soldiers sat in the trenches, often stripped to the waist, just a few hundred yards from our house. I often wondered what they were really doing there. Surely they were not placed there to fire rounds of ammunition for just two or three hours a day. I watched them from our attic, watched how they moved from trench to trench. I heard them sing and laugh. I saw them

229

shave and clean their guns. *'Jawohl, Fraulein. Schnaps?'*

Ten days had passed since they had requisitioned the room for *Kommandant mit Adjutant*. They still hadn't arrived. What had happened?

We had to make an opening in the back fence; we were not allowed to walk through the meadow or near the tank. Mother and aunt Olga ventured to the shops, hoping to get something to eat; but the whole escapade proved useless. All the shops were shut.

I told Janowski I had used his sugar and prepared myself to defend my action, although I knew it was wrong. But there was no need; he took it well. He only asked me not to go below the three-quarter level mark, as he had children, too. I told him about the flour, which I had been using for some time now, pretending to have borrowed it from a neighbour who ran away.

'Have you used it all?'

'Not yet.'

'Then I suppose I had better take what is left home with me.'

I took it down and returned it to him. I felt humiliated and regretted confessing my crime. We had only a few pounds of grain left.

Vitek tried to keep our minds occupied, digging deep into family history. He told us of an uncle who didn't like the girl he was being forced to marry; and of how he took a bike and hid in the woods on the wedding day; and of how they found him and brought him to the side of his wife-to-be; and of how they got married, had four children; and of how his wife never forgave him. 'He was afraid to say boo. She never stopped nagging him.' It was all very interesting, even charming; but not on an empty stomach.

Marek, especially, was very hungry. He had lost a lot of weight and, as a result, his face became smaller and his eyes bigger.

Where was our *Kommandant*? Where was his *Adjutant*?

230

From the attic we could see the evacuees. At a distance we saw them marching under escort, some loaded with belongings, others empty-handed. Cows, goats, children and dogs were all moving at what seemed a slow pace. They would disperse to the sides of the road on sighting a plane, or when the shelling started — especially when the Russians sent a daily ration of rockets which made a frightening, prolonged sound like a herd of cows about to be slaughtered. They were officially called 'Stalin's organs'; which drove us to the conclusion that Stalin loved peculiar music.

The authorities evacuated the entire population from the other side of the railway lines. Every family on our side housed a few evacuees; every family, that is, except us. The risk of being denounced, even in those last stages of the War, was too great to take. Janowski agreed and came to our rescue. He spread the word that he, as an Underground commander for the district, wanted Boyarski's house to be used for a different purpose.

Aunt Olga exchanged two of our rabbits for a kilogram of potatoes. We ate the potatoes, skin and all, and wondered why the vegetable had never been mentioned by historians who studied Lucullus' banquets.

Marek was visibly hungry; so, in the morning, I announced that I would go to our milk-woman to get something to eat. Nobody paid much attention to what I said. When I left the house I wasn't even sure that they had noticed my departure.

I left through the opening in the back fence. So far, so good. I knew more or less where Madalinska's village was; but only just. She had always been good to us. Before the front line reached us she would deliver milk to us daily; she was always loaded with heavy milk containers — one on her back, two hanging in front of her. She would give a just measure and, from time to time, would give us an option on a chicken, or on cottage cheese.

Janowski was digging a shelter in his backyard.

'In case of a Russian offensive: Where are you going?'

'To Madalinska. How far is it?'

'About five kilometres. If I was you, I wouldn't go. Knowing you, I know you will. What else can I say? Keep clear of the main road. Use the country lanes and fields instead. When you come to the sixth crossing you will see a roadside chapel. Turn to the right. Keep going for about half a kilometre; turn right again. The name of the village is Slomka. And everyone knows Madalinska.'

Janowski looked in the direction of Warsaw. 'No news; we are completely cut off.'

He pointed to a black pillar of smoke, a smoke-screen.

'Do you realise the uprising is going into its third week?'

'The Ghetto uprising lasted six weeks.'

'The Russians; it's all their fault. They are waiting till we bleed to death. If they had wanted, they could have speeded up their offensive.'

'Where are the English? Are they coming?'

'Sometimes I wonder if you are plain stupid, or just pretend to be in order to get on my nerves. Take a piece of advice from me. Start on an outdoor shelter. Sooner or later, and I think sooner, we will find ourselves in the very centre of the front line.'

'Thanks for the advice. We'll take it into consideration.'

The day was so still, the sky so high, the air clean. The cornfields were of pure gold, pregnant with grain. The fields and the country lanes were deserted. The field flowers were in abundance. I promised myself I would gather them on the way home.

It was so peaceful. I couldn't believe I was only a few kilometres from the front line. Maybe there was no war. Perhaps I had just awakened from a nightmare. I was

232

fifteen again, walking through the country. Soon the peasants would come to the fields, for the corn was heavy and ready for the harvest. They would bring sickles, wooden pitch-forks and their songs. And they would greet each other with, 'Blessed be your toil'.

But I wasn't fifteen any more. My father wouldn't be waiting for me when I returned home. My whole world had collapsed. Irma, my Irma; would I ever see her again? That boy who used to come and get soup from us — why was he destined to perish? I thought of all the people in my life; those I had loved and those I had never loved. I cried for them all, for I realised that the basic right to live couldn't be measured by personal preferences. I wondered if those few Russians had managed to break through the Herman Goering division without coming to any harm. I remembered the German soldier who had helped the Jewish boy over the Ghetto wall; was he still alive? I wondered about Italians sent to freeze in the plains of Russia. How they must have longed for their sunny Italy. O sole mio.

I buried myself among the swaying corn, among the field flowers. I chewed corn, sweet and hard and earthy. I looked from a distance at the girl I once was. I had learned how to steal; I had hardened. No-one could stay unmarked in times like this; contamination was widespread.

I drifted with the corn. The flowers were rich blue and red. The leaves curled in the sun; some petals had faded already. There was a nagging sensation in my stomach. Hungry; I was hungry and my people were hungry. And I was wasting time instead of trying to get some food; I sat up and found myself facing the towering black smoke over Warsaw.

All those people; all those people! And I thought of Marek back home — skinny and dark — and Vitek with his arsenal of family anecdotes.

I got up and, before long, passed the roadside chapel

and reached Madalinska's village. A dog barked, then another. A peasant with a single tooth and white messy hair directed me to Madalinska's cottage.

'My golden miss', she greeted me. 'What are you doing here?'

'We have no food left; do you have any to spare?' I almost cried. She was wiping her huge hands on her enormous apron.

'Oh, we had food, plenty of it. Now it's all gone, taken by the Army. Hardly any left for us.'

'Never mind, Mrs. Madalinska', I said; which was a lie, because I did mind. 'I'd better be going back. Hope to see you after the War.'

'Wait.' She stopped me and went out of sight. She came back with half a bottle of milk and two pieces of home-made bread. 'For you.' She pushed the goods into my hands, and when she noticed that I was reaching for my purse she became agitated.

'Oh my', she tossed her head. 'D'you think it's for sale? Nothing is for sale now. I'm giving it to you, d'you understand? God keep you all in his mercy. Take care. A young miss like you shouldn't be walking around. Soldiers everywhere. If this war ever ends there will be a lot of German bastards.'

A thunder; a cannonade?

'You'd better stay with us till it calms down.' She was already tying a kerchief over her head, as if preparing to run or hide.

'Thanks, Mrs. Madalinska, but I must go back.'

'As you wish.'

I started on my way back home. First one, then another prolonged boom rolled over my head. It wasn't thunder. The sky was blue; only the white puffs of an anti-aircraft barrage hung in the air. The road in front of me was empty; when I looked back I couldn't see Mrs. Madalinska's village any more.

Shells burst open nearby, spitting fire and scattering

metal. I tried to protect my head with my arms, then threw myself to the ground. A long procession of ants crawled past me. They carried their tiny eggs, unperturbed by what was going on. It seemed obvious that they had a better chance of surviving than I.

'Oh God', I said aloud, 'if I have to be killed, let me reach aunt Olga's garden first.'

If I were killed in the fields, nobody would ever know what had happened to me, and Marek would never eat the bread and drink the milk I had managed to get for him.

One of 'Stalin's Organs' roared over my head. I heard shrapnel and a plane cutting through the sky. I decided to wait. It shouldn't last long; normally it lasted an hour or so. But what good would it do, staying in one spot? One could be killed lying down, walking, crawling, or even while screaming to high heaven begging God for life. So what was the use? I wanted to be home, to see my loved ones; urgently, immediately. I wanted to be good to them, and to bring Marek bread and milk so he could listen to family history on a full stomach for a change.

Home; home. I was frightened, cold, hot, confused. One moment I was running; the next crawling; maybe weeping, maybe screaming.

I came across the trenches; I must have taken a wrong turn. I crawled carefully, holding the precious food, never letting it go. The guns were being loaded; the soldiers next to them moved swiftly. There was a blaze, an explosion. Clouds of earth erupted. I ran; I tripped. The milk! The milk. It was still there, but some had sunk into the soil. I got back on to my legs. There were trenches to be crossed. I was all wet, scared, muddled. The soldiers waved at me. 'Fraulein, Fraulein, come here', they called. I ran and ran and fell to the ground and ran again until I couldn't hear them any longer, for I didn't want to give birth to a German bastard. I wanted to give birth to Julek's child. I wanted my child to be born when all this madness was at an end. And my child would live in times when he wouldn't have to steal sugar; he would play in the fields and wouldn't know what a barrage meant.

I think I cried and ran, ran, ran and, just before I went past Janowski's place, the bombing stopped.

'Did you find Madalinska?'

'Yes, I did.' I ran past.

'What's your hurry? Can't you stop for a while?'

I didn't answer. Our garden. Our home. At last. They must have worried about me; my only loved ones.

Someone opened the door. Everybody was upstairs. Our *Kommandant mit Adjutant* hadn't arrived yet.

'Where have you been?', asked mother.

'At Madalinska's. Look: bread, milk. I spilled half of it. It's for Marek.'

'How clumsy of you', remarked Tania. 'It was hardly worth the effort.' I put my goods on the table.

And that was all they ever said. They hadn't noticed. They hadn't even been worried.

Marek drank the milk, ate one slice of bread, and divided the second slice among the rest of us.

We stood guard, Julek and I. I told him how it had been on the way back and I cried. He kissed my hands; he kissed my face. He said he was sorry and that they didn't realise how bad it was, that from the inside the shelling wasn't any worse than on any other day, so they didn't really know. He whispered and he kissed me and he cried too. When it became darker, the shelling and bombing continued, and we thought we heard Russian voices.

But in the morning all was as before; the Herman Goering division and the well guarded trenches were in front of us.

——21——

A general evacuation was proclaimed. People assembled, disassembled, ran in circles. Some were already on the road, under escort.

Janowski's wife, who was pregnant, haemorrhaged. She needed an operation. Janowski arrived; he had spoken to a German doctor who had agreed to operate. Janowski suggested that, for safety reasons, the operation should take place at aunt Olga's house. The officer in charge agreed. Aunt Olga and mother were to assist; Zofia was to look after Janowski's children. Tania and I were also exempted from the evacuation, for some unknown reason.

Janowski brought his wife to our place. We covered the dining table with a clean sheet. We boiled the water. The doctor was efficient and looked normal without his uniform. He said he was willing to operate but he was not going to use any anaesthetic because he would need all he had for his soldiers. Janowski's wife smiled and said it would be all right; she didn't really mind. Her cheeks were flushed.

Mother, Tania and I stayed in the kitchen. I couldn't bear to hear Mrs. Janowski cry and couldn't stop from listening. It had never occurred to me that someone might need an operation during an evacuation. She didn't cry once. She had her operation performed to the constant rolling bombardment; it was so bad that once the doctor even left her and went down to the cellar. He stayed there with our rabbits, never suspecting our prisoners' presence over the wall.

Janowski came. Zofia was with his boys. The whole area was deserted; the only people left were those who had been exempted. He had seen the houses being methodically plundered, some being set on fire.

'They must be desperate', he said. 'It won't be long now. Maybe a day, or two. My poor child. I wanted him to be born in free Poland. Now he is being butchered by a German.' He turned his back on us.

'Don't think like this; the German is saving your wife's life.'

'I can't help it. I am frightened.'

The operation took about half an hour. The doctor washed himself in our bathroom. 'Wonderful.' He changed back into his uniform, and urged Janowski to look after his wife, to feed her well. Apparently she had lost a lot of blood. She was not allowed to move.

Later, food arrived from the doctor. Mrs. Janowski didn't want to touch it and pleaded with her husband to give it to their boys. She was pale and, from time to time, searched for Janowski's hand. 'Sorry', she kept saying.

Aunt Olga carried the bucket out. She took a spade and buried what was left of Janowski's child.

We suggested that Mrs. Janowski should be told of Vitek and the others, but Janowski objected, pointing out that it might be too much of a shock. He stayed with her, but didn't allow Zofia and the boys to come over.

'At least my sons will stay alive if your family is discovered.'

The night turned bright as day. The bombing never stopped, and Shelminka refused to go out. She hid under Vitek's bed and, before long, urinated.

I went to the attic with my mother. We saw Russian planes dropping flares, then bombs. I wished one of the planes would land in the garden and take us all behind the front line.

There was a lot of movement in the trenches. The guns spat fire. The tanks rolled from their holes and we heard orders being given. Mother told me how much she loved me and how happy she was seeing me happy with Julek, and urged me to be cautious and not to become pregnant before the War ended.

This was my mother; full of love and compassion to start with, but always managing to end on a false note. I told her I loved her too and not to worry.

Just then we heard an incredible roar and rumble. A formation of tanks sped towards the German line. I stood fascinated and couldn't believe I was witnessing a battle. A small piece of shrapnel pierced the roof and landed near us. My mother put her arm around me, and together we followed the movements of the tanks. And while we did, mother told me of her aunt who had lived on a large estate. During the season when the village girls were helping in preparation of fruit for bottling, the aunt ordered the girls to sing, so they wouldn't eat too many fruits. 'It was before the Russian Revolution', mother added.

Why was she telling me all this? The noise was deafening; the tanks were facing each other, charging, backing, pointing guns, firing, twisting, changing formation. I wondered how it would all end. There was so much commotion; one burst of a gun and our house would cease to exist. Mother kept on talking. Between one barrage and another it came out that she was telling me about my father and how he had bought a guitar instead of food, when both of them were just about starving. It was shortly after they were married. 'During the Russian Revolution', my mother concluded. 'Are you hungry?' she asked.

'No.'

The shelling was constant; the air was full of smoke. One of the tanks burst into flames and a few burning figures jumped out. I didn't know if they were Russians or Germans. They cried in inhuman voices which were saturated with pain; they rolled to the ground, crept around until they were shot, and then they didn't move any more. Their stillness petrified me. After a while I started to shake all over.

It happened during the Second World War.

My mother was cool; she told me it would be better to go downstairs. And then we heard shouts in Russian coming from everywhere. Mother hugged me and said that the German occupation must be over. Suddenly there was a prolonged whistling sound which grew louder and louder; the whole house shook on its foundations. I thought the roof was falling in on us. Instead, it was a rocket which had shot through the roof and landed near us. I couldn't move. It must be the end, I thought; but my mother picked it up and while I was shouting: 'Leave it. Don't touch it!', she threw it through the window — whereupon it exploded. I shook and shook, and couldn't stop; and then I thought that Janowski's method wasn't as stupid as it seemed. I even managed to smile. I wondered how his wife was.

The shelling stopped; the tanks were moving this way and that way. Mother sent me down. 'You'd better go and see how Vitek and the others are feeling. We haven't seen them for the whole day. I'll be fine; don't worry. Go.'

So I went down. Janowski was sitting next to his wife. It was decent of him to keep her company with all the shelling. She was motionless; Janowski was holding her hand. There was a dark puddle on the floor.

'Mr. Janowski . . .'

'It's all over', he said.

I asked him if he had heard Russian voices, too, and he answered that he hadn't; and then he wept and wept.

'In the afternoon I lost my child; now I have lost my wife. My precious ones. They will never see independent Poland.'

The floor was covered with glass; the window was smashed. What was there to do? I wanted to close the shutters.

'Don't', said Janowski. 'I want to be able to see her.'

The tanks and the guns clattered, blasted, roared, and then the morning came and it was quiet. The Herman Goering division was digging itself in again.

The burned-out tank stood in front of the house and the sentries dug a long grave to bury their dead. A Red Cross truck carried away the wounded.

The air was heavy in the cellar. I told them the War surely would have to end soon; we had heard Russian voices during the night, which meant the offensive must have started. Their only response was to look at me. I told them about Mrs. Janowski. They turned their heads away and Inka cried.

Janowski carried his wife to his house. Mother and aunt Olga went with him. They buried her in the garden. And then the gendarmes rushed from house to house, announcing that all men were subject to evacuation. I had just managed to wash the thick blood from the floor when Janowski came. He asked our permission to hide with our family. Zofia was to look after his children; she was good with them.

'Welcome to the criminals' circle', I said.

He looked at me and I think he understood. I felt ashamed.

Vitek walked over to him and shook his hand; so did Inka, Julek and Marek.

Marek whispered into my ear, 'What a pity I'm not a rabbit; they feed on grass, twigs, anything.'

Our supply of 1939-vintage rusks was coming to an end, and nobody tried to get rid of the innocent little worms any more.

Another hellish night passed, full of Russian voices and 'Stalin's organs'.

We slept upstairs. Janowski hardly spoke; he didn't

241

even tell us what size bullets were flying over our heads. Tania and aunt Olga kept guard.

In the morning we were back to normal, if one could call our situation normal.

And then Tania noticed first one German, and then another one, on the spot where we had buried the grenades. They stood for a while, spoke to each other and left with some hesitation.

Aunt Olga grabbed the floor runner and a small shovel. Someone must have noticed. Our only chance was to remove the grenades before they returned with reinforcements. Otherwise they would execute us and burn the house down. As soon as we reached the spot aunt Olga started her tricks: shaking the rug, rolling and unrolling it. The shovel dropped, I bent down and began to dig. The soil was all wet — that's funny, I thought. The soil was quite mucky, and so were the spade and my hands. I lifted them to my nose. There was no mistaking the strong smell. I laughed.

'It is no time for stupid jokes'. Aunt Olga reprimanded me, and went back to her tricks.

'Aunt, you don't understand; they used the spot to urinate.'

'Are you sure?'

'Look for yourself.'

Aunt Olga dropped the runner and bent down. After a thorough examination, she agreed. But we took the grenades back, anyway; it seemed less risky to have them hidden with us. Even Janowski approved.

We endured another long, mournful night. Janowski cursed the War and the German butchers. Outside all hell broke loose. There were no more windows left in the house. A huge shell landed in front of the cellar window, almost touching the sand-bag. I went to investigate and took Shelminka with me. She whimpered and didn't urinate until we came back inside. She did it in safety

242

under her kitchen stool. We decided to leave the shell where it was, trusting it not to explode.

Tania did a good job; she cleaned the rabbit cages. The air in the cellar had become vile and hard to breathe. We lined the cages with twigs and dry branches; there was not much grass left and we decided to keep it as feed for our very hungry protectors.

Janowski gave me permission to dig into his suitcase, where I found a block of chocolate. He instructed me to go to his place and ask Zofia to give us a glass of milk, for they had a goat. He gave the milk to Marek and divided the chocolate among us all.

Next morning the Herman Goering division was nowhere to be seen. The meadow and trenches were deserted, except for some pipes sticking up to the sky. From above they must have looked like anti-aircraft guns. The Russian planes circled, scanning the area for a long time.

Fritz was his name; I couldn't help knowing it.

The screaming order, 'Out, get out', came at the same time as a banging on the door. Aunt Olga's hands lost all their steadiness, and it seemed time stood still until she finally unlocked the door. Mother, Tania and I waited as if paralysed.

They burst in, pointing their guns at us. They rushed through the house knocking down whatever was in their way; when the younger one apologised, the older one roared, 'This is an evacuation, understand?' The young one saluted, or rather half saluted, 'Yes, Fritz.'

That was how I learned his name.

That was how we learned that we were still under German occupation; that the War hadn't ended with the Herman Goering division leaving the trenches.

'How much time do we have?', asked mother.

'Time?' Fritz laughed. 'No time. You have to go now,

immediately.' Aunt Olga grabbed the suitcase and I ran down to the cellar. I opened the trapdoor, and pushed in what was left of our rusks. 'Evacuation, we're leaving now. See you before long.' I didn't even see them.

I placed the rabbit in the cage and secured the door. The young German appeared and shouted for me to hurry, and demanded to know what was going on. I pointed to the rabbits, and he said 'Quickly, quickly', because the Bolsheviks could arrive at any moment. That was why the Germans wanted us to evacuate; they wouldn't like us to be left to the Russians and to be killed by them. The German was talking, and his words were like a balm to my confused soul. So, at long last, the Germans were withdrawing. What a pity we hadn't hidden. It had all happened so quickly that it hadn't been possible. At least my loved ones were safe. And Mr. Janowski.

They marched us away. Aunt Olga dragged a suitcase. How she had managed to pack it during those few chaotic minutes, I wasn't sure. Shelminka refused to walk, so I carried her.

One could feel autumn all round. We saw sharp, long shadows, and swallows sitting on the telegraph lines trying to decide whether of not it was time to migrate. If only we had been birds, we could have stayed away from Poland during the War years. It had been hard to notice the summer, and I wasn't even sure when it had passed.

Early this morning things had felt great. The meadow in front of us had been empty, and even Janowski had said it must have been a total German defeat and the Russians shouldn't be long. Last night we had seen German tanks in retreat, and we were sure the War had ended.

Later that morning Fritz and his men had combed their hair, buttoned their uniforms, polished their boots and checked their guns ready to evacuate us.

——22——

We reached the roadway. Storm-troopers had methodically emptied house after house. The country road, uneven and dusty, was filling rapidly with people who were constantly hurried along. Orders were barked out and occasionally people were jostled with rifle butts.

Zofia and Janowski's sons walked in front of us, leading their goat. I heard Fritz's voice in front of me, and then behind me; and whenever his voice levelled with me I froze and quickened my steps. His square helmet was tilted and the oval number plate around his neck shone to perfection.

I thought that somewhere there must have been girls who wanted to be with him, who thought him handsome and good company. Maybe even now they were looking at his photo, remembering, and saying, 'That is my Fritz'.

I thought, It's warm; why don't the birds sing? I was thirsty; my feet hurt. What was I doing there?

I walked within myself.

Aunt Olga was breathing heavily beside me, her face sprinkled with a mixture of dust and perspiration. I took the suitcase, and almost fell to the ground.

'What on earth have you put in it?' I asked. She stopped for a moment.

'Who knows? I took a few things. Who knows?' she mumbled.

Mother and Tania, where were they? They had been

next to me just a moment ago. Where were they? I couldn't see them. What had happened?

Distant artillery thundered, and Fritz kept on firing periodically, straight into the air. If he wasn't shooting, he was setting houses on fire. If he wasn't setting houses on fire, he was screaming at us.

Cottages and haystacks were in flames. And we marched. From time to time I would catch a glimpse of mother's hair, appearing then disappearing.

Peasants led cows and children, goats and old people. They pushed wheelbarrows, and balanced huge loads on their backs. One skinny man with bouncing legs walked as a circus clown walks on a tight rope.

Clouds of smoke shifted, dimming and tarnishing the sky and the sun.

'Quickly, quickly!'

I couldn't see mother's head any more. I had lost sight of them both. What should I do now? I had planned to return home, given an opportunity; now I wouldn't be able to break away. 'See you before long', was what I had said before we left.

On and on and on. My feet blistered. I almost dropped the suitcase, but aunt Olga wouldn't let me.

'Mummy', cried a little girl, Muu-ummy!' She had mottled, very blonde hair. She pressed her fingers to her eyes, then wiped her hands on her once clean, sun-bleached caftan. Her face was smeared with tears and dust, her nose was running, and her sobs were sporadic and shuddering, like artillery fire. She had corn-flower blue eyes with such a depth of pain and bewilderment that I turned my head away.

On and on and on.

'Holy Virgin, Mother of the Polish Crown', someone intoned.

'Have mercy on us', invoked eager voices.

So many voices were mixed up, praying and crying, cursing and comforting.

How were our prisoners, I wondered? We had to go back; but first I had to locate mother and Tania.

'Halt.' I recognised Fritz's voice. 'Rest', he snapped. People squatted wherever they were. An old man kept on standing, patting his cow. He was as scrawny as his animal. What was he doing here? He should have been somewhere in the field with his animal. Both of them should have been left in peace, warming their dry bones in the sun and chewing the cud.

I spotted mother and Tania; I urged aunt Olga not to move. She held on to her suitcase, as others did to whatever they possessed.

I stumbled over legs and heads, over children and dogs. I pushed my way like a tank, disregarding whomever I hurt, ignoring curses and abuse. But, on the way back, after all the hugging and crying, we walked cautiously, carefully, finding time for, 'Excuse me,' and other luxuries; for we were together again.

I tried to locate the little girl but I couldn't; there were so many children crying, 'Mummy'.

Aunt Olga was exactly where I had left her. The tears carved straight, clean lines on her dusty face. She smiled at us, but cried again when I suggested we leave the suitcase behind, because it was beyond anybody's strength to carry it further.

I opened the wretched suitcase.

'Don't throw anything away', aunt Olga begged. 'It might prove to be all we possess.'

Inside was an iron with two cast-iron heaters; this was absolutely necessary in case we wanted to freshen up our clothes. Apart from Uncle's portrait, there was also toothpaste, a wall mirror, a cooking pot and a crystal vase. All this surely was needed, for we might feel like throwing a party for Fritz and Co.

'Quickly, quickly; get up; march!' Fritz, or maybe somebody else, shouted the order.

I selected a few pieces of clothing, dumped the rest

and, with Tania's assistance, helped aunt Olga up and
forward.

'Quickly, quickly!'

'We must find some way to get back', I whispered to
mother.

'How?'

'I don't know yet, but we must.'

'Don't be hasty.'

'If you are frightened, I'll find the way myself.'

'We are not going to be separated, that's for sure.'

'Shut up', snapped the sentry.

There were no planes in sight but everyone looked at
the sky; a vibrating drone made everyone nervous.

'Don't worry; calm yourself, folks', shouted a young,
one-legged man. 'The planes are ours, on a reconnaisance mission. Don't panic.' He lifted his crutch up and
waved at the sky. And he smiled gaily, joyously.

'Damn swine!' Fritz knocked him down. I didn't really
see it; it happened so quickly. But I saw the young one
getting up, swaying, and wiping the blood off his face.
He forced a smile. 'Bloody bastards; desperate, that's
what they are. Their breeches are full of shit. Won't be
long folks!'

The sun was getting hotter, and the plane which
circled above us glistened from behind a smoke screen.

Fritz's parents, I was sure, must have been thinking of
him all the time, must have been proud of him. His
photograph must have been somewhere in their home,
in a place of honour, always looked at, dusted every day,
standing on a hand-crocheted doily. 'Yes, that is our son.
God be with him.'

'Quickly, quickly!'

We kept on moving forwards. My lips were parched.
The people around me dragged their feet; some of them
limped. Their hair and clothes were all dull and dusty.

There was a constant din, with cows mooing; people shouting; goats bleating; dogs yapping; children crying; and soldiers screaming — all this against the never-silent, distant cannonade.

Shelminka behaved herself. I even think that she enjoyed her outing. She followed us, and only when a shell exploded did she refuse to go on, forcing us to carry her.

All of our theories and discussions, including the plan to take Marek and Julek with us, had now resolved themselves. Julek couldn't have come anyway; there were no young men in sight, except for the one-legged one. That tight mass, that crowd, consisted of women, children and old people. Even the animals were old.

An explosion deafened us all and the guards ran and screamed, forcing us to hurry, pointing their guns with more urgency.

'Apparently a goat . . .'

'No, not a goat. It was a dog . . .'

'Ran away, followed by its owner . . .'

Nobody knew who it was, though some crossed themselves and swore on their lives that it was a child.

'Not a child! That old man got bashful all of a sudden. Went to the side to piss. Saw it with my own two eyes, so help me God. Stumbled over a wire and phew . . . straight up to heaven.'

A mine, they said.

'Holy Mother, full of Mercy . . .'

A woman walked in front of me. Her steps were steady, ageless. Her head was covered by a kerchief, and her long, ragged skirt was full at the bottom. She walked barefoot, carrying a brightly painted clay statuette of a saint in her arms. She prayed incessantly, calling on all the saints and calling to God for guidance. She must have left her shoes at home, so that, when she returned home one day together with her saint, she could put on

249

her shoes, dress herself properly, and then go to church again, to thank God for all his mercies.

Her feet were rough, her steps automatic, and I felt she was capable of walking like this to the end of the earth, as long as she was holding her saint to her breast. I envied her.

We walked to the sound of a distant barrage, all of us reduced to a passive, anonymous mass.

The burnt-out houses were ugly. I hated seeing the fields ploughed by tanks and guns. But mostly I hated an old tree which withstood it all, standing there in red and yellow, green and gold.

Towards evening we dragged our feet. We searched for a way out, but wherever we looked the houses were burnt out and we were cordoned by evenly spaced guards. Perhaps we should have approached them? Surely they had mothers and sweethearts somewhere, and homes they would like to return to? But they looked so unapproachable, uniform, faceless. And they were under orders, and must have believed that it was absolutely necessary to drag that mass of people with them, to burn houses, to shoot, to scream.

There was no way out.

It was dark. We were passing alongside a fence, which aunt Olga said belonged to someone called Gorski. And then she disappeared through a hole in the fence and Tania followed her. Nobody noticed . . . Good. My heart beat quickly. Now for another broken plank . . . Come on! Where, where? The fence was sturdy. The guard next to us was going forward, turning around.

'Now!', whispered mother, 'You next!'

'You.'

'You.'

I could see it; an opening. I went for my life, through to the other side of the fence. Shelminka whimpered. Shshshshshhh. A shadow loomed; someone breathed hard.

'Mother? . . . Mother?. . .'

'Shshshshshshshsh!'

There were no stamping feet, just the wooden fence, and the world changed. Tania, aunt Olga . . . and mother, mother was there! So we had made it after all.

We moved cautiously, slowly, our eyes getting used to shapes.

'This way.' Aunt Olga led the way. 'The house; in front.'

A white structure emerged. The moon appeared and hung in the sky like a huge, bright lamp.

We heard steps; someone was coming towards us.

'What do you want here?'

'Mr Gorski? Olga Boyarski. Remember me?'

'Mrs. Boyarski! Not much of a welcome; not like in the old times.'

'Could we stay here?'

'Of course. We were given permission to stay till 4 a.m. The village folk were allowed to stay with us and many have, so you can pretend you belong with them. When were you evacuated?'

'This morning, without warning. We want to return to my place.'

'I understand. We would love to stay behind, if possible. Zofia Borowska arrived not long ago with Janowski's boys. How tragic; his wife, I mean.'

'Yes.'

He took us to the communal shelter where family groups were sleeping, squatting, talking. We sat in the corner and agreed to go back as soon as the moon went down. The artillery started again, more vicious than ever. It was hard to breathe. People crossed themselves, whispered 'Our Father' and 'Holy Mother'. They were full of enduring resignation.

Zofia appeared.

'Mr. Gorski told me you were here. Warsaw is still burning. What are your plans?'

'We'll try to return home, once it's dark.'

'I don't know what to do — to try to reach Warsaw, or to stay with the boys. Maybe the boys should stay with the Gorskis? I don't know. Mrs. Gorski put them to bed and they didn't mind. I would love to be somewhere near my husband . . . if he is still alive. On the other hand, he wanted me to be with the Janowskis till it was all over. I don't really know.'

'I can't possibly help you, I'm sorry', said aunt Olga. 'If you decide to return with us, we will be glad to take you with us. Mr. Janowski needs his boys badly now; he needs you.'

'Would you consider taking the boys with you?'

'Janowski left them with you.'

'Please understand me. I don't know yet, but it would be cruel to drag the boys away from their father, as you said.'

'If necessary, I will take the boys.'

'What about the goat? Mr. Janowski asked me to take the goat wherever we went; the boys need milk.'

'We will see.'

I took Shelminka and went outside. The moon was slowly going down. My stomach rumbled. I had to speak to the Gorskis. The garden was devastated, chopped to pieces. Hardly any trees were left. Mrs. Gorski was in the stable, attending to the wounded. She looked as though she had been taken straight from some patriotic picture, tall and blonde, gentle and aristocratic, bringing comfort to those less fortunate than herself. Despite her lack of sleep she managed to look beautiful and composed. Her clothes were still fresh and her face serene. She made me feel shy. My dress stank; my hair was in a mess.

'Yes?' She smiled at me.

'I wonder if you could do me a favour, Mrs. Gorski?'

'That depends on what you want of me, my child.'

'Our dog. We can't take her with us. We intend to go back home. Could she stay with you? Till you go yourselves? Please?'

'And then what?' A slight change in her face.

'Before you go, let her off the leash. She might manage to find her way home. I hope she will. Oh, I'm certain she will.'

'I hope you know what you are doing.'

'Mrs. Gorski, there is no other way.'

'Very well.'

'Thank you, Mrs. Gorski.'

'What is your dog's name?'

'Shelminka.'

Mrs. Gorski told me where to leave Shelminka and I tied her to a beam in the stable. She shivered all over and cried. And when I kissed her she licked my hands and face. 'You'll come back to us, won't you?', I begged her, and I nearly cried when I left.

The moon had almost disappeared. Zofia decided to come with us, and aunt Olga was relieved. She wanted to take her suitcase and what was left in it, but we persuaded her to leave it behind. Before we left we took the suitcase to the house and Mrs. Gorski lifted her eyebrows in a characteristic way. 'Why worry, Olga, everything that is left behind will be looted anyway.' That was exactly what her predecessors would have said.

We started on our way back, first travelling through the Gorski's property. Mother, aunt Olga, Tania and I were followed by Zofia pulling the goat and two very frightened boys. The goat bleated, the boys cried and complained, and Zofia threatened that if they didn't stop, she would be forced to leave them as they were and go on her own; besides, they had better learn how to control themselves, because otherwise the Germans would find us all and would kill us before we even had time to finish the Pater Noster.

The open road was in front of us. I was angry that we had left Shelminka behind, because the goat bleated all the time anyway. The goat was needed for the boys, I was continually reminded.

I don't really know how we reached aunt Olga's

house. The road and the fields were full of army men, tanks and vehicles, infantry, trenches, guns. And our small group pushed against the torrent, falling to the ground, crawling, with the goat bleating and the boys whimpering. I felt hot and cold, and every time I saw a burnt-out house, I feared that aunt Olga's house would be reduced to cinders too.

I don't know how long it took us. Neither do I know why we were never spotted. I only know that, when we came to the meadow and saw aunt Olga's house intact, we ran towards it. The door had been smashed down and the whole house ransacked, but we found our prisoners all well. We told Janowski that Zofia and the boys and the goat were well, and already hiding in his shelter.

'Thank God.' He wanted to know more but there was no time to be lost. We secured the doors with planks, we closed all the shutters, and only then did we sit in the cellar and tell everyone what we had been through. And they told us their story: how, as soon as we had left, Janowski and Julek had gone to the attic, because Janowski had suddenly remembered that he had a few more blocks of chocolate and wanted to bring them down, as well as some of the sugar to share with everyone. And when they were in the attic they saw a small contingent of military policemen running towards the house; so they grabbed the sugar and hurried back to the cellar. Even before they had time to hide, the Germans had knocked down the door and were inside.

Just at that moment Tania pointed to the window. 'Oh, not again', she exclaimed. 'Look; hide, quickly', she said. I caught a glimpse of military boots passing by. We pushed our way into the hideout. There was no time to place the rabbit in the 'go-through' hutch. But we all managed to hide. Janowski was at the far end, and next to him were Olga, Marek, mother, Tania, Inka, Vitek, Julek and I.

254

——23——

They banged and they cursed, and the door came
down with a loud thud. We heard their heavy steps just
above our heads, and I prayed once more that if we had
to die, it would not be at their hands. We heard more
shouting, banging and cursing, and then footsteps coming down. We froze.

'So many coats.'

'Look, rabbits. How many d'you want — two, three?'

'Three'll do.'

Their footsteps went back up.

How stupid we all were, leaving our coats, securing
the door of a house which had been plundered and left
open, probably by these very men. Julek pushed something into my hand. It was a cool, rounded, familiar
grenade. I pressed it against my body; at least we were
armed. But I didn't know how to use the damned thing.

We heard them smashing and shouting, banging and
laughing.

Julek's stomach rumbled.

'Stop it', urged Inka. 'You are endangering our lives.'

'Can't help it; sorry.'

'They might hear it, it's so loud.'

'Oh, stop it, mother', whispered Marek.

'Vitek, it's time you did something about your son.
The way he speaks to me is deplorable. Do something;
you are his father.' Inka's whisper made more noise than
Julek's rumbling.

'We will discuss it later, darling.' Vitek breathed hard.

And then Tania declared she was hot and might suffocate if not let out. And, besides, she had left father's scissors upstairs and would hate to lose them. 'Father always used them. Remember?'

Tania tried to push her way through. 'Scissors', she repeated.

'If you move one step further, I'll hit you. Sit down', I warned my sister in a friendly whisper; and she sat down.

There were more noises: clattering; banging; clangour; swearing; and footsteps just above our heads.

'They're chopping the furniture up, can't you hear?' exploded Janowski. 'They're going to burn us alive.'

'How d'you know?'

'Can't you hear? They're pouring the kerosene over the floor. Can't you smell it?'

'As a matter of fact I can't', I said, and then I thought that I could.

We heard more smashing, more banging, more cursing.

'Shshshshshsh, listen.'

'I've had it. Lydia, as your commanding officer, I order you to go out and tell those barbarians not to burn us down.'

'Oh, you shut up; if you want to go out, go out yourself', whispered Marek.

'See what I mean?', lamented Inka. 'He has no manners left at all.'

'Be quiet, all of you', implored Vitek, and we all obeyed.

We sat still. All those sounds of chopping and smashing and laughing drilled into my mind. Now, when liberation was so near, we were doomed and nobody would ever know that we had existed. All the stories from the past would be lost; and Marek would never run in the sun, would never meet a girl. The child I longed for would never be born.

'Stalin's organ' was roaring, playing the death tune. We heard whistling rockets; a cannonade; bombs. The whole house shook.

'It must be a 187 millimetre firing.'

It was hard to breathe, and we took it in turns to move next to the vent. Inka begged Marek to stay there but he didn't want to.

The smashing upstairs had stopped. Had it stopped? Or were they still there, waiting for us to crawl out from the hideout? For they must have known that somewhere in the house there was someone hiding.

'As your superior officer', Janowski was at it again, 'I command you to find out what's going on, Lydia'.

'Shouldn't we wait till the barrage stops?'

'It might prove too late; someone has to find out what's going on.'

I asked for a gun; not that I knew how to use it, but I felt it would give me some sense of security. Nobody really protested when I crawled out; Julek touched my hand. 'Take care!', he said.

I was out of the cellar. So far, so good. As I went up, step by step, the stairs creaked. The doors were smashed again. There was no sign of fire; no sign of Germans. And it was so good to breathe; oh, how good it was. The air, the air! I went through one room, then another. What a mess. All that was left of the loungeroom was scattered around, and Boyarski's sword was missing. My breathing was still troubling me. Steady, I told myself; the Germans have left. Steady . . .

I went outside; there was no need to open the door. I stepped on to the porch and went down the stairs one, two, three. I fell, fell, fell, until I reached the bottom of what, I suddenly realised, was the tank ditch. Trust me to forget a thing like that. I sat there while the bombardment went on: a continuous blast; a continuous barrage. I

257

sensed somebody's presence. It couldn't be. I wanted to live. Something moved. It was dark in the ditch and the sky above was dark, too. My family was waiting for me; they were breathing hard and worrying about me. I should have gone, but somehow I stayed as I was. I couldn't move. I wasn't hurt, I could move my arms and my legs; I wasn't dead because I was reasoning. I was sure there was something close by. My breathing surely couldn't have been so noisy. That other breathing was coming closer, closer. I pressed my back against the side and the dirt fell all over me and I shut my eyes . . . Shelminka! Shelminka; my brave, little friend. I hugged her and she squealed and licked me all over. Shelminka, who had never before ventured outside the Boyarski's property, who was frightened of bombs, had come back to us. Her coat was dusty and sticky, and when I hugged her she cried.

I got up and ducked again because of the blast and then I went inside. I had to let my people out before they suffocated. And before that I had to see Janowski's children and have a good look around to see if there was any immediate danger which might prevent my loved ones from leaving the shelter.

Shelminka didn't follow me. I thought she would be immune to shelling by now. She whimpered; she howled. I lifted her up and she cried. I carried her inside. Her cushion; that was the answer. But where was it? Surely, they hadn't taken a dog's cushion? It wasn't in its proper place and I just couldn't see; everything was so dark. I stumbled and Shelminka cried. Her coat was all sticky. She licked my face. There must be a pillow somewhere; any pillow — mine, mother's, Vitek's, for all I cared. Something soft. There it was; a pillow. I wanted to rearrange it, and instead ended up with feathers in my mouth. They had slashed the bedding.

'Stay here.' I wanted to go; I had to go. But Shelminka

didn't want to stay; she dragged herself towards me. I picked her up and carried her to the cellar.

I opened the trapdoor. 'The house is clear and not burning', I called out. 'The doors have been knocked down again. You might just as well come out. Be careful.'

'What took you so long?'

'Shelminka's back. I think she's injured. I'll come back soon.'

I left before they were all out. I was frightened; I was breathing normally but my heart was leaping. My hands were sweaty and cold, but this time I remembered the ditch.

A blast brought the outline of houses back for a moment and showed me the way. There was constant thunder with a continuous, flaring blaze. And my heart beat in my throat.

I went through the hole in the fence, around the back. I had to hurry. The sky was covered by flickering flames and the earth trembled.

I reached Janowski's shelter. 'It's me.' I banged on the door. Zofia opened up.

'Thank God. Are you all right?', she asked.

'We are all well.'

'You should've seen the Germans; they were furious. I was petrified they were going to find you and then . . . '

'How are the boys?'

'Asleep.'

'Could you spare us something to eat?'

She went inside and came back with a small bag.

'1939 Rusks, if you want them.'

'Thanks. Many thanks.'

So we would eat; suddenly, I felt very hungry. I had to hurry home. I rushed through blasts and roars, and a glowing sky, but it didn't matter any more. I hadn't seen a single German and I had something for all of us to eat.

At last I was in the cellar. Everybody looked at me.

'How are things?', Janowski asked.

'The boys are asleep and well. Look what Zofia gave me; rusks!'

'I hope she left enough for my sons.'

Aunt Olga took the bag and divided its contents.

We ate; we actually ate. Crunch, crunch. Tania brought some water: how good it was, how good it felt.

'How's Shelminka?'

'Something's wrong with her hind leg. We'll wait till morning and then we'll see.'

If morning ever came.

I gave Shelminka some water. She drank it — a good sign. She shared her rusk with me.

Tania and mother brought what was left of our bedding. We all stretched out; wall-to-wall people.

Aunt Olga and Janowski decided to go to the attic. 'One has to assess the situation', explained Janowski as he went up. 'See you in the morning.'

If morning ever came.

I cuddled next to Julek. Marek was already asleep; Vitek's arm was around Inka; mother's arm was around Tania. My family.

It was dawn. The light reached the cellar and the rabbits started the daily inspection of their dwelling. Shelminka's nose was dry and her thigh was covered with blood; dried blood. It didn't seem to be a bullet wound. I brought water down and washed the blood away. She licked my hands, and let me do it. She was a good little friend. It didn't look too bad; someone must have kicked her while she was running to us, frightened. Brave, trusting friend.

We ventured upstairs one by one to freshen up. As long as the bombing was heavy we could take the risk; the Germans were nowhere to be seen. We didn't feel very secure, as the whole house was wide open. It was impossible to keep a proper guard in the attic, and we were frightened of being cut off from the hideout.

I stood in the doorway and watched. The entire district was empty, as far as I could see.

It was going to be one of those perfect days when the sun was caressing; when the wind brought awareness of being; when the light highlighted beauty. It was going to be a golden Polish autumn day, tarnished by bursts of smoke, fire and cannonade.

My country was still being tormented.

The barrage was growing in volume. We should have been back in the cellar. Shelminka hadn't even bothered to leave our sanctuary. She was sore but her nose was less dry, so she must have been feeling better.

'Excuse me.' Janowski pushed his way through, went to the attic and came back with a cupful of groats, straight out of his horn of plenty. He gave me the cup.

'Something warm would be nice before we die.'

'Something warm might help us to stay alive.'

He dismissed what I said with an impatient wave of his hand and descended to the cellar. Only Inka and I stayed upstairs to cook. The attack was in full swing; so the chances of Germans descending on us were minute. Nobody could possibly notice the rising smoke from our chimney; or so we hoped.

Inka washed the groats, or rather caressed them. She smiled. The fire was already burning. She placed the pot on the stove in the place of honour. The grains absorbed water and swelled, and their vapour tantalised us. We watched over them as if bewitched.

Voices; where were they coming from? There was shouting, a drumming of feet . . .

'Listen . . . '

Louder and louder it came. Oh, not again; not now, not before we fill our bellies. Not now. Please. Not now.

Inka ran to the door.

'They are heading straight towards our place.' She screamed. 'Hide everybody! Quick, hide!'

I was holding the pot and didn't know where to put it.

261

Panicky noises from the cellar died down. So they must have managed to hide. And now the pot; we had to concentrate on the pot. Shelminka yelped. Inka grabbed my hand. 'We have to go down!' she yelled, and our meal-to-be ended on the floor.

'How could you?'

I went on my knees and Inka was next to me, and we scooped the grains back into the pot. We blew and waved our hands, and tapped them and blew on them again.

Suddenly, we heard banging and a single shot; and then heavy boots were stamping over our meal.

But the men were not in uniforms.

Who were they?

Inka; Inka was exposed — not that it mattered now.

'We were told that you're hiding a man', the short one said in Polish.

I looked at them from the floor; all six, seven, eight of them. They were blocking the light. I couldn't see them very well.

'We want a man named Janowski; we must have him.'

'Janowski, you said? I know him, he lives two houses down from here. But, as far as I know, he was evacuated with the others.'

'What about you; weren't you evacuated?'

'We had to stay. My aunt hurt her leg and couldn't walk. So we took the risk.' I was amazed at my own voice; it was so smooth. But my nerves were pulling in opposite directions, ready to snap.

'Give us Janowski', another one barked from the back line. 'We must have him.'

'Sorry; can't help you.'

'Stop playing games. This is serious. We know he's in this house somewhere, so you'd better call him.'

Aunt Olga appeared from down under.

'Mrs. Boyarski: we must have Janowski.'

'Who are you?'

262

'Surely you know me. I work for Janowski. Remember me?'

'As a matter of fact, I don't.'

'Are you going to call Janowski?'

'How could I; he is not here.'

'Come out Janowski'; they all started to yell.

'Out you come or else.'

'Janowski, come out; the Russkis are here!'

'Janowski; no need to hide any more!'

'W-what d-d-do you mean?' Inka lifted her tormented face.

'What I said. It was meant to be a joke; understand? A surprise; understand?'

Janowski's head appeared and his mates helped him up. They all shouted and laughed and shook hands.

'Is it really over?' Janowski's voice came from the centre.

'Sure, as God is my witness. Let's go; there's plenty of work to do.'

'I'll see you later', Janowski said, and left with them.

The barrage still went on.

Some joke; some surprise.

Inka cried; aunt Olga put her arm around her.

'We made it. Free; free at last.' She cried, too, and ran down to the cellar with Inka following her.

I ran out to the ditch. I sat in the deepest end and wept. I felt very small. They had cheated us; the liberation shouldn't have been sprung on us like this.

'Irena.' My mother called me, but I didn't respond. 'She is impossible. Never around when she's wanted. Where are you; can't you answer?'

Julek called me, too, and Marek. But I couldn't face them; I couldn't stop crying. And I needed to be alone. Irma and Stokowski's sons were with me; and the boy who stopped coming for soup; and the hostages whose names had been pasted all over so many walls. I remembered two: Zalewski and Slowon — why those two out of so many, I didn't know. They were names without faces.

Where were you, my friends?

'Where did she go? Not even one moment of peace.' Mother wasn't angry, only concerned. I felt really bitchy. Jadwiga would have said, 'Quiet, quiet'; or nothing at all.

Vitek; yes it was Vitek's voice, asking someone to go and check if it was true. For all we knew it could have been a few tanks again.

'We will go', said aunt Olga, 'as soon as Irena comes back'.

And then the cannonade gained in strength again; the War was not over yet. The planes flew over low.

I couldn't hear Vitek's voice any more. They must have gone to the cellar. It was all clear for me. I crawled out, went to the attic, and from there I could see the main road. Tanks and army trucks were filling up every space. There were so many soldiers, and they were definitely not Germans. So we were free. I cried and laughed, and I was so very sad. Why sad, I wondered; but, yes, I was sad.

I climbed down to the cellar ready to go with aunt Olga. Vitek was really worried, because our hideout wasn't safe any more.

'Who knows if the Germans won't return again.'

And then he sat next to Marek and told him how my father had set a chair on fire because he had wanted to see the fire brigade in action. He was six then, and nobody had wanted to take him to the fire station.

We left, aunt Olga and I, and mother followed us.

'I want to see it, too, and kiss the first soldier I come across.'

'I hope the Germans don't come back. I feel very tired.' Aunt Olga was sad, too; more like her old self.

It was not easy to cross the meadow; there were so many ditches, and barbed wire and pieces of army junk were scattered everywhere. It seemed we were the only people left; not one other person was in sight. There were so many burnt-out houses, with all their windows smashed. The fences and the trees were all flattened. We could hear motors running and, at the crossroads, there were trucks blocking the path.

They were Russian; Russian, as far as the eye could see, with tanks, a field kitchen, and ambulances. Someone was singing a strange, haunting song. Small detachments marched this way and that, and mine searchers branched from the main road with long probing poles. Trucks were speeding by.

Mother ran to the first group and kissed a young officer. 'Thank you, thank you', she sobbed.

He looked a bit embarrassed but pleased.

'Don't worry little mother', he smiled. 'This time we're here to stay.'

'What's all this shelling?'

'We're still advancing. You should know.'

'How far is the front line from us?'

'You want to know a lot, little mother', he laughed. 'Four, five kilometres.'

'My God', said aunt Olga.

We waved good-bye and started on the way back.

'Hey, little mother; wait, wait!' The Russian ran towards us and gave us a whole loaf of bread.

Aunt Olga cried.

'They are here to stay', reported mother. 'It's not a matter of a few tanks; it's the whole Army; masses of them everywhere.'

'Bread!' Marek jumped around.

We ate the Russian bread. What a delicacy; what a texture; what a taste. What a gift.

'We must move farther from the Front. Five kilometres isn't much of a distance; the front line might change.'

The day we were liberated, Marek ran out from the house, and his legs seemed to be even more skinny than when he had been inside.

He ran a few steps as though he were on stilts; and then he stopped and looked back, all puffed-out and happy. Vitek swayed and fell to the ground, weeping.

And when we started on our way the Russians were all over us.

'What's happened to you? And what about the boy?'

We told them, and they gave us cod-liver oil for Marek and some bread. We dragged ourselves through a deserted township. We were free but not exactly happy; because how could anyone be happy amidst so much devastation?

And then we came across our first group of liberated Poles. They looked at us and said, 'It's not even two hours since the Russkis came, and here we have our Jew-boys again'.

The Russian patrol led us through a mine-field. They shared their food with us, including even some wild pears, and in the end were offended because neither Tania nor I wanted to make love with them. But they took us to the village they had recently left, which was some twenty kilometres from the Front.

A peasant let us use his barn, where we slept in the hay. In the morning we were awakened by the sun's piercing rays and by swallows circling and chirping over our heads. We were happy. Then we started to itch, because the barn had also been used by the Russian army; and apart from everything else, they had left thousands of very hungry lice behind.

We ate, and couldn't stop wolfing down all that good farm food, until we all made ourselves sick.

Shelminka soon recovered, and had a litter of four healthy pups. We even returned to Lodz; but we never went back to our flat, because we couldn't face the past any more. But we kept on searching and searching for old friends, and found very few survivors.

One day Kazia came and did all of our washing — even though she was working full time in a factory by then. She was looking after a German family. 'Who needs war?' she said. 'The poor woman was left behind with three kids and a mother; an old, stupid witch. She doesn't even know if her husband is alive. Nice kids . . .'

Kazia.

Marek started school and lost two front teeth in a fight, but never disclosed the cause of the scuffle. Vitek was the only one who didn't question Marek, although he agreed with us that there could be only one explanation: Marek was a Jew.

But things were on the move; Vitek was back in the Department of Reconstruction. With so many ruins around, a time to rebuild had arrived. Vitek was able to put his dreams to good use.

The day the War ended we spent with our family. We talked more of the futility of war than of victory. On the way home we walked through dark streets. People bumped into each other; some sang; some were drunk; some laughed. Gun shots bounced from street to street: people were celebrating the end of six years of war by firing guns.

I went to Warsaw and my heart almost stopped. I saw a group of men working on the demolition of ruins, and I was sure they were Jewish slave-labourers as I remembered them during the German occupation. But they were not Jews; they had swastikas painted on their backs, and they moved painfully and cautiously. I stared at them and remembered how, during the War, the Germans used to bring Jews from the Ghetto and make them demolish ruins or clean the snow. We were doing the same to them; except, perhaps, they had a chance to survive, which my people had not. What was going through their minds while they worked there in the snow, among the ruins which were their doing? How would they have reacted if I had told them that I had mistaken them for Jews? For all persecuted people looked like Ghetto Jews to me.

I visited Majdanek, where the wind howled, the cabbages grew, and where I realised that what we had gone through was only a tiny speck of dust in comparison with mountains of spectacles and shoes; I stood in front of them in silence and in sorrow.

I became pregnant, and during my pregnancy Jadwiga arrived to congratulate us, and brought along a small dish of lollies. 'Symbolic', she said. 'It looks like a cradle with something sweet inside'. The point was, she had dug out the dish from under the ruins of her house.

It was summer again. More than two years had passed since the Russians had liberated us. The Second World War had ended. I had a baby, and we managed to rent a small place in the country. Julek was working in the city but spent every Sunday with us.

The country air was good for my son; he was putting on weight and beginning to stand up. And he laughed a lot.

Every evening I walked two miles to get some milk for him; fresh, rich milk, direct from the cow. While I did this my mother looked after our son; for she had come to spend her summer holiday with us. I didn't torture her any more; maybe it takes a mother to understand a mother.

The sun was setting over the forest, tinting the tree-tops bright orange. It was quiet. The fields and the meadows became darker, and I couldn't distinguish the colours any more. The frogs croaked.

I stop. There is no wind tonight; the air is moist and

warm. Not even a blade of grass moves; I, too, want to be still. I have the vast sky for a roof, like a huge colander where every hole is plugged up with a bright star. The lights flicker in the distant village, and the dogs bark; one here, one there. It's easy to breathe. It's great to be alive; better to be free. For now Julek and I have learned the joys of walking together, whenever we wish.

Suddenly, the wind moves through the fields and sends the trees bending and tossing. The moon, a half-moon, appears from behind the forest, staring at me with one cold eye.

My mother is waiting for me; and my son.

The wind whispers, agitates, laments, comforts, tantalizes, stimulates. I neither walk nor drift. My body fills with fresh air, kinder thoughts, timid optimism. I let myself be carried towards my son, half running, half dancing, trying to keep in step with nature. For tomorrow the sun will rise again.